Introductory Transformational Grammar of English

Second Edition

MARK LESTER

Culture Learning Institute
The East-West Center

Holt, Rinehart and Winston

New York   Chicago   San Francisco   Atlanta   Dallas
Montreal   Toronto   London   Sydney

To my parents

Library of Congress Cataloging in Publication Data

Lester, Mark
   Introductory transformational grammar of English.

   Includes index.
   1. English language–Grammar, Generative.
I. Title.
PE1112.L46   1976   425   75–42366

ISBN 0–03–088345–8

Preface

Introductory Transformational Grammar of English is intended to give the reader a great deal of information about English grammar. It uses transformational grammar as the vehicle for presenting that information, but the theory and machinery of transformational grammar are treated as means to an end rather than ends in themselves. Furthermore, the book assumes an audience that has had little or no background either in English grammar or in linguistic theory.

After finishing this book, the reader should be equipped to do the following: read and understand the applications of transformational grammar that appear in the language arts journals; evaluate and teach the commercial grammar programs now available in a thorough and professional way; modify and supplement existing language programs with confidence; use quite different types of reference works on English grammar, such as Jespersen's *Essentials of English Grammar* and Quirk, Greenbaum, Leech and Svartvik's *A Grammar of Contemporary English*; and, most important of all, look at nearly any English sentence with a fair amount of insight about how it is put together.

The content of the book focuses on the main grammatical features of English: (1) the major constituents of simple sentences; (2) how active sentences can be turned into passives, statements into questions, positive sentences into negative sentences, and unemphatic sentences into emphatic sentences; (3) how simple sentences are combined to produce more complex sentences. The theoretical approach adopted is a simple and basic form of transformational grammar. The book concentrates on those areas of transformational grammar that have provided insights that have stood the test of time. Accordingly, it avoids those areas (such as the relation of the lexicon to the grammar) where there is considerable dispute among linguists. It also avoids any special terminology or notational system that is tied to one particular theoretical camp.

Perhaps the most distinguishing feature of this book is the pedagogical approach. There is a lengthy introductory essay on what transformational grammar is, how it differs from structural linguistics, and how it works, complete with a mini-grammar so that the reader can see how the phrase structure and transformational rules fit together. Each chapter begins with an overview of the main points covered. Every point is illustrated with multiple examples and has one or more sets of exercises (with answers provided) for readers to test their understanding. Each chapter concludes with a review exercise that incorporates all points taught in the chapter and deliberately pulls in material covered in previous chapters. There is a compilation of all phrase structure rules at the end of Part I, and there is an appendix that gives a chapter-by-chapter summary of all rules introduced, with examples of all transformational rules.

The second edition of this book, like all revisions, is partly similar to and partly different from the first edition. It was quite clear from the comments of users that the most satisfactory aspects of the book were its general organization around rule types (phrase structure rules, simple transformational rules, and sentence-combining rules) and the copious examples and exercises. Most criticisms were of specific pieces of analysis. In the second edition I have kept the same basic organization and have expanded the number of examples and exercises (actually, there are more than twice as many exercises in the revised edition). The actual text itself has been substantially rewritten; in fact, about 75 percent of the text is new material. I have incorporated a number of new insights gained in the interval since the first edition was published. However, probably the most important factor in the revision was Quirk, Greenbaum, Leech and Svartvik's *A Grammar of Contemporary English*, which provided me with a great deal of data. On the whole, the second edition covers generally the same material as the first edition but in greater depth. Occasionally this means greater complexity and more rules, though sometimes a clearer analysis is both more complex and more simple (for example the treatment of tag questions).

There appear to have been three main ways in which the first edition was used. One way was to use the book as the main text for the course, usually supplemented by discussion or lectures on other grammatical approaches or applications, depending on the purpose of the course. A second way was to use it in conjunction with another text, usually either another grammar book or a book of readings about language. A third way was to use it as a self-teaching supplementary text not dealt with during class time. In my opinion, this second edition will continue to be useful in the same three ways. The only difference is that the second edition is somewhat longer and will take a little longer to cover than the first edition.

My thanks to these people whose detailed criticisms and suggestions were so helpful to me: Professors Irene Brosnahan, Robert H. Canary, Millard C. Dunn, Elizabeth Eddy, Robert J. Geist, Ralph J. Goodell, William B. Hunter, Jr., and Lee Little. I would also like to thank Victor Askman, Karen Shiroma, and Donna Sugihara for help in preparing the manuscript.

M.L.

Contents

Part II
Simple Transformational Rules 137

Part III
Sentence-Combining Rules 213

INTRODUCTION

An Elementary Transformational Grammar of English

The great Danish scholar of the English language Otto Jespersen wrote the following paragraph in the introductory chapter of his book *Essentials of English Grammar:*

> The chief object in teaching grammar today—especially that of a foreign language—would appear to be to give rules which must be obeyed if one wants to speak and write the language correctly—rules which as often as not seem quite arbitrary. Of greater value, however, than this *prescriptive* grammar is a purely *descriptive* grammar which, instead of serving as a guide to what should be said or written, aims at finding out what is actually said and written by the speakers of the language investigated, and thus may lead to a scientific understanding of the rules followed instinctively by speakers and writers. Such a grammar should also be *explanatory*, giving, as far as this is possible, the reasons why the usage is such and such. These reasons may, according to circumstances, be phonetic or psychological, or in some cases both combined. Not infrequently the explanation will be found in an earlier stage of the same language: what in one period was a regular phenomenon may later become isolated and appear as an irregularity, an exception to what has now become the prevailing rule. Our grammar must therefore be *historical* to a certain extent. Finally, grammar may be *appreciative*, examining whether the rules obtained from the language in question are in every way clear

(unambiguous, logical), expressive and easy, or whether in any one of these respects other forms or rules would have been preferable. (Jespersen, pp. 19–20)[1]

Jespersen draws a distinction between two different kinds of grammar. One kind, the prescriptive, gives non-native speakers a set of rules that they must follow in order to use the new language correctly. In other words, a prescriptive grammar tries to modify the learner's linguistic behavior. Jespersen obviously has considerable reservations about the value of prescriptive grammars for native speakers. Instead, he would prefer the second kind of grammar, the descriptive, which does not aim at changing behavior, but rather tries to discover what, in fact, the speaker's linguistic behavior actually is. Furthermore, a descriptive grammar may become the basis for more sophisticated investigations which will enable us to understand and explain the instinctive rules that underlie the speaker's linguistic behavior.

The need to distinguish between the two types of grammar can hardly be overemphasized. There is no need to apologize for linguistic prescriptivism as long as the basis for correction is understood by all parties concerned. In a beginning foreign language class, for instance, the views of the learner about what should or should not be said in the new language are worthless: the role of the teacher is purely prescriptive.

When dealing with native speakers of a language, the situation is naturally quite different. Children do not go to school to learn their own language in the same sense that they go to school to learn a foreign language. They "know" English in a way that they will never "know" any foreign language, no matter how much they are schooled in it. At this point we must distinguish sharply between two kinds of "knowing": conscious and unconscious. Most speakers, adults as well as children, do not know much about their language consciously. They do not know its history or why it works the way it does. This book is an attempt to give readers a conscious awareness of some aspects of their own language. Unconscious knowledge is what all speakers of a language share, namely, the ability to produce, understand, and make judgments about the grammaticality and structure of sentences in their language. By the time children come to school they already have a vast unconscious knowledge of their language.

However, their unconscious knowledge is immature as compared to that of adult speakers in at least two ways. The most obvious way is vocabulary. The vocabulary of even an illiterate adult is much greater than that of a child. If we broaden the meaning of vocabulary to include the grammatical properties of the word as well as its literal denotation, the difference between adults and children is even greater.

A second way that adults' unconscious knowledge is greater than children's is in the area of what we might call role playing. Throughout the course of a day

---

[1] From *Essentials of English Grammar* by Otto Jespersen, published in 1933 by George Allen & Unwin Ltd. Reproduced by permission of the publisher. (Whenever Jespersen is cited throughout this text, the reference is to *Essentials of English Grammar*.)

each of us shifts linguistic gears as many times as we enter into different personal and professional relationships. It is a mistake to think of the changes as being along a single axis that ranges from formal to informal. We have many different axes. We can range from shop talk to baby talk; from intimate to highly impersonal; from solemn to facetious. We talk one way to superiors, another way to subordinates; we talk one way to our children, another way to our parents; we talk one way to men, another way to women. Young children know a few of these roles and the linguistic conventions that go with them, but their repertoire is naturally quite limited. Some of the linguistic conventions they will learn as a direct result of their schooling (for instance, the ones that pertain to some of the conventions of written English), but most they will learn as a sheer function of growing up and taking part in the various roles.

Since the publication of Jespersen's *Essentials*, the United States has seen the evolution of two new and quite different schools of language study. The first school had its roots in the 1930s, but did not gain wide recognition until after World War II. This school is commonly known as *structural linguistics*. The second new school can be dated from the publication by Noam Chomsky in 1957 of a monograph entitled *Syntactic Structures*. This school is usually referred to as *transformational grammar*. What are the main claims of these new schools, and how do they differ from each other and from what had gone before?

Both of these schools consider themselves scientific revolutions, so perhaps a good way to begin is to examine what it is that they are revolting against. The tradition that preceded structural linguistics is called *traditional grammar*. This term means different things to different people. At its worst, it means a confused blend of prescriptive and descriptive grammars aimed at changing linguistic behavior along the most artificial lines. At its best, however, it means the work of a scholar such as Jespersen. His *Essentials of English Grammar* belongs to a long and honorable tradition, and one that is still alive. The following passage on reflexive pronouns from Jespersen's *Essentials of English Grammar* is a good example of the best kind of traditional grammar. The passage is taken from a chapter that deals with the "relations of verb to subject and object."

When the subject and object are identical, we use for the latter a so-called reflexive pronoun, formed by means of *self, e.g. I defend myself*. The pronouns are the following:

(I) myself	(we) ourselves.
(thou) thyself ⎱ (you) yourself ⎰	(you) yourselves.
(he) himself ⎫ (she) herself ⎬ (it) itself ⎭	(they) themselves.
(one) oneself (rarer one's self).	

A few verbs are always used reflexively:

She prides herself on her good looks.
He absented himself from all committee meetings.

There is a tendency to get rid of these pronouns whenever no ambiguity is to be feared:

> I washed, dressed and shaved, and then felt infinitely better.
> He is training for the race.
> He drew back a little.
> The army retired in good order.
> The disease spread rapidly.
> You must prepare for death.

Sometimes a difference is made, or may be made, between the fuller and the shorter expression; *behave oneself* is often used of good manners and breeding, while *behave* is used for action generally: the troops behaved gallantly under fire.

> He settled himself comfortably in an easy-chair | They settled in Australia.
> No opportunity offered | He offered himself as an interpreter.

Sometimes there is an element of exertion in the reflexive use: *We kept ourselves warm by walking to and fro* is more deliberate than *we kept warm*, etc.; cf. *the soup did not keep warm* very long. *He proved himself a fine fellow* emphasizes his endeavours, while *he proved a fine fellow* merely means that people saw that he was.

It is natural that the tendency to use verbs without the reflexive pronouns is stronger in English, where these pronouns are heavy and cumbersome, than in other languages where the corresponding forms are short and light (French *se*, German *sich*, etc.).

The reflexive pronouns are also used after prepositions:

> He looked at himself in the glass.
> He lives by himself in an old cottage.

But if the preposition has a purely local meaning, the simple forms without *self* are used:

> Shut the door behind you!
> I have no change about me.
> She stood, looking straight in front of her.
> They had the whole afternoon before them. (Jespersen, pp. 111–112)

From the purely descriptive standpoint of presenting accurate information about the usage of the reflexive, this passage would be hard to improve on. Note that the explanations Jespersen gives are almost always concerned with the meaning of the usage; for example, the reflexive can be deleted from the sentence when "no ambiguity is to be feared" or when the reflexive follows a preposition of "purely local meaning." Jespersen also points out that the presence or absence of a reflexive sometimes changes the meaning of the verb. For Jespersen, a descriptive grammar describes usage, and usage can be explained in terms of its effect on meaning.

THE STRUCTURAL REVOLUTION

The one book written from the viewpoint of structural linguistics that has probably had the greatest impact on the teaching of English is Charles Carpenter Fries's (pronounced *freeze*) *The Structure of English*. Let us look at the main ideas in this book in some detail in order to see how a leading structural grammarian viewed the structural revolution. Bear in mind, however, that there were other structural linguists besides Fries, and that what is true for Fries may not be necessarily true for them. No field of study is perfectly monolithic.

At the end of the first chapter, Fries states that the purpose of his book is to

challenge anew the conventional use of "meaning" as the basic tool of analysis in the area of linguistic study in which it has had its strongest hold— sentence structure and syntax. (Otto Jespersen insists, for example, "But in syntax meaning is everything." *A Modern English Grammar* (Heidelberg, 1931), IV, 291.) [Fries's footnote.] (Fries, p. 7)[2]

In this quotation we see one of the key ideas of structural linguistics. Linguistics cannot use meaning as a tool in the analysis of language, a position diametrically opposed to the basic ideas of traditional grammar. The structuralists argued that the goal of linguistic analysis is to see how meaning is conveyed. Since meaning is the goal, it cannot at the same time be a means used to reach the goal, or else the discovery process is completely circular: meaning is discovered by the use of meaning. For Fries, language is a physical, observable phenomenon that must be studied objectively.

Fries criticizes traditional grammar for providing analyses that merely label the elements in a sentence but do not explain how meaning is conveyed.

In the usual approach to the grammatical analysis of sentences one must know the total meaning of the utterance before beginning any analysis. The process of analysis consists almost wholly of giving technical names to portions of this total meaning. For example, given the sentence *the man gave the boy the money*, the conventional grammatical analysis would consist in attaching the name "subject" to the word *man*, the name "predicate" to the word *gave*, the name "indirect object" to the word *boy*, the name "direct object" to the word *money*, and the name "declarative sentence" to the whole utterance. If pressed for the basis upon which these names are given to these words, one would, in accord with the traditional method, say that the word *man* is called "subject" because it "designates the person about whom an assertion is made"; that the word *gave* is called "predicate" because it is "the word that asserts something about the subject"; that the word *boy* is called "indirect object" because it "indicates the person to or for whom the

---

[2] From *The Structure of English* by Charles Carpenter Fries, copyright 1952 by Harcourt Brace Jovanovich, Inc., and reprinted with their permission. (Whenever Fries is cited throughout this text, the reference is to *The Structure of English*.)

action is done"; and that the word *money* is called "direct object" because it "indicates the thing that receives the action of the verb." The sentence is called a "declarative sentence" because it "makes a statement." The whole procedure begins with the total meaning of the sentence and consists solely in ascribing the technical terms "subject," "predicate," "indirect object," "direct object," and "declarative sentence" to certain parts of that meaning. "Knowing grammar" has thus meant primarily the ability to apply and react to a technical terminology consisting of approximately seventy items. It is this kind of "grammatical knowledge" that is assumed in the usual discussions of the value of "grammar" for an effective practical command of English, or for English composition, or for mastery of foreign language. It is this kind of grammatical analysis, this starting with the total meaning, *and the using of this meaning as the basis for the analysis*—an analysis that makes no advance beyond the ascribing of certain technical terms to parts of the meaning already known—it is this kind of grammatical analysis that modern linguistic science discards as belonging to a prescientific era. (Fries, pp. 54–55)

Fries begins his analysis of the sentence *the man gave the boy the money* by distinguishing between two different kinds of meaning. One kind of meaning is *lexical meaning*. The lexical meaning of *man*, for instance, is the dictionary definition of the word: it tells us what the word *man* refers to in the real world. However, what the dictionary cannot tell us is how the word *man* is used in the sentence quoted above. In the sentence *The boy gave the man the money*, the function of the word *man* is quite different from its function in the first sentence. The grammatical function of a word in a sentence is called the *structural meaning* of the word in Fries's terminology. Thus, in order to understand a sentence, we must know both what its words mean (the lexical meaning) and their grammatical function within the sentence in question (the structural meaning).

Fries next addresses himself to the question of how we recognize structural meaning. He argues that structural meaning is "signalled by specific and definite devices. It is the devices that signal structural meanings which constitute the grammar of a language. *The grammar of a language consists of the devices that signal structural meanings*." (p. 56) When the appropriate structural signals are absent from a sentence, the sentence will be ambiguous because we can assign it more than one possible structural meaning. Fries illustrates this point with the sentence

Ship sails today.   (Fries, p. 62)

The sentence is ambiguous because both *ship* and *sails* could be either a noun or a verb. However, if the appropriate structural signals were present, the sentence would not be ambiguous; for example,

The ship sails today.
Ship the sails today.

In this case, *the* signals the structural meaning of *ship* and *sail* in the two sentences.

One of the deeply held tenets of structural linguistics is that the recognition of structural meaning is independent of lexical meaning. In other words, speakers of a language do not depend on the meaning of the word in a sentence to tell them what its grammatical function is. In support of this position, Fries makes up sentences with words that have structural meaning but no lexical meaning, for example, *Woggles ugged diggles.* (p. 71) The fact that we know that *woggles* and *diggles* are nouns and that *ugged* is a verb means that we identify parts of speech without reference to meaning.

Fries also discusses the inadequacy of the traditional definitions of parts of speech. Again, the basis of his objection to traditional definitions is not that their classification is faulty, but that their definitions are not really defining:

> What is a "noun," for example? The usual definition is that "a noun is the name of a person, place, or thing." But *blue* is the "name" of a color, as is *yellow* or *red*, and yet, in the expressions *a blue tie, a yellow rose, a red dress* we do not call *blue* and *yellow* and *red* "nouns." We do call *red* a noun in the sentence *this red is the shade I want. Run* is the "name" of an action, as is *jump* or *arrive. Up* is the "name" of a direction, as is *down* or *across.* In spite of the fact that these words are all "names" and thus fit the definition given for a noun they are not called nouns in such expressions as "We *ran* home," "They were looking *up* into the sky," "The acid made the fiber *red.*" The definition as it stands—that "A noun is a name"—does not furnish all the criteria necessary to exclude from this group many words which our grammars in actual practice classify in other parts of speech. (Fries, p. 67)

However valid Fries's criticism of certain kinds of traditional grammars may be, it is not a valid criticism of sophisticated traditional grammarians like Jespersen. In his *Essentials of English Grammar*, Jespersen makes no attempt to define nouns, either by meaning or otherwise. He simply gives a list of typical types of nouns with the following comment: "It is practically impossible to give exact and exhaustive definitions of these [part of speech] classes; nevertheless the classification itself rarely offers occasion for doubt and will be sufficiently clear to students if a fair number of examples are given. . . ." (Jespersen, p. 66)

Fries also rejects the traditional meaning-based definitions of such functional relationships as subject, direct object, indirect object, appositive, and the like. Instead, he identifies these relationships in terms of formal signals of structure. For example, "subject" is defined as being that noun which is "tied" to a verb by agreement, that is, by the change in the form of the verb that is correlated with the number of the preceding noun; for example:

The boy *loves* ice cream.
The boys *love* ice cream.

Other functional relations are defined in terms of linguistic formulas or patterns. For example, given the pattern

determiner–noun–verb–determiner–noun

the second noun, by definition, is a direct object.

Fries's task is to identify the structural signals by which speakers actually recognize the speech class of a word. Here are structural signals by which Fries claims that speakers recognize a noun to be a noun:

1. Contrast of form between nouns and other parts of speech. For example, noun/verb: *arrival/arrive, defense/defend*; noun/adjective: *bigness/big, truth/true*.
2. Compounds ending in *-one, -body, -thing, -self/selves*. For example, *someone, somebody, something, myself*.
3. Contrast of singular versus plural forms marked by "s." For example, *boys/boy, desks/desk*.
4. Irregular contrasts of singular and plural forms. For example, *men/man, children/child*.
5. Possessive "s." For example, *man/man's/men/men's*.
6. Position after determiners. For example, in the following phrase the italicized words are nouns because they follow determiners:

   The *poor* and the *rich*, the very *lowest* and the very *highest* are. . . . (p. 118)

7. Position after prepositions. For example, *at school, by telephone*.
8. Recognition of the other parts of speech in the sentence. Fries gives an example of this category the following newspaper headlines: (p. 119)

   Bus Fares Cheap in Emergency
   Bus Fares Badly in Emergency

We recognize *Fares* to be a noun in the first sentence and a verb in the second sentence because we recognize the part of speech of the word following *Fares*.

The formal characteristics of nouns that Fries gives above break down into two types: characteristics of the form of the word (groups 1–5) and characteristics of position within the sentence (groups 6–8). These two basic types of characteristics are also used in the characterization of the other three parts of speech.

At the risk of dreadful oversimplification, structural linguistics (as represented by Fries's *The Structure of English*) may be described as a revolutionary departure from traditional grammar in terms of what there is in language that needs to be explained. For Jespersen, explanation means discussion of how a certain form or construction came to be used the way it is. The explanation can be semantic or purely historical. For the structural linguist, the basic question of linguistics that needs explanation is a psychological one: How does language convey meaning? The structuralists' answer to this question is, I think, fairly summed up in this quotation from Fries:

The total linguistic meaning of any utterance consists of the lexical meanings of the separate words plus such structural meanings. No utterance is intelligible without both lexical meanings and structural meanings. How, then, are these structural meanings conveyed in English from the speaker to a hearer? Structural meanings are not just vague matters of the context, so called; they are fundamental and necessary meanings in every utterance and are signalled by specific and definite devices. It is the devices that signal structural meanings which constitute the grammar of a language. *The grammar of a language consists of the devices that signal structural meanings.* (Fries, p. 56)

For the structuralist, two basic conclusions follow from the position just stated:

1. There is a one-to-one tie between structural signals and meanings. The language learner comes to associate certain meanings with certain forms. As Fries puts it:

> One of the earliest steps in learning to talk is this learning to use automatically the patterns of form and arrangement that constitute the devices to signal structural meaning. So thoroughly have they become unconscious habits in very early childhood that the ordinary adult speaker of English finds it extremely difficult not only to describe what he does in these matters but even to realize that there is anything there to be described. (Fries, pp. 57–58)

2. Linguistic analysis needs to distinguish between the kind of information available to the user and the kind of information that is not. The former will have relevance to the acquisition and use of language, while the latter will not. Historical information about the English language may be of interest to the specialist, but it is obviously irrelevant to any examination of how language conveys meaning, since the typical speaker does not have historical information available. From this point of view, Jespersen's excursions into the history of the language are irrelevant to the central topic of how language conveys meaning.

THE TRANSFORMATIONAL REVOLUTION

For the structural grammarian, the goal of linguistics is to account for linguistic behavior. The basis of the transformational revolution is ultimately the simple observation that explanations of our linguistic behavior cannot account for the extent of our linguistic knowledge. For example, Fries demonstrates the importance of structural signals by showing that if these signals were omitted from a sentence (as in newspaper headlines), the resulting sentence would be ambiguous. Chomsky points out that there are other kinds of ambiguity that have nothing to do with structural signals. A well-known example from *Syntactic Structures* is the phrase

The shooting of the hunters

This phrase can mean either (1) the hunters shot something, or (2) someone shot the hunters. Here we have one form with two different meanings. However, unlike the ambiguity of *ship sails today*, it is very difficult to see how the phrase can be made unambiguous by adding structural signals. In other words, the ambiguity of *the shooting of the hunters* is not due to a confusion as to the proper part of speech classification. There is no doubt that *shooting* is a gerund (a verb changed into a noun by the addition of *-ing*) and that *hunters* is a noun. Even knowing this, the sentence is still ambiguous.

One possible solution from a structural standpoint would be to argue that the ambiguity is due to the function word *of* in that particular pattern. In other words, when we have the sequence

gerund—of—noun

the sequence will be ambiguous in the same way that *the shooting of the hunters* is. The problem with this solution is that it does not work. Chomsky cites two phrases that appear to have exactly the same structure as *the shooting of the hunters*:

The growling of lions
The raising of flowers

Neither one of these phrases is ambiguous in the sense that *the shooting of the hunters* is. This is a fact that native speakers of English simply know. Furthermore, we know that the relation of the gerund to the noun in the two phrases above is not alike. In *the growling of lions* the relation of *lions* to *growling* is similar to the relation of *hunters* to *shooting* in the first meaning of *the shooting of the hunters*, namely, the lions growled and the hunters shot. In *the raising of flowers*, the relation of *flowers* to *raising* is similar to the relation of *hunters* to *shooting* in the second meaning of *the shooting of the hunters*, namely, someone grew flowers and someone shot the hunters.

Another frequently cited pair of sentences that illustrate the discrepancy between the information contained in the structural signals and what we actually know is the following:

John is easy to please.
John is eager to please.

In terms of sentence structure, these two sentences are identical. However, every native speaker of English knows that these two sentences are really totally different. The first sentence states that John is an easy person to please, while the second sentence states that John is eager to please us. There is nothing in the sentence structure of these two sentences that could account for the difference in the way we understand them. A possible explanation could be that the difference is in the lexical meaning of the two adjectives *easy* and *eager*. We can show that this is not the case, however, by substituting other adjectives into the same position. For example, we know that *John is difficult to please* is like *John is easy to please*, while *John is anxious to please* is like *John is eager to please*. Consequently, the difference between the two sentences is more basic than just the lexical meanings of *easy* and *eager*.

Ambiguity results when one form has two or more meanings. The opposite of ambiguity is when one meaning is embodied in two or more forms. For the sake of a term, let us call the opposite of ambiguity *paraphrase*. The classic instance of paraphrase in English is the relation between the active and passive versions of the same sentence; for example:

Active: The detective saw the accident.
Passive: The accident was seen by the detective.

In structural terms, the two sentences above are totally unrelated. The subject noun of the active sentence is *detective*, while the subject noun of the passive is *accident*. The verb of the active sentence is *see* in the past tense. The verb of the passive sentence is *was* plus *see* in the past participle form. The object of the active sentence is *accident*, while in the passive sentence it is *detective*. Despite these obvious differences, every speaker of English knows that in a very profound sense these two sentences are basically the same. Furthermore, we all know that the passive is a kind of alternative version of the active, and not the other way around. Paraphrase relations are a second way in which our knowledge of the language cannot be accounted for in terms of lexical meanings of words and structural signals.

We may represent the connection between form and meaning by the following diagram:

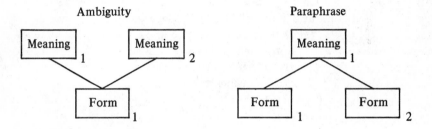

For example, the phrase *the shooting of the hunters* is ambiguous because the one form has two meanings:

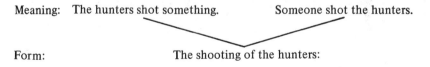

The paraphrase relation between the active and passive results from one meaning with two forms:

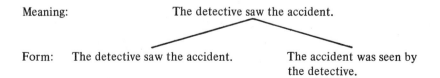

For the transformational grammarian the basic goal of linguistics is to account for what speakers know about their language. The transformational revolution is a radical shift in the kinds of questions that linguists deal with, just as the structural revolution was a radical shift away from the questions that traditional grammarians concerned themselves with. A scientific revolution is not so much a matter of changing the answers, but changing the relevant questions.

We have already seen that native speakers of a language are aware of ambiguity and paraphrase relationships beyond what can be accounted for in terms of structural signals. What kind of knowledge does this awareness imply? For one thing, it implies that a speaker of a language, in some unconscious, intuitive way, "knows" the internal structure and the relationship of one part with another of all the sentences in his language. This knowledge does not depend on any prior exposure to each particular sentence, nor does it necessarily depend on the meaningfulness or appropriateness of the sentence to some situation. Chomsky illustrates both of these points in *Syntactic Structures* with the following pair of nonsense sentences:

Colorless green ideas sleep furiously.
Furiously sleep ideas green colorless.

When Chomsky first made up these sentences, it is safe to assume that neither had ever occurred in the history of the English language. Both are unique, and both are meaningless. Yet every speaker of English knows that the first sentence, no matter how witless, is a grammatical sentence in English and that the second sentence is not. We may characterize native speakers' knowledge of their language as the ability to make judgments about sentences: they can decide whether a sentence is grammatical or not (more accurately, they can decide if two sentences are equally grammatical, equally ungrammatical, or one more grammatical than the other); they can decide whether two sentences mean the same thing or not (paraphrase); they can recognize which sentences have more than one meaning (ambiguity); they can decide if the relation of the parts to the whole in one sentence is the same as or different from the relation of the parts to the whole of another sentence. In short, the transformational grammarian is interested in linguistic knowledge.

In crude terms, a transformational grammar is a system or device that duplicates the kinds of judgments people make. This system is what transformationalists call a grammar. A transformational grammar of English is a device that mirrors the judgments a native speaker of English would make. In a very basic sense, a transformational grammar cannot do anything that a speaker of English cannot do. In other words, the grammar is an attempt to make explicit and conscious what the speaker of English does intuitively and unconsciously.

At this point we might consider an old riddle. What has two eyes like an Indian, two arms like an Indian, two legs like an Indian, and looks exactly like an Indian, but is *not* an Indian? The answer, of course, is a picture of an Indian. A transformational grammar is a picture or model of our linguistic ability to make judgments about our language. However, it is not that ability itself; it is a device that duplicates the kind of judgments people make about their own language, and *not* a direct statement about what goes on between people's ears.

WHAT IS TRANSFORMATIONAL GRAMMAR?

Grammar is a way of talking about how words are used to make units that communicate a meaning. As Fries points out, this meaning is greater than the lexical meaning of the individual words that make up the unit. Words are elements or units that enter into relations with other words to form new units, which in turn enter into relations with other units to make more complex and abstract units, which may in turn enter into relations with still other units to make even more abstract units, and so on. Thus, all grammars are basically attempts to make statements about linguistic units and their relations. For example, let us compare the different statements that traditional grammar, structural linguistics, and transformational grammar make about the simple sentence

The detective saw the accident.

In traditional grammar, the analysis would look something like this:

<u>The detective | saw / the accident.</u>

The vertical line indicates that the material to the left is the complete subject of the sentence and the material to the right is the complete predicate. The slanted line indicates that the material to the left is the verb and the material to the right is the object. The individual words would be identified by part of speech; for example, *detective* and *accident* would be classified as nouns, *saw* as a verb, and *the* as an article (although terminology differs here).

In structural linguistics the analysis would indicate that the sentence in question is an instance of an English sentence pattern of the form

Det–Noun–Verb–Det–Noun

where Det stands for determiner. The first noun in this pattern functions as the subject, while the second noun functions as the object.

In transformational grammar, the analysis would look like this (in a simplified form):

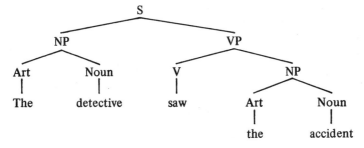

The S stands for sentence, NP for noun phrase, VP for verb phrase, and Art for article. We may "read" the analysis from the top down in the following way: The sentence (S) consists of two elements in this order: a noun phrase (NP) and a verb phrase (VP). The noun phrase consists of two elements in this order: an article (Art) and a noun. The article is the word *the* and the noun is the word *detective*. The verb phrase consists of two elements in this order: verb and noun phrase. The verb is the word *saw*. The noun phrase consists of two elements in this order: article and noun. The article is the word *the* and the noun is the word *accident*.

We may also "read" the analysis from the bottom up in the following way: *the* is an article, *detective* is a noun, *saw* is a verb, *the* is an article, and *accident* is a noun. Articles and nouns combine to make up noun phrases. The verb and the following noun phrase combine to make up the verb phrase. The initial noun phrase and the verb phrase combine to make up the sentence.

Although the information given in the three different analyses is essentially identical, the three grammars differ substantially in their mode of presenting the information. In a traditional grammar sentence diagram, the relation between words is highlighted. That is, the words are grouped into units whose relative function is indicated by the lines in the diagram. In the sentence above, for example, the five words are grouped into three units, *the detective, saw*, and *the accident*. Notice that the sentence diagram does not itself further identify the elements that make up the units. The structural sentence pattern is almost the opposite. It directly identifies the basic units by part of speech but does not itself directly indicate the relations the words enter into to form larger units. The transformational analysis is more complicated than either the traditional sentence diagram or the structural pattern because it directly identifies the part of speech of the individual words (*the* is an article, *detective* is a noun, and so on) and at the same time shows the abstract units formed by relations between words (*the detective* is a noun phrase, *saw the accident* is a verb phrase, and so on).

If there were no more than this to transformational grammar, the kind of analysis presented above would be merely a somewhat more sophisticated version of traditional sentence diagramming that directly incorporates part-of-speech information into the diagram. However, transformational grammar is fundamentally different from both traditional grammar and structural linguistics in two ways. First, a transformational grammar provides a two-stage analysis. The analysis we have seen so far is the first stage. The second stage applies to the analysis provided by the first stage. The second stage may add new elements to the string of words in the first analysis, it may delete words from the string, or it may rearrange the words of the string into a new order. These changes are called *transformations*, and it is from these changes that the name *transformational grammar* is taken. One group of transformations changes certain types of active sentences into a corresponding passive sentence. For example, we can transform the first-stage string given in the above analysis for *The detective saw the accident* into this passive sentence:

The accident was seen by the detective.

This group of transformations has reversed the two noun phrases, added the verb *be*, changed the verb *see* from the past tense form to the past participle form, and added the preposition *by*. Thus, one of the basic ideas of transformational grammar is that more than one second-stage sentence can be produced from a single first-stage analysis.

The string of words given in the first stage (and the analysis that goes with the string) is called a *deep structure*. The deep structure analysis, as we have said before, not only provides part-of-speech information about the individual words but also shows the way words are related to form more abstract units. The finished product of the second stage of analysis is called *a surface structure*. For very simple sentences (such as *The detective saw the accident*) the deep structure and the surface structure are nearly the same. Sometimes, however, as in the case of the passive, the deep structure and the surface structure may differ radically from each other.

One of the basic reasons for proposing transformational rules is that they can show how surface sentences that have a systematic semantic and formal relation to each other are grammatically related. For example, every speaker of English knows that the sentences in the following pairs are somehow the same sentence, despite their superficial differences:

(a) John looked up the word.
     John looked the word up.
(b) John gave the ball to Mary.
     John gave Mary the ball.

Furthermore, certain sentences seem to differ from other sentences in a systematic way. For instance, the following pairs of statements and questions are obviously related:

(c) John can come.
     Can John come?
(d) John is here now.
     Is John here now?
(e) John answered the question correctly.
     Did John answer the question correctly?

In a transformational grammar, the connection between two closely related surface sentences is explained by deriving both from a single underlying deep structure sentence. The difference in form between the two sentences is explained by the use of transformations.

When we first began discussing the transformational revolution, we said that one goal of transformational grammar was to explain ambiguity and paraphrase relationships. In the terminology of transformational grammar, an ambiguity results when two different deep structures happen by accident to end up with exactly the same surface structures. For example, by different transformations the two unrelated deep structure sentences *The hunters shot something* and *Someone shot the hunters* can have the same surface structure, *The shooting of the hunters*. Examples (a) and (b) above and the active/passive pair *The detective saw the accident* and *The accident was seen by the detective* are instances of paraphrase relations between sentences. In a transformational grammar, a paraphrase relation results when one deep structure sentence can be turned into two (or more) different surface sentences by applying different transformations. In example (a) above, there is an optional transformation that allows the preposition in verb-plus-preposition units to be moved after the following noun phrase. In example (b) above, there is an optional transformation that permits deep structure sentences that have two noun phrases following the verb to reverse the two noun phrases and put the preposition *to* between them when they are transformed into surface sentences.

There is another form of paraphrase that we might call sentence building. Compare the following:

> (a) The children ate everything in sight. The children were hungry after their long hike.
> (b) The children, who were hungry after their long hike, ate everything in sight.
> (c) The children, being hungry after their long hike, ate everything in sight.
> (d) The children, hungry after their long hike, ate everything in sight.

It seems clear that sentence (d) is a highly compressed paraphrase of the two sentences in (a). A very important aspect of transformational grammar is its ability to show that longer and more complex surface sentences are built up out of two or more simpler deep structure sentences.

To summarize the key points so far, one of the two main differences between transformational grammar on the one hand and traditional grammar and structural linguistics on the other is that a transformational grammar has two stages of analysis. The first stage produces an analysis called a deep structure. The deep structure shows both the part of speech of the individual words and the grouping of the words to form more abstract relations or units. The second stage of analysis changes or transforms the deep structure into a surface structure. The transformations may add to, delete from, or rearrange the units in the deep structure, or even combine two or more deep structures to produce a single complex surface sentence or structure. The main advantage to this two-stage analysis is that it better mirrors our intuitive knowledge of ambiguity and paraphrase relations between surface sentences.

HOW DOES A TRANSFORMATIONAL GRAMMAR WORK?

A grammar is a way of talking about how words are used to make units that communicate a meaning. When we analyze a sentence we are showing how the words are related in making up the abstract unit we call a sentence. It is very important to understand that the grammaticality of the sentence does not depend on our analysis. That is, the sentence is grammatical whether we analyze it or not. It is easy to slip into the mistaken notion that an analysis of a sentence "proves" that the sentence is grammatical. Just the opposite is true. When we analyze a sentence we are "proving" that our system of analysis is adequate to give a conscious, explicit explanation of the relations we intuitively know to exist in the sentence.

All grammars have the same goals in analyzing sentences. However, we have already seen that transformational grammar is different from other grammars in having a two-stage system of analysis. It also has a second important difference: it has an explicit, well-developed theory on where the analysis comes from. In this respect, transformational grammar is very much like geometry. Plane geometry, for example, is a way of talking about the abstract relations inherent in figures on a plane. The kinds of statements that can be made are restricted by an explicit, well-developed theory based on two sets of axioms. The first, more general set governs not only plane geometry, but many other fields of mathematics. An example would be the axiom that the whole of a quantity equals the sum of its parts. The second set of axioms, called postulates, are restricted specifically to plane geometry. An example of such a postulate would be that through a given point not on a straight line, one, and only one, straight line may be drawn that is parallel to a given line.

The statements that can be made in a transformational grammar are also restricted by a theory based on two sets of axioms. The first set is a general one about the analyses of all languages. An example would be that in the deep structure analysis of any sentence, all words in the bottom line of the analysis must be connected by a line to some abstract class (such as noun or article), which in turn must be connected through other abstract classes to *Sentence*. The second set of axioms is a set of postulates specifically for the analysis of English. Each language would have its own set of postulates. An example for English would be that a noun phrase consists of an article and a noun. This postulate would not be true of the many languages that do not have articles.

The study of the first general set of axioms for transformational grammar has become a rich and complex branch of mathematics in its own right. In this book, however, we will be concerned almost exclusively with the postulates for analyzing English sentences. There are actually two sets of postulates, one set that produces the deep structure analysis of individual sentences and a second set that transforms the deep structure into the surface structure. Let us deal with the deep structure set first.

The deep structure postulates are a set of rules that rewrite symbols. Here is a highly simplified set of rules (often called *phrase structure rules*) that will produce the sentence *The detective saw the accident* (plus a few other sentences):

GIVEN: S

(i) $S \longrightarrow NP \frown VP$

(ii) $NP \longrightarrow Art \frown Noun$

(iii) $VP \longrightarrow \begin{Bmatrix} V \frown NP \\ V_i \end{Bmatrix}$

(iv) $Art \longrightarrow \{the, a\}$

(v) Noun ⟶ {*accident, detective*. . .}

(vi) V ⟶ {*saw*. . .}

(vii) V_i ⟶ {*laughed, smiled*. . .}

Rule (i) says that the given symbol S (for sentence) is rewritten as noun phrase followed by verb phrase. Rule (ii) says that the noun phrase symbol is in turn rewritten as article followed by noun. Rule (iii) is more complicated. It allows for a choice of how the verb phrase symbol is to be written. The symbol { } means, "pick one of the enclosed options." We can pick either the top line and rewrite VP as verb followed by a noun phrase *or* we can pick the bottom line and rewrite VP as V_i. (Can you guess what V_i stands for?) Rule (iv) says that the abstract symbol article is to be rewritten as either *the* or *a*. Notice that rule (iv) is the first rule that produces actual words. The first three rules rewrite one abstract symbol as one or more abstract symbols. Rule (v) says that the abstract symbol noun is to be rewritten as an actual word. The three little dots . . . mean that the list given is not exhaustive; that is, there are other nouns besides the ones given on the list. Rule (vi) says that the abstract symbol verb is to be rewritten as an actual word. Rule (vii) says that V_i (which stands for intransitive verb) is to be rewritten as an actual word.

Let us now follow through the actual production or derivation of a deep structure sentence following the rules. The given S is like an axiom in geometry— its existence is accepted without proof. By Rule (i) S is rewritten as NP⌢VP. By Rule (ii) NP is rewritten as Art⌢Noun. In Rule (iii) we will choose the first option and rewrite VP as V⌢NP. In Rule (iv) we will rewrite Art as *the*. In Rule (v) we will rewrite Noun as *detective*. In Rule (vi) we will rewrite V as *saw*. We cannot apply Rule (vii) because we did not pick the bottom line of Rule (iii), which is the only source of the abstract symbol V_i.

The deep structure diagram (often called a *phrase structure tree*) is a record of the actual choices we made in the derivation of a particular sentence. Let us go through our use of the phrase structure rules again, rule by rule, and see what the resulting phrase structure tree looks like.

BY RULE (i)

S ⟶ NP⌢V̄P

BY RULE (ii)

NP ⟶ Art⌢N

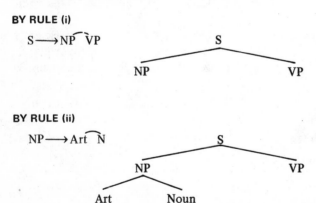

BY RULE (iii)

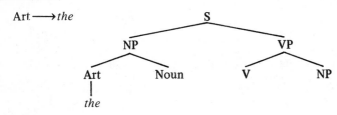

BY RULE (iv)

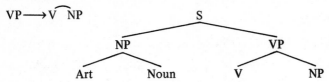

BY RULE (v)

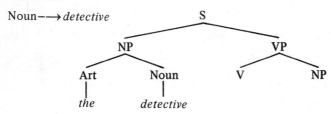

BY RULE (vi)

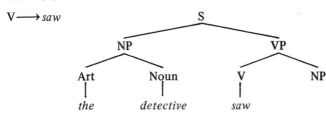

As you can see, even though we have gone through the rule system once, we have not rewritten the second NP because the second NP was produced by Rule (iii), which follows the rule [Rule (ii)] that rewrites the NP. The solution is quite simple. The general axioms that underlie the operation of the phrase structure rules do not require that the rules be executed in any particular sequence. In other words, the numbering of the rules is for convenience of reference, not for indicating a necessary ordering of application. The general axiom is that any phrase structure rule can be applied any time that a symbol on the bottom of a phrase structure tree branch is the same as a symbol on the left-hand side of a phrase structure rule. So, we merely reapply Rule (ii).

BY RULE (ii)

NP ⟶ Art Noun

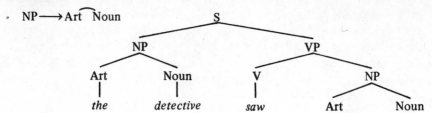

BY RULE (iv)

Art ⟶ *the*

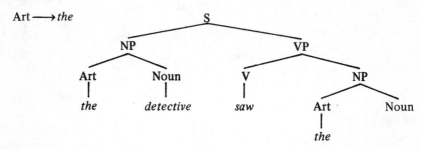

BY RULE (v)

Noun ⟶ *accident*

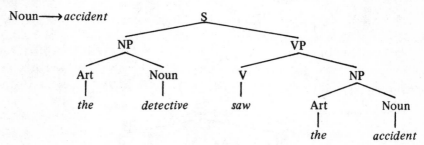

As an exercise, the reader should derive the same sentence but applying Rule (iii) before Rule (ii). What difference is there in the phrase structure diagram? How would you derive the sentence *The detective smiled*?

The phrase structure tree (or diagram) is the specific application of the phrase structure rules to the production (equivalently *generation* or *derivation*) of an individual deep structure sentence. A complete set of phrase structure rules for English would produce all possible deep structure sentences. To use a fancy metaphor, the phrase structure rules are a road map that shows all possible routes. The phrase structure tree is the record of one particular trip.

We have now seen an example of where the analysis of a deep structure sentence comes from—from specific choices taken within the phrase structure rules. Where do the phrase structure rules themselves come from? The answer is very simple: from nowhere. That is, they are simply made up—just as the postulates in geometry are made up. A rule is valid to the extent that it plays a necessary role in producing analyses that are intuitively correct. A secondary consideration is the generality of a rule. Given two rules that do essentially the same thing, we would prefer the rule that applies without restriction throughout the grammar over the rule that can be applied only in special circumstances. Like the postulates in geometry, the rules of transformational grammar have no claim on any reality in their own right. They are artifacts created to provide a model of reality.

The phrase structure rules are used to produce analyses of deep structures. The deep structures are transformed into surface structures by a second set of rules known as transformational rules. All transformations can be broken down to one or more elementary transformational operations: the addition of a new element into the deep structure, the deletion of an element from the deep structure, or the rearrangement of elements within the deep structure. Each of these operations is governed by a separate transformational rule. Transformational rules differ from phrase structure rules in the following four ways:

1. All phrase structure rules are obligatory; that is, if the rule can be applied, it must be applied. Some transformational rules are also obligatory, some are optional (that is, whether the rule is applied or not, the resulting surface sentence will be grammatical—the passive rules are a case in point), and some are obligatory in certain situations and optional in other situations.

2. The phrase structure rules can apply only to the abstract symbols at the bottom of phrase structure tree branches. Transformational rules, on the other hand, can apply to any abstract relation within the tree that has been given a label. We have already seen an example of this in our earlier discussion of the passive, where we pointed out that the rule that reverses *detective* and *accident* actually applies to the noun phrases that *detective* and *accident* are in, not just to the nouns themselves.

3. Phrase structure rules do one thing at a time—rewrite single abstract symbols either as one or more abstract symbols or else write them as actual words. Transformational rules, on the other hand, particularly the rules that rearrange the elements in the deep structure, can bring about many changes by the application of a single rule. An example would be the rule that switches the subject and object noun phrases in deriving a passive sentence.

4. Phrase structure rules and transformational rules have quite different functions. Basically, phrase structure rules account for the grammatical relations that are inherent in the sentence. The deep structure contains both the words and their grammatical relations. In other words, the deep structure accounts for the basic *meaning* of a sentence. The transformational rules, on the other hand, play only a marginal role in determining meaning. Their main function is to determine the *form* of the surface sentence. The transformational rules that convert a deep structure into a passive are again a case in point. By the application of these transformational rules the deep structure is considerably altered in form, but not in basic meaning.

To recapitulate: ambiguity and paraphrase demonstrate that there is not a simple one-to-one connection between the meaning and the form of sentences.

In transformational terms, the meaning of a sentence is accounted for by a tree diagram, which is a representation of the deep structure of the sentence. The tree diagram shows the relation of the words to each other and to the abstract relations that make up the sentence. The tree diagram is produced by the phrase structure rules. The deep structure is converted into actual form, that is, the surface structure, by the application of transformational rules. Thus the output of one set of rules serves as the input for the next set of rules. If there were no transformational rules, we could not account for the differences between form and meaning, that is, for ambiguity and paraphrase.

A transformational grammar has two goals: (1) to generate all the sentences of a language, and (2) to provide for every sentence an analysis which conforms to our reaction to that sentence, that is, to distinguish grammatical sentences from ungrammatical ones and to analyze the internal structure of the sentences in a way that accounts for our intuitive understanding of the sentences and their relation to other sentences.

These goals are achieved (to the degree that they are achieved at all) by means of a system of rules. In order to guarantee that the system of rules will even approach the two goals, the system of rules must conform to a variety of different restraints. As there are different kinds of restraints, there are different kinds of rules conforming to those restraints. Each of the different rule types has a very definite area of the grammar as its province. Accordingly, this book is organized according to the different types of rules and their provinces. Part I deals with simple phrase structure rules; Part II, with transformational rules that apply to single sentences; and Part III with the transformational rules that join two or more deep structures together to form a single surface sentence.

PART I

Phrase Structure Rules

OVERVIEW

The basic idea of transformational grammar is that all grammatical sentences (surface structures) of English are derived from a set of elementary sentences (deep structures). The phrase structure rules produce the set of elementary sentences. The first phrase structure rule is written this way:

$$S \longrightarrow NP \frown Aux \frown VP$$

The *S* means the class of all elementary sentences in English. The arrow means that this class "may be rewritten as" or "consists of the following subclasses in this order." The *NP* means Noun Phrase, the *Aux* means Auxiliary, and the *VP* means Verb Phrase. The $\frown$ means "joined together in this order." The first rule means that all elementary sentences in English (S) are made up of a Noun Phrase, an Auxiliary, and a Verb Phrase (and in that order). Put another way, to show that an elementary sentence is a well-formed English sentence, we must be able to trace its component parts back to a Noun Phrase, an Auxiliary, and a Verb Phrase. It is important to understand that NP, Aux, and VP are themselves symbols for a class of abstractions. These classes will be broken down into their component classes until actual words are reached. In Part I there are three chapters, one for each of the three abstract classes produced by the first phrase structure rule: the Noun Phrase, the Auxiliary, and the Verb Phrase.

The Noun Phrase (Chapter 1)

There are several different roles that noun phrases play: subject, direct object, indirect object, and object of a preposition. Chapter 1 deals with the internal structure of all noun phrases, no matter what their role in the elementary sentence is. All noun phrases, for example, contain a noun and are either singular or plural in number. In addition, some types of noun phrases have articles (*a, the*), while other types, first and second person pronouns, for example, do not normally take articles.

The Auxiliary (Chapter 2)

The Auxiliary is a class symbol for the source of the past and present tense markers and for the three classes of "helping verbs" that can be used in front of the main verb: the modals (*will, can, etc.*), the perfect "tense" *have*, and the progressive "tense" *be*.

The Verb Phrase (Chapter 3)

The verb phrase consists of three main elements: the main verb, the complement, and the adverbial. The first element, the main verb, is self-explanatory. The complement is the source for whatever noun phrases, adjectives, prepositions, or adverbials are necessary to make a complete, grammatical sentence. The third element, the adverbial, is the source for optional adverbials of time, place, and manner. By definition, the grammaticality of sentences is not affected by the addition or deletion of adverbials derived from this third element.

CHAPTER 1

The Noun Phrase

OVERVIEW

The noun phrase is broken down into three main types: (1) noun phrases containing a common noun, (2) noun phrases containing a proper noun, and (3) noun phrases containing a first or second person pronoun (*I, we, you*).

Noun phrases containing a common noun also contain articles and number. Articles are broken down into three subclasses: (1) specified, in which the article indicates that the identity of the common noun is known or can be established (*the boy*, for example); (2) unspecified, which indicates that the identity of the common noun is not known or is unimportant (*a boy*, for example); and (3) the null article Ø, which acts as a place marker for articles that do not appear on the surface (as in the noun phrase *boys*, for example).

The number in a noun phrase containing a common noun can be either singular or plural with one important class of exceptions. There are a large group of common nouns that can only be used in the singular. These nouns are often called *uncountable* or *mass* nouns.

Proper nouns differ from common nouns in that proper nouns do not have articles (the *the* that some proper nouns have is treated as part of the name itself and not as an article, as in the noun phrase *the Alps*) and do not have a choice of being either singular or plural (for example, we cannot make *the Alps* singular).

The first and second person pronouns have number, i.e., they can be either singular or plural, but they do not have articles. The third person pronouns are treated as substitutions for entire noun phrases. The selection of the correct third person singular pronoun (*he, she, it*) depends on the "gender" of the noun in the noun phrase.

The chapter also includes a discussion of the compatability (or co-occurrence) of subject nouns with certain verbs. This co-occurrence is described in terms of a set of inherent properties (or features) that all nouns have.

THE NOUN PHRASE (NP)

$$
NP \longrightarrow \begin{Bmatrix} Article \; Noun \; Number \\ Proper \; Noun \; \begin{Bmatrix} Singular \\ Plural \end{Bmatrix} \\ Person \; Pronoun \; Number \end{Bmatrix}
$$

$$
Article \; (Art) \longrightarrow \begin{Bmatrix} Specified \\ Unspecified \\ \emptyset \end{Bmatrix}
$$

$$
Specified \; (Spec) \longrightarrow \begin{Bmatrix} \textit{the, this, that, these, those}; \text{possessive} \\ \text{nouns and possessive pronouns; numbers} \end{Bmatrix}
$$

$$
Unspecified \; (Unspec) \longrightarrow \begin{Bmatrix} \textit{a/an, some, a few, a couple, several,} \\ \textit{much, many} \ldots \end{Bmatrix}
$$

$$
Noun \longrightarrow \{\textit{boy, tree, idea, elephant} \ldots\}
$$

$$
Proper \; Noun \; (Nprop) \longrightarrow \begin{Bmatrix} \textit{Mr. Brown, Mary, America, the Alps, the} \\ \textit{Colorado River, the Hawaiian Islands} \; .. \end{Bmatrix}
$$

$$
Number \; (No) \longrightarrow \begin{Bmatrix} Singular \\ Plural \end{Bmatrix}
$$

$$
Personal \; Pronoun \; (PPn) \longrightarrow \textit{I, you}
$$

Note: { } means "pick only one of the enclosed elements."
 . . . means that the list is not complete.

ARTICLE (Art)

In the analysis given here, the article is made up of three different and mutually exclusive subclasses: the specified article, the unspecified article, and the null (or zero) article.

The Specified Article (Spec)

The specified article consists of the definite article *the*, the four demonstrative pronouns *this, that, these,* and *those,* and all possessive nouns and possessive pronouns (*John's, the school's, my, our,* for example). All specified articles limit the meaning of the noun they modify to some specific or specified group. For example, when we use *the boy* or *the boys,* we make the assumption that the hearer or reader knows which particular *boy* or *boys* we are referring to, either directly or through context. Similarly, a possessive noun or possessive pronoun specifies the noun by identifying the owner; for example, *John's car, my car.*

The demonstrative pronouns specify which of several possible referents the speaker means. *This* and *these* indicate objects relatively closer to the speaker; *that* and *those* indicate objects relatively closer to the hearer (or relatively farther away from the speaker). This spatial distinction for physical objects is extended metaphorically for abstract nouns, for example, *this idea* and *that idea.*

The specification of nouns in terms of their physical location relative to the speaker and hearer is quite common throughout the languages of the world; some languages even make such specification obligatory for every concrete noun. English, of course, does not go that far, but the same distinction pops up in some verbs; for example *go* and *take* imply motion away from the point of reference, while *come* and *bring* imply motion toward the point of reference:

Go!
Go away and take your dog with you!

Come!
Come here and bring your hammer with you!

While the point of reference is typically the speaker, it can be the hearer, for example:

He will come to you asking for more money.
If all else fails you will then go to me for further instructions.

At one time English also made the same distinction in a pair of adverbs: *hither* "toward this place" and *thither* "toward that place."

Unspecified Articles (Unspec)

When we use a noun with an unspecified article, for example, *a boy,* we imply that it is not important that the hearer know exactly which particular boy we are referring to. The unspecified article does not necessarily mean that we could not identify which boy we had in mind; it only means that his identity is not relevant to what we want to say about him at the moment.

With the exceptions of *a/an* and *much,* the unspecified articles are used with plural nouns; for example,

many rugs
a few elephants
several houses

A/an, often called the indefinite article, is used only with singular nouns because it comes from the number *one* (as you might guess from the form *an*). *Much* is used only with a special group of nouns that can be used only in singular. This group of nouns, called uncountable or mass nouns, is discussed in the section on number.

The Null Article (Ø)

The concept of a null article is borrowed from mathematical logic. Perhaps the best way to think of it is as a place marker. In mathematics the null is zero (*0*). The difference between the number *1* and the number *10* is a zero. In this case zero is a very real part of the number. It is a place marker, indicating that the number consists of two digits. In exactly the same way, the null article Ø is a place marker, indicating the position of the article within the noun phrase. The null article often has a special meaning. Compare the italicized noun phrases in the following pairs of sentences:

He loved *many books*.
He loved *Ø books*.
Some cigarettes are in the desk.
Ø cigarettes cause cancer.
The candy is delicious.
Ø candy is hard on your teeth.

These nouns with null articles seem to be generalizations about the whole class of objects the nouns refer to, generalization about all books, all cigarettes, and all candy. Just to give this use of nouns a name, let us call it the "generic" use.

NOUN

In the Introduction (p. 8) there is a lengthy discussion about how we recognize part of speech classes, using nouns as a specific case in point. If that discussion is not fresh in your mind, it would probably be worthwhile to review it at this point.

As you have probably guessed, the *Noun* symbol that occurs in the phrase structure rule with *Article* on one side and *Number* on the other side really stands for common noun. To say the same thing in a different way, in this book a common noun is a noun that takes an article and (usually) can be either singular or plural. As we will see below, proper nouns (usually) do not have articles and the ability to be either singular or plural. The distinction between common and proper nouns, though real, is a technical and limited one. In this book, we will use the word *noun* to mean all nouns, whether common or proper. If it is necessary to specify which type of noun we are talking about, we will use the term *common noun* or *proper noun*. For our purposes, the defining characteristic of common nouns is that they can be freely used with articles and with either the singular or plural number.

Number

When we use a common noun, we must attach number to it. In English we have two numbers: singular and plural (meaning two or more). Some languages have more than two numbers; even English used to have three numbers for the personal pronouns—singular, dual, plural (that is, three or more).

The singular ending in English is not overtly marked. In linguistic terminology, it is null ($\emptyset$). The plural marker in English takes various forms. The most common is spelled either *-s* or *-es*, as in *day:days; picnic:picnics; box:boxes*. Since this *-s/-es* ending is by far the most common ending for the plural, it is considered to be the regular ending. English also has a number of less common (and therefore "irregular") plural endings. Almost all of these endings come from one of two sources: (1) borrowed foreign words that have kept their foreign plurals; for example, *one analysis—two analyses; one phenomenon—two phenomena*; or (2) historical survivals of older ways of making the plural; for example:

one foot—two feet
one tooth—two teeth
one mouse—two mice
one child—two children
one man—two men
one woman—two women
one ox—two oxen

There was a small group of nouns in Old English that made their plural without any change in the form of the word. Some modern survivals of that group are

one deer—two deer
one fish—two fish
one sheep—two sheep

In Modern English the names of most fish form their plurals this way:

one tuna—two tuna
one bonito—two bonito
one perch—two perch
one angelfish—two angelfish

Oddly enough, most other marine creatures form their plurals in the regular way:

one whale—two whales
one crab—two crabs
one eel—two eels
one shrimp—two shrimps

Even apparent exceptions to this generalization,

one guppy—two guppies
one shark—two sharks

turn out to follow the generalization, because guppies and sharks are not true fish (guppies are live-bearers and sharks do not have skeletons—true fish lay eggs and have skeletons). The use of plurals conforms amazingly to the technical biological definition of fish.

So far we have been talking about the singular and plural endings as though we always had the liberty of choosing the number of common nouns. Usually, of course, we do have that liberty. However, there are some common nouns that can be used only in the singular or only in the plural. The first examples that might occur to you are the small number of common nouns that must be used in the plural: *scissors, pants, trousers, pliers, tweezers,* and so forth.

A much larger and more important group, however, are the common nouns that cannot be used in the plural. The peculiarity of this group of common nouns can be shown by comparing two common nouns that mean nearly the same thing: *assignment* and *homework*.

> I just got a new assignment.
> *I just got a new homework.[1]
> Do you have many assignments?
> *Do you have many homeworks?
> The teacher gave them one assignment for the whole month.
> *The teacher gave them one homework for the whole month.
> The class was given two assignments.
> *The class was given two homeworks.

Homework belongs to a group of common nouns that cannot be used in the plural. A more accurate way of describing this group of nouns is to say that they cannot be counted; that is, we cannot say *one homework–two homeworks.* Since the article *a* historically means "one," we cannot say *a homework* either. There are many kinds of things that by their very nature cannot be counted: the names of gases and liquids (*one air–*two airs; *one oxygen–*two oxygens*), things that occur in particles (*one dust–*two dusts; *one sand–*two sands*), things that occur as groups (*one wreckage–*two wreckages; *one junk–*two junks*), the names of raw materials (*one zinc–*two zincs*), and certain kinds of abstractions (*one fun–*two funs*).

Words like *homework* are often called *uncountable* or *mass* nouns. In a very real sense, these common nouns do not have any number at all. However, since they are used with a third person singular form of the verb, they are usually treated as being singular. Thus, we can divide common nouns into two mutually exclusive feature groups: *countable nouns/uncountable nouns.* Countable nouns occur with number; that is, they can be either singular or plural. Uncountable nouns have the form of the singular without being singular in meaning.

Feature systems like these are often graphically represented as a kind of upside-down tree:

---

[1]The asterisk * is used to denote that what follows is an ungrammatical expression.

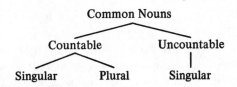

· The difference between *countable* and *uncountable* is inherent within the common noun; that is, some nouns are *countable* and some are *uncountable*, and you just have to know which is which. The choice between *singular* and *plural*, however, is not inherent within the *countable* noun. Each time we use a countable noun we must decide whether to make it *singular* or *plural*, depending on the situation.

The distinction between countable and uncountable nouns is valid enough, but there are two more wrinkles to be straightened out. Some nouns can be either countable or uncountable (with a change in meaning). Here are some fairly clear-cut examples with the uncountable use first:

Tea is something to drink, but *a tea* is a party.
Youth is the state of being young, but *a youth* is a young man.
Iron is an ore, but *an iron* is for pressing clothes.
Lamb is meat, but *a lamb* is a baby sheep.
Room is space, but *a room* is part of a house.
Glass is a material, but *a glass* is something to drink out of.

The second wrinkle is a special use of -*s* with uncountable nouns to mean something completely different from "plural." Most people would interpret the -*s* in the following words to mean not "more than one" but "different kinds of":

A turf specialist knows a lot about *grasses*.
The company produces dozens of *inks*.
They export *fruits* mostly to canneries.
The supermarket carries *soups* I have never even heard of.

Here are some sample phrase structure trees for noun phrases:

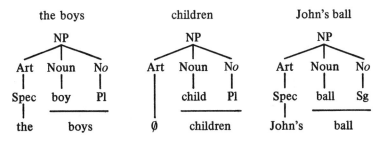

The first set of branches indicates that the class of noun phrase consists of three subclasses in a fixed order. These subclasses (Art, Noun, No) are called "nodes." Each of the three nodes is broken down into its subclasses until we reach the level of actual words. The phrase structure tree is a record of which choices were made among the options allowable in the grammar. In the derivation of a particular sentence, you know both your point of origin (the abstract class "sentence") and your destination (the actual sentence that you are trying to produce).

In the example given above, we are working with a part of a sentence, but the principle is the same. We are given a sequence of words that we intuitively recognize to be an instance of an abstract class we call a "noun phrase." Our task is to show exactly how this abstract class is embodied in this particular string of words in a way that will reveal both the relations of the whole to the parts (the noun phrase to each of the words), and the relation of the parts to each other. The net result is that we have an explicit statement that (hopefully) mirrors our intuitive understanding of the words in question and gives us a way of comparing this particular string of words with other strings of words so that we can make explicit the ways in which we feel the two strings to be similar and dissimilar.

The horizontal line drawn under the Noun and N*o* nodes indicates the operation of a set of rules that converts terminal elements into their proper form. For instance, this set of rules converts the plural node after *boy* to -*s*, but converts the Pl after *child* to -*ren*. These same rules would also govern the pronunciation of the surface forms. For example, the rules would indicate that *child* when followed by a singular node is pronounced with a long *i*, but when followed by a plural node is pronounced with a short *i*. We will assume the proper operation of these rules without comment.

EXERCISE 1.1   **Phrase Structure Trees for Common Nouns**[1]

Draw phrase structure trees for the following noun phrases:
1. two questions
2. an orange
3. these ideas
4. some sand
5. his uncle
6. glass
7. many glasses
8. the sheep (singular)
9. the sheep (plural)
10. several women

Proper Noun

Proper nouns are often defined as being the names of persons or places. Although it is true that all proper nouns are the names of persons or places, the definition can be misleading because it does not really define what *name* means. For example, in the following sentence,

The nurse came into the ward and turned white.

---

[1] Answers to exercises may be found at the end of each chapter.

is the word *nurse* a common noun or a proper noun? You could argue that *nurse* is a proper noun because it is the name of the particular person responsible for the patients in that particular ward. However, this argument is false because *nurse* is the name of a *class* of people, not the name of an individual member of the class, as in the following sentence:

Ms. Thwackum came into the ward and turned white.

From the standpoint of formal grammar, *nurse* is not a proper noun in the sentence above because it meets all the formal conditions for a common noun; it has an article in front of it and it could be made plural without changing the basic meaning of the rest of the sentence:

The nurses came into the ward and turned white.

Moreover, we can use other articles with the same noun:

A nurse came into the ward and turned white.
Some nurses came into the ward and turned white.

From a formal standpoint, proper nouns are really frozen noun phrases: they can take only the article *the*, and usually not even that; and they have a fixed number. The names of people or places are singular, while the names of mountain ranges and island chains are always plural. Since we have no freedom of choice in picking an article to go with a proper noun, the phrase structure rules do not show Proper Noun occurring with Article, because if it did, it would mean that proper nouns have the same freedom of usage with articles as common nouns have. For this reason, when a proper noun like *the Alps* has the article *the*, the *the* (if you are still with me) is treated as part of the proper noun itself and is not derived from the Article node. Here are some sample derivations of noun phrases containing proper nouns:

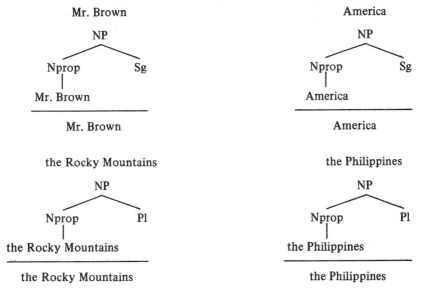

Now that we have made the difference between common and proper nouns perfectly clear, there is only one problem left: sometimes proper nouns can be used as common nouns. Here are some examples:

The Fred that I know lives in Chicago.
Several Bill Smiths answered your ad.
I met a John Brown yesterday too.

Admittedly these sentences require special circumstances, but within context they are perfectly grammatical. The *Freds, Bill Smiths,* and *John Browns* in the example sentences are names for classes of people having these names instead of individuals uniquely identified by their names as they usually are.

EXERCISE 1.2   **Common Nouns and Proper Nouns**

Draw phrase structure trees for the following noun phrases:
1. several answers
2. many people
3. Ralph
4. some leaves
5. the Panama Canal
6. two trout
7. the bank
8. the First National Bank
9. the judge
10. the jet set

The Co-occurrence of Nouns with Verbs

The semantic ties that bind the subject noun and the main verb together are very strong: *birds sing, fish swim, batters bat, pitchers pitch, catchers catch.* We know from our experience in the world that certain nouns "go" with certain verbs. It is possible to reflect in the grammar some of the more general semantic ties between nouns and verbs by use of features of co-occurrence. Compare the following noun phrases:

The idea surprised me.
The rock fell off the table.
The celery was flourishing.
The dog sneezed.
The girl wrote out a check.

Some verbs can co-occur with any subject noun. *Surprise,* for example, can be used with all five nouns:

The idea
The rock
The celery ⎬ surprised me.
The dog
The girl

Notice, however, that when we try to use all five nouns as subjects for the second sentence, *idea* is not an acceptable subject:

*The idea
The rock
The celery ⟩ fell off the table.
The dog
The girl

With the third sentence, *idea* and *rock* are not acceptable subjects:

*The idea
*The rock
The celery ⟩ was flourishing.
The dog
The girl

With the fourth sentence, *idea, rock,* and *celery* are not acceptable:

*The idea
*The rock
*The celery ⟩ sneezed.
The dog
The girl

Finally, with the last sentence, only *girl* is an acceptable subject:

*The idea
*The rock
*The celery ⟩ wrote out a check.
*The dog
The girl

These facts suggest that as far as the co-occurrence of subject and object nouns with verbs is concerned, there is a kind of hierarchy of noun features:

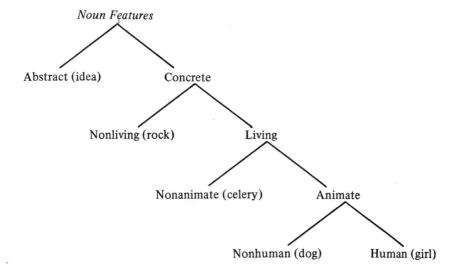

The great advantage to this type of hierarchy is that it can clearly show the similarities as well as the differences between any two nouns. For example, *girl* and *dog* differ in that *girl* is human and *dog* is nonhuman. However, they share all the other features in the hierarchy; that is, they are both animate, living, and concrete. Therefore, we can predict that despite their differences at the lowest level of the hierarchy, *girl* and *dog* will both be acceptable subjects for a verb like *fall* (*off*), which requires only that the subject be a concrete (as opposed to an abstract) noun. To take a new example, the verb *breathe* requires an animate subject, but it can co-occur with either a human or nonhuman animate noun.

What happens when a subject noun and verb do not co-occur? Is the sentence then ungrammatical? When this happens, we are aware that the sentence is not acceptable in any literal interpretation. What we usually do is make the sentence grammatical and acceptable by giving it a metaphorical interpretation. For example, we know that the following sentence is not true in any literal sense:

The idea breathed new life into them.

However, it is not ungrammatical nor meaningless. We interpret the sentence by giving the noun *idea* the property of an animate noun—we even have a special name for this: personification. This type of violation of the normal co-occurrence relations is very common, but it is meaningful only because we know what the correct co-occurrence relations are supposed to be. If we did not know the correct relations, the whole effect of deliberately violating them would be lost.

EXERCISE 1.3   **Noun Features**

Using the same five noun phrases (*the idea, the rock, the celery, the dog, the girl*), indicate for each noun phrase whether or not it is an acceptable subject for the following sentences (no fair pretending you are watching a science fiction movie):

1. _____ was drowned in the river.
2. _____ was just what we wanted.
3. _____ was badly hurt in the accident.
4. _____ could tap dance while whistling "Dixie."
5. _____ has grown quite a bit.
6. _____ is still in the car.
7. _____ was diseased.
8. _____ has mass and occupies space.
9. _____ answered the questions carefully.
10. _____ was quite an improvement over the first one.

Personal Pronoun

The following chart gives the subject forms for the personal pronouns *I* and *you*:

	1st person	2nd person
Singular	I	you
Plural	we	

The *I—you* relationship is defined automatically: *I* means the speaker, *you* means the hearer. *We* is the plural form of *I*. It does not mean that two or more people are talking in chorus. It means that the speaker is speaking not just for himself as an individual, but as the spokesman for some group of people. Similarly, *you* can mean not just a single listener, but the group that the listener represents.

One of the oddities about the English pronoun system is that the distinction between the singular and plural forms of the second person has been lost: both are *you*. Historically, there were two different second person pronouns, one for the singular and one for the plural. However, in the thirteenth century, a completely different use of the second person pronouns became established. The singular forms were used in addressing children or persons of inferior rank, while the plural forms were used as a mark of respect in talking to a superior. By the sixteenth century it was considered impolite or even insulting to address anyone with the singular forms, so these forms simply dropped out of the language and everyone used the plural on all occasions.

The third person pronouns (*he, she, it, they*) are completely different from the first and second person pronouns because the third person pronouns are *substitutes* for whole noun phrases. For example, in the sentence

The boy hit the ball.

we can substitute the appropriate third person pronouns for the two noun phrases:

He hit *it*.

The first and second person pronouns are not substitutes for anything else but are noun phrases in their own right, as in the sentence

I hit *you*.

For this reason, our grammar treats the first and second person pronouns as part of the basic noun phrase, while third person pronouns must be derived by a rule that substitutes them for a noun phrase. Here is a chart for the subject forms of the third person pronouns:

	3rd person		
Singular	he	she	it
Plural	they		

The third person pronouns differ from first and second person pronouns in another important respect: they have a three-way distinction based on the "gender" of the noun in the noun phrase that the third person pronoun is a substitute for. Nouns that can be replaced by *he* are said to be "masculine," nouns that can be replaced by *she* are "feminine," and nouns that can be replaced by *it* are "neuter." These terms are as good as any, but they do give rise to a serious confusion when they are applied to certain European languages. In some European languages the nouns have several different sets of endings. In order to put the correct ending on the noun and on the adjective and articles that modify the noun, the speaker must know which set of endings the noun takes. Usually there is no particular pattern to which nouns go with which set of endings; consequently, a person learning the language must simply memorize the ending along with the noun. Unfortunately, these endings are also termed "genders." In some languages there are two genders (French, for example) and in other languages there are three (German, for example). Consequently, there are two completely different meanings of the term *gender*: (1) the English use, in which gender is based on the sex (or lack thereof) of the object the noun refers to, and (2) the use in certain European languages, in which gender means a particular set of endings attached to nouns and to words that modify nouns, but which have no necessary connection with the sex of the thing referred to.

In the English use of gender, an object that is not animate is automatically neuter and replaced by the pronoun *it*. Also, animate nouns, if the speaker does not know (or does not care) whether the creature is a male or female, are sometimes replaced with *it* (even though mothers of small children have been known to become quite angry when asked, "What is its name?").

Many animate nouns have a built-in gender. *Bull* is masculine, *cow* is feminine, *waiter* is masculine, *waitress* is feminine. *John* is a boy's name, *Mary* is a girl's name. When we do not use the first name, the use of the titles *Mr., Miss, Mrs.*, and *Ms.* tells the gender of the person. However, many animate nouns do not specify gender, for example *cook, teacher, student*. In a fine display of male chauvinism, the English language treats these unspecified animate nouns as masculine; that is, if we are forced to use a third person pronoun to replace a human noun when we do not know (or care about) the gender of the person referred to, we usually use *he*.[1] Here are some example phrase structure trees showing the replacement of a noun phrase by a third person pronoun:

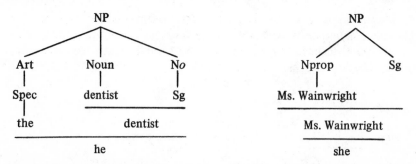

---

[1] This practice has come under increasing attack, since the change in women's status has focused attention on the usage as seeming to deprive women of equal status. As a result, many people now try to avoid this generic *he* by using the plural or some other rephrasing.

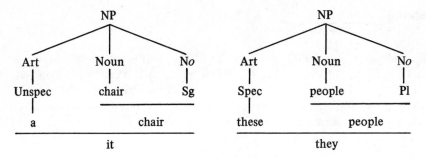

Suppose you heard this sentence out of context:

She has answered it.

We do not know what person (or creature) *she* is a substitute for, nor do we know what the *it* has replaced—telephone, letter, question, or the call to dinner. However, we do know that *she* has replaced a feminine-gender animate noun and that *it* has replaced an inanimate noun. We can envision third person pronoun substitution in terms of a feature tree:

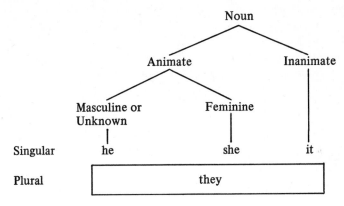

Since the grammar can never tell us what we do not already know (either consciously or unconsciously), we are not able to draw a phrase structure tree for a complete noun phrase when we do not know what was in the noun phrase. In the example sentence above, we do not know what noun phrases *she* and *it* have replaced. Therefore, our phrase structure tree can only reflect what we do know, namely, that *she* has replaced a singular, feminine, animate noun, and that *it* has replaced a singular inanimate noun. Let us agree to represent *she* (when we do not know what actual noun phrase it is replacing) in the following way:

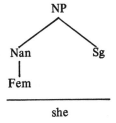

where *Nan* = /animate noun
   Fem = feminine gender

We know even less about *they*. *They* is the replacement for a noun phrase with plural number, but we do not know whether the noun is animate or inanimate. However, we do know that the noun phrase does not contain the first or second person pronoun because it is impossible to substitute a third person pronoun for a first or second person pronoun; for example, we know that

They know John.

is not a substitute for

We know John.

Let us agree, then, to represent *they* when we do not know what *they* stands for in the following way:

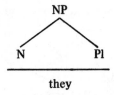

where *N* = either a common noun (with its article) or a proper noun.

As with the co-occurrence restrictions between nouns and verbs, pronoun restrictions can be violated. The most common instance of using an apparently incorrect replacement of a pronoun for a noun is the use of *she* for nouns that would normally be replaced by *it*. This is usually done as a mark of affection or familiarity. For example,

The *ship* will be recommissioned, and then *she* will be reassigned.
Our *Country*, right or wrong, but may *she* always be right!
She's a grand old *flag*, *she's* a high flying *flag*.

EXERCISE 1.4   *He* and *It*

Now that you have seen how we will represent *she* and *they* when we do not know what they stand for, how do you think we should represent *he* and *it*?

Pronoun Case

Another type of feature needs to be mentioned for pronouns. We have seen that the proper substitution of a third person pronoun for a noun phrase depends entirely on the intrinsic gender feature of the noun and upon the number. There is another kind of feature that is not intrinsic to the noun: case. The

English pronoun system changes the form of the personal pronouns according to the function the pronoun plays within the particular sentence. For example, in the surface sentences

I saw him.
He saw me.

I and *He* are in the "subject" case, *me* and *him* are in the "object" case. Pronoun case depends on the pronoun's function in the surface structure of the sentence, not the deep structure. A clear illustration of this is in the passive transformation. When the active sentence

I saw him.

is transformed into the passive

He was seen by me.

the subject in the deep structure ends up in the object case on the surface, and the object in the deep structure ends up in the subject case. Since the determination of the case of a pronoun seems to be a feature of surface structure, all pronouns in the deep structure are written in the subject case form.

We will conclude with a few general remarks about noun features. There are several different ways by which the features are determined. Some features are built into the noun; that is, when we pick the noun the features come along as a package deal. *Brick*, for example, is inherently common (as opposed to proper); countable (*as opposed to uncountable*); concrete (as opposed to abstract); and inanimate (as opposed to animate). Two other features, however, are not part of the package. We can make the word singular or plural at our pleasure; that is, number is not inherent in most countable nouns. The other feature that is not inherent in the noun is case. If we substitute a pronoun for *bricks*, the case of the pronoun (*they* or *them*) is not inherent in the noun, nor is it a matter of our free choice. Instead, the choice of case is entirely dictated by the grammar of the surface sentence.

EXERCISE 1.5   **Review**

Draw phrase structure trees for the following noun phrases:
1. she
2. the Isle of Man
3. seventy-six trombones
4. many people
5. we
6. it (where *it* means *the airplane*)
7. homework
8. Inspector Dover
9. a coke
10. them

Answers to Exercise 1.1   PHRASE STRUCTURE TREES FOR COMMON NOUNS

1.   two questions

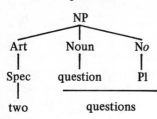

2.   an orange

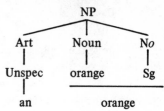

3.   these ideas

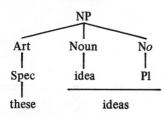

4.   some sand

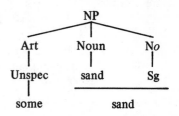

5.   his uncle

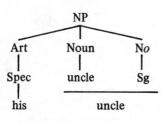

6.   glass

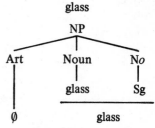

7.   many glasses

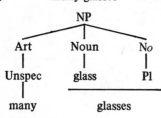

8.   the sheep (sg)

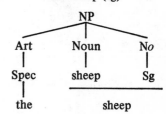

9.   the sheep (pl)

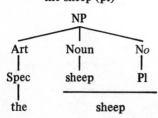

10.   several women

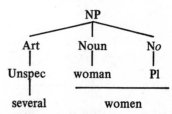

Answers to Exercise 1.2   COMMON NOUNS AND PROPER NOUNS

1.   · several answers

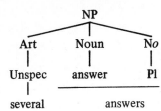

2.   many people

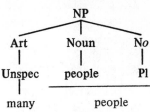

3.   Ralph

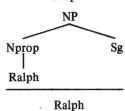

4.   some leaves

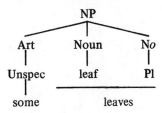

5.   the Panama Canal

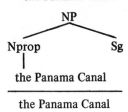

6.   two trout

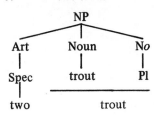

7.   the bank

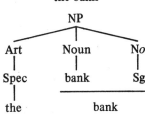

8.   the First National Bank

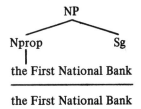

9.   the judge

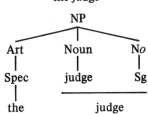

10.   the jet set

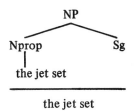

Answers to Exercise 1.3 NOUN FEATURES

1. *The idea
   *The rock
   *The celery } was drowned in the river.
   The dog
   The girl

2. The idea
   The rock
   The celery } was just what we wanted.
   The dog
   The girl

3. *The idea
   *The rock
   *The celery } was badly hurt in the accident.
   The dog
   The girl

4. *The idea
   *The rock
   *The celery } could tap dance while whistling "Dixie."
   *The dog
   The girl

5. *The idea } (acceptable as a metaphor)
   *The rock
   The celery } has grown quite a bit.
   The dog
   The girl

6. *The idea
   The rock
   The celery } is still in the car.
   The dog
   The girl

7. *The idea
   *The rock
   The celery } was diseased.
   The dog
   The girl

8. *The idea
   The rock
   The celery } has mass and occupies space.
   The dog
   The girl

9. *The idea
   *The rock
   *The celery ⟩ answered the questions carefully.
   *The dog
   The girl

10. The idea
    The rock
    The celery ⟩ was quite an improvement over the first one.
    The dog
    The girl

Answers to Exercise 1.4 *HE* AND *IT*

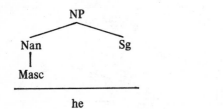

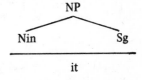

where *Masc* = masculine noun
      Nin = inanimate noun

Answers to Exercise 1.5 REVIEW

1.

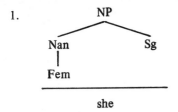

2.

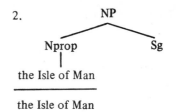

3.

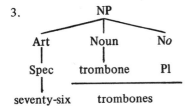

4.

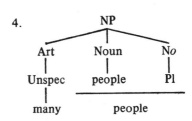

5.
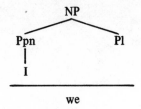

```
        NP
       /    \
    Ppn      Pl
     |
     I
   _____
       we
```

6.
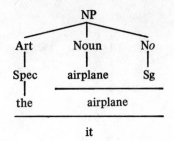

```
              NP
        /      |      \
     Art     Noun      No
      |        |        |
    Spec    airplane    Sg
      |    _____
     the        airplane
              _____
                  it
```

7.
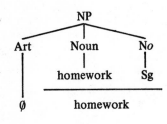

```
           NP
      /     |     \
   Art    Noun     No
    |       |       |
         homework   Sg
    |    _____
    Ø      homework
```

8.
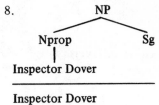

```
              NP
          /        \
      Nprop         Sg
        |
  Inspector Dover
  _____
  Inspector Dover
```

9.
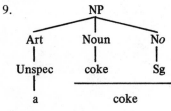

```
           NP
      /     |     \
   Art    Noun     No
    |       |       |
  Unspec   coke     Sg
    |    _____
    a        coke
```

10.
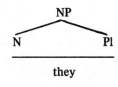

```
        NP
      /    \
    N       Pl
   _____
       they
```

CHAPTER 2

The Auxiliary

OVERVIEW

In somewhat simplistic terms, the auxiliary is everything in the underlying sentence from the end of the subject noun phrase to the beginning of the main verb. The auxiliary is composed of tense, either present or past, as well as various kinds of "helping" verbs, which may or may not be present in any particular sentence. This grammar deals first with tense, and then with three types of "helping" verbs: modal auxiliaries, the perfect, and the progressive.

Tense

In this grammar (as in most transformational grammars), the meaning of tense is restricted to the present and past inflectional endings. Tense does *not* mean time. Every language can make the distinction between past, present, and future time, but there is no obligation for the distinction to be carried solely by the inflection of the verb. Many Asian languages have no verb inflection at all. They convey time relations by adverbs. Some European languages make subtle time distinctions in the verb inflection (Latin, for example). English and the other Germanic languages are mixed: they have a few verb inflections that partially correlate with time, but also rely on adverbs to express time relations.

In the deep structure sentence, tense is generated as the leftmost element of the auxiliary. Although at first this placement seems odd, it actually captures an important generalization. The tense marker (the past or present inflectional ending) is always carried by the leftmost verb, no matter what that verb is. If there are no "helping" verbs, the tense is attached to the main verb, because that is the leftmost verb; for example, *John laughed*. However, if there are any "helping" verbs in the sentence, the main verb is no longer the leftmost verb, and consequently does not carry the tense marker. For example, if we add the modal verb *may* to the sentence above, the past tense marker will attach to *may*, not *laugh*, producing *John might laugh*.

Since the tense is generated to the left of whatever verb it will eventually be attached to, we must have some way of moving the tense marker from the left side of the verb to the right side of the verb so that it may be attached as a suffix. As you have already learned, rules that switch the order of two elements are called transformational rules. This particular transformational rule is used so often that it has a special nickname: the flip-flop rule. One of the striking things about the transformational treatment of the auxiliary is that different parts of the auxiliary seem to require the same basic flip-flop rule.

Modal Auxiliaries

In this grammar, the modal auxiliaries are nine "helping" verbs (often called modals) that can occur in front of the perfect: *can, may, must, shall,* and *will* in the present tense, *could, might, should,* and *would* in the past tense. One of the most difficult points in understanding the modals is what the past tense means with them. Obviously, in a sentence like

It might rain tomorrow.

might is past tense in form but not past in time.

Perfect

The important thing to remember about the transformational treatment of the perfect is that the perfect really consists of two parts: the verb *have* and the past participle marker which is attached to the following verb by a flip-flop rule. In this grammar we use *-en* as the symbol for the past participle marker, even though in most cases the past participle form of the verb is the same as the simple past.

Progressive

The progressive also consists of two parts: the "helping" verb *be* and the present participle marker *-ing*, which is attached to the following verb by a flip-flop rule. An important point that follows the discussion of the progressive is the distinction between "active" and "stative" verbs. In a sentence containing an active verb, we may think of the subject as performing some action. In a sentence containing a stative verb, the verb describes or defines the subject, rather than the subject's doing something.

There are two important formal differences between active and stative verbs: (1) active verbs can be used in the progressive, while stative verbs cannot—for example, *I am looking at you* (active verb) versus **I am seeing you* (stative verb)—and (2) active verbs cannot normally be used in the simple present tense, while stative verbs can—for example, **I look at you* (active verb) versus *I see you* (stative verb).

THE AUXILIARY

Auxiliary (Aux) ⟶ Tense (Modal) (Perfect) (Progressive)

Tense ⟶ $\begin{Bmatrix} \text{present} \\ \text{past} \end{Bmatrix}$

Modal ⟶ *can, may, must, shall, will*

Perfect ⟶ *have* -EN

Progressive ⟶ *be* -ING

The second element in the deep structure of sentences is the auxiliary. The auxiliary is the source for the past and present tense markers and for all the "helping verbs" that can be put in front of the main verb. We will use the term *verb* in the same general way as we used the term *noun*. For our purposes, *verb* means any word that can have a tense marker attached to it. The term thus includes both "helping verbs" and main verbs.

The auxiliary is made up of four components: the first obligatory, and the next three optional. The obligatory element is called "tense." Since this word means different things to different people, the sense in which it is being used here needs to be clarified. For the purposes of this grammar, tense means the present and the past inflectional ending of verbs.

Present Tense

The present tense ending takes two forms: one form is written as *-s* or *-es*. This form is used when the subject noun phrase can be replaced by a third person singular pronoun; for example,

John sings.
He does.
Mary usually washes the dishes.

The other form of the present tense ending is null ($\emptyset$). This form of the ending is used when the subject noun phrase cannot be replaced by the third person singular, for example,

They sing$\emptyset$.
I do$\emptyset$.
The girls usually wash$\emptyset$ the dishes.

When we try to capture these generalizations about the form of the present tense in a phrase structure rule, we encounter some difficulties. The phrase structure rules that we have used so far are basically a set of instructions to rewrite one thing as something else. If we try such a rule for present tense, i.e.,

$$\text{Pres} \longrightarrow \left\{ \begin{matrix} \text{-}s/\text{-}es \\ \emptyset \end{matrix} \right\}$$

the results are ungrammatical. This rule will produce such sentences as *John sing, *I does,* and *Mary usually wash the dishes* because the rule does not make any connection between the subject noun phrase and the form of the present tense ending. The rule the way we have written it is an *unconditional* rule; that is, it allows us to rewrite present tense as either *-s/-es* or $\emptyset$ without any consideration of the subject noun phrase. We need a *conditional* rule that will rewrite present tense as *-s/-es* under certain conditions and $\emptyset$ under other conditions. We use conditional rules all the time. We take an umbrella only if we think it might rain; otherwise, we do not bother. On the form we use for figuring our taxes, Internal Revenue Service Form 1040, line 23 says "If line 20 is larger than line 22, enter balance due," while line 24 says "If line 22 is larger than line 20, enter amount overpaid."

Basically, conditional rules are *if* rules. If this happens, then do one thing, but if that happens, then do another thing. It is easy to write conditional rules as *if* rules. If the number in the subject noun phrase is plural, we know that the present tense is rewritten as $\emptyset$; for example,

The windows rattle.
The Alps spread over several countries.
They watch TV all the time.

Now, how do we state this generalization in terms of a phrase structure rule? First we need to state the conditions for the rule's application, namely, that the subject noun phrase is plural and the tense is present. If that condition is met, then present is rewritten as $\emptyset$. Here is a simple way to write the rule (there are other ways that are just as good):

IF Pl Pres, THEN Pres $\longrightarrow$ $\emptyset$

Notice that we have not used the term "subject noun phrase" in the rule because by definition the subject noun phrase is always the first component in the deep structure of all sentences. Moreover, the number node for noun phrases is always the rightmost element within the noun phrase whereas the tense node is always the leftmost node within the auxiliary. Therefore, number and tense are always next to each other.

EXERCISE 2.1　**Present Tense with Singular Nouns**

Now that you know how to write conditional rules, see if you can write the conditional rules that are necessary for rewriting present tense with singular nouns. These rules are more complicated than the one above for plural subject nouns because you have to distinguish between those noun phrases that can be replaced by a third person pronoun and those noun phrases that contain a first or second person pronoun.

Past Tense

One of the characteristics of all Germanic languages (including English) is that they have two basically different ways of making the past tense. One way, which we think of as being the "regular" way because it is the most common in Modern English, is to add on a suffix spelled -ed; for example,

We walk*ed* to school yesterday.
He color*ed* the picture black.
They paint*ed* the house.

The other way, which we think of as being "irregular," is to mark the change from present tense to past tense by changing the vowel of the verb, for example,

come–came
dig–dug
find–found
run–ran
wring–wrung
drink–drank
see–saw
take–took

In Modern English the vowel changes look pretty chaotic. However, in Old English it is possible to see quite definite patterns in the kinds of vowel changes that took place. Some of these patterns have come into Modern English largely intact, for example, the *sing–sang–sung, drink–drank–drunk* pattern. This pattern can even be traced back into the prehistoric period before German, English, Latin, Greek, and Sanskrit appeared as separate languages.

There are a few groups of verbs that reflect survivals of the older patterns. One group is a hybrid: the past tense is formed with both a "regular" ending and a vowel change; for example,

flee–fled
hear–heard
sell–sold
tell–told

Another hybrid group adds *-t* instead of *-ed*; for example,

feel–felt
keep–kept
sleep–slept
think–thought

Still another group has a null (∅) form of the past tense; for example,

I cut∅ my finger yesterday.
He shed∅ some light on the subject.
Jones hit∅ the ball into left field.

Some more examples of this last group are

bet–bet
cost–cost
hurt–hurt
put–put
quit–quit
set–set
spread–spread

From the standpoint of the phrase structure rules, it is immaterial what actual form the present or past tense endings take. For our purposes we will assume that the actual form is always correctly selected. Thus, we can indicate the tense of verbs in the following way:

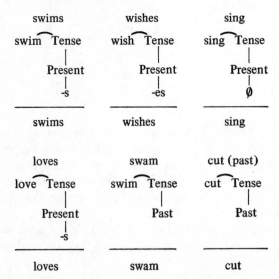

EXERCISE 2.2   **Tense**

Draw phrase structure trees to show the derivation of the following verbs:
1. thought
2. says
3. tore
4. answers
5. did
6. whisper
7. took
8. cost (present)
9. lend
10. went

The Flip-Flop Rule

The auxiliary rules generate tense as the first (and only obligatory) component of the auxiliary sequence. Below are two sentences generated with the minimal development of the auxiliary, that is, with just tense:

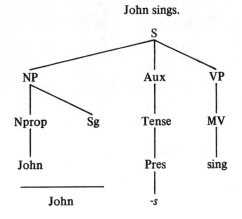

John sings.

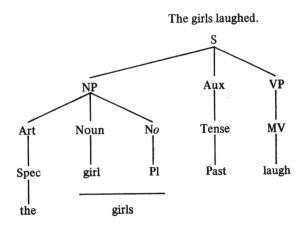

The girls laughed.

Notice that the tense is generated to the left of the main verb (MV). In order for the pieces to come out in the right order, the tense will have to be moved to the other side of the main verb by a transformational rule. This rule, known as the "flip-flop" rule, may be formulated this way:

Tense‿Verb $\Longrightarrow$ Verb‿Tense

[*Note:* Transformational rules are written with a double-shafted arrow.]

This rule changes *John‿-s‿sing* into *John‿sing‿-s* and *The‿girls‿Past‿laugh* into *The‿girls‿laugh‿Past* with tense correctly attached to the verb as a suffix.

At this point the reader has every right to object. Why is tense placed on the left side of the main verb? After all, tense is a suffix, not a prefix.

Despite this obvious objection, there is a good reason why tense has to be generated in front of the main verb. You recall that tense is an obligatory element in the auxiliary; that is, every sentence must contain tense, either present or past. The other three elements in the auxiliary are optional. A sentence can have any one of the three elements, any two of them, all three of them, or none of them. Here is a sentence that has just the past tense:

John cried.

Notice what happens when we add the progressive (one of the three optional elements):

John was crying.

The main verb *cry* has now changed from the past tense form to the present participle form. The verb that now carries the past tense is the auxiliary verb *be*. Next, notice what happens when we add another optional element, the perfect:

John had been crying.

The main verb is still a present participle, but the auxiliary verb *be* has changed from the past tense to the past participle form. The perfect auxiliary verb *have* now carries the past tense ending.

Finally, adding a modal auxiliary, the remaining optional element, we get the following sentence:

John might have been crying.

This time *had* has changed back to the uninflected form *have* and the past tense ending has shifted forward to the modal auxiliary *may*, changing it to *might*.

The generalization that holds for all four sample sentences is that tense is always attached to the *first* verb. The first verb may be any one of the three optional elements, or if none of the options are picked, the main verb. As far as the rules are concerned, it does not make any difference which, if any, of the options are exercised: tense is always attached to the first verb. The function of the flip-flop rule is only to attach the tense to whatever verb follows it.

We often talk about the past tense or present tense *form* of a verb; for example, *wish* and *wishes* are the present tense forms of the verb *wish*, while *wished* is its past tense form. There is nothing wrong with this terminology as long as we understand that the expressions "past tense form" or "present tense form" describe verbs after tense has already been attached. From the standpoint of how we combine words to make up grammatical sentences, the present and past tense markers do not "belong" to the verb. They are assigned to particular verbs by phrase structure rules. In other words, it is a matter of history what the shape or form of a verb is when we add the past tense or present tense marker to it, but it is a matter of grammar as to which verb gets the tense marker to begin with.

Since this is our first example of a transformational rule, it might be a good idea to think back to the differences between phrase structure rules and transformational rules. A phrase structure rule is basically a classifying rule. That is, it breaks an element down into the parts that make it up; for example, it breaks NP down into Art Noun No. A transformation rule does one of three things: it adds something, it deletes something, or it rearranges the order of the elements in the sentence. Obviously, the flip-flop rule does the last-mentioned. It re-arranges the order of the tense and the verb. There is another major difference which is not quite so obvious. Phrase structure rules can only apply to bottom-most nodes in a derivation. That is, once we have rewritten NP as Art Noun No, there is no way that the phrase structure rules can refer back to the original NP. However, a transformational rule can do exactly that. Instead of having to have two separate flip-flop rules, one for the present tense and one for the past tense, it refers back to the node *above* present and past. In other words, transformational rules have the ability to look back up into the phrase structure tree and see where things come from. As you can imagine, this gives the transformational rules great flexibility. Finally, notice that the flip-flop rule is not limited just to main verbs, but will apply to both main verbs and helping verbs.

Here is a sample derivation employing the flip-flop rule:

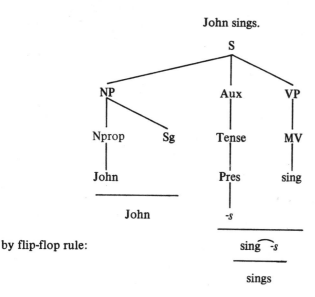

John sings.

In the convention used throughout this book, the transformation rules will be listed along the left margin in the order of their application. The actual result of the application of the rule will be shown on the same line as the name of the rule. Notice that a line has been drawn over the *sing -s*. This line is a way of indicating the part of the tree diagram that the transformational rule applies to. In other words, *-s sing* has been transformed to *sing -s* by the application of the flip-flop rule.

EXERCISE 2.3   Tense and Main Verb

Draw phrase structure trees and show the application of the flip-flop rule for the following sentences:
1. The girl laughed.
2. The doorbells rang.
3. My shoelace broke.
4. Some children cried.
5. John lisps.

MODAL AUXILIARIES

We will deal with five modal auxiliary verbs: *can, may, must, shall,* and *will*. All of these verbs are highly irregular in form. A "regular" verb has four distinct forms, for example, *walk, walks, walked, walking*, Many "irregular" verbs have five distinct forms, for example, *sing, sings, sang, sung, singing*. The verb *be* has the greatest number of distinct forms, eight: *be, am, are, is, was, were, been, being*. The modal auxiliary verbs, however, have only a two-way contrast of form:

Verb:	can	may	must	shall	will
Present:	can	may	must	shall	will
Past:	could	might	—	should	would

Notice that there is no contrast between the third person singular and the other present forms. That is, we do not add a third person singular *-s*: **he cans, *he mays, *he musts, *he shalls, *he wills*. Of course *can* and *will* can be used with a third person singular *-s*, but in a totally different meaning. For example,

He cans tuna.
He wills his entire estate to charity.

The fact that the modals have a ∅ instead of the expected *-s* for their present tense in the third person singular means that we must adjust the rules we have made about forming the present tense.

EXERCISE 2.4 **Present Tense with Modal Auxiliaries**

Using the format developed for Exercise 2.1, write a conditional phrase structure rule that produces the proper ending for present tense modals. Assume that this new rule will apply before all the other rules for present tense.

Past Tense with Modal Auxiliaries

The past tense of four of the modals are of the hybrid type that add an ending and also change the vowel. *Must* does not have any historical past tense. If it is necessary to convert a sentence containing *must* into the past, an entirely different verb must be used as a semantic substitute. For example,

Present: John *must* go home now.
Past: John *had* to go home then.

The past tense forms of the modals have a range of meaning beyond what past tense means with other verbs. Consequently, it is possible to use modal auxiliaries that are past tense in form but not in meaning. For example,

He *could* come back tomorrow.
It *might* rain tomorrow.
I *should* feel better tomorrow.
They *would* go tomorrow if they could.

The past tense of modals is a clear illustration of the need to separate form from meaning. The phrase structure rules generate an abstract element that is necessary to account for the proper form of verbs; the name of the element has no intrinsic significance. The element means various things depending (in this particular case) on the type of verb that it is attached to. Attached to modal auxiliaries the element means one thing; attached to most main verbs, the element means something else. The name "past tense" was picked for the element because it is suggestive of the most common use.

The difference (if any) between the present tense modals *will* and *shall* has been known to cause a certain amount of anxiety among native speakers. Historically, *will* and *shall* (like many other pairs of modals) have long had partially overlapping meanings. In 1653 a grammarian by the name of John Wallis decided to do something about the wishy-washy distinction between *will* and *shall*. In his book *Grammatica Linguae Anglicanae (Grammar of the English Language)* he proposed that the first person use of *shall* would mean a simple, factual statement about future action, while the first person use of *will* would mean "promising" or "threatening" some future action. However, in the second and third persons, the two meanings would be exactly reversed: *will* would mean simple futurity; *shall* would mean promising or threatening. As far as we know, Wallis's distinction was not a very accurate reflection of the then current usage of *will* and *shall*, and certainly it is not an accurate description of present-day usage. Nevertheless, Wallis's distinction was enshrined as a rule of the language by later grammarians, and has been used ever since to frighten children. For most speakers of American English (including this writer), *will* and *shall* mean exactly the same thing in statements. In questions, though, they do contrast. For example, compare these two questions:

Will we dance?
Shall we dance?

The first sentence is a genuine question that asks for information. The second sentence means something like "Let's dance." Here are two sample derivations involving modals.

She may laugh.

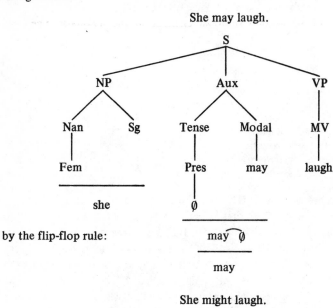

She might laugh.

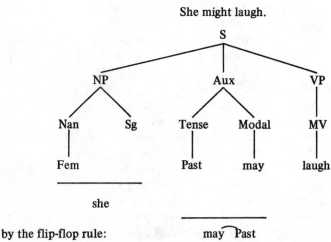

EXERCISE 2.5 **Tense and Modal Auxiliaries**

Draw phrase structure trees and apply the flip-flop rule for the following sentences:
1. The day will come.
2. She should resign.
3. Dogs can swim.
4. You (plural) must leave.
5. A dollar would help.

PERFECT

The *perfect* is the second optional element in the auxiliary. The perfect always consists of two pieces: the helping verb *have* plus the past participle marker, *-en*. Compare these two sentences:

I wrote a letter to my parents.
I *had* writt*en* a letter to my parents.

Notice that when the perfect is part of the auxiliary, the form of the verb after *have* is the past participle form. The *-en* was chosen as the symbol for the past participle ending because *-en* is the most common distinctive past participle marker; for example:

bite–bit–bitt*en*
break–broke–brok*en*
choose–chose–chos*en*
eat–ate–eat*en*
ride–rode–ridd*en*
shake–shook–shak*en*
steal–stole–stol*en*
write–wrote–writt*en*

The next most common way of marking a difference between the simple past and past participle is by a vowel change alone; for example:

begin–began–begun
drink–drank–drunk
sing–sang–sung
sink–sank–sunk

However, for many irregular verbs and for all regular verbs, the form of the past participle is identical with the form of the simple past; for example:

tell–told–told
leave–left–left
bleed–bled–bled
find–found–found

shoot–shot–shot
work–worked–worked
play–played–played
dance–danced–danced

The perfect, then, consists of *have* plus the fact that the following verb is always in the past participle form (even though most of the time the past participle form looks the same as the past). We have captured this generalization by writing the phrase structure rule for the perfect this way:

Perfect ⟶ have⌢-EN

Like tense, *-en* must be attached to the right-hand side of the verb that follows it. Consequently, we must invent another flip-flop rule that will put the suffix *-en* in the correct place:

-EN⌢verb ⟹ verb⌢-EN

Here are some examples of the application of this flip-flop rule:

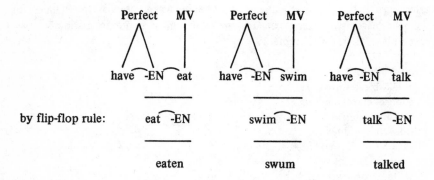

When a sentence is generated without a modal, but with the perfect, the tense will then attach to the helping verb *have*, since it is the first verb that follows the tense. When the present tense is attached to *have*, the whole construction is sometimes called the "present perfect tense"; when the past tense is attached to *have*, the construction is sometimes called the "past perfect tense." Here are three sentences with the past perfect tense:

He *had lived* a full life.
Mr. Smith *had chosen* to ignore the whole thing.
He *had left*.

Here are some sample derivations of the perfect:

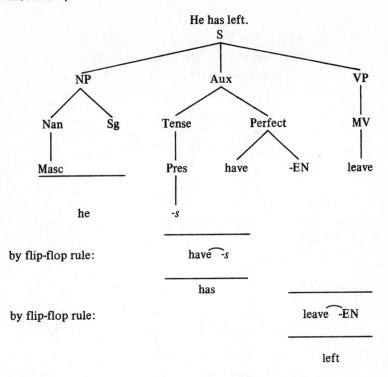

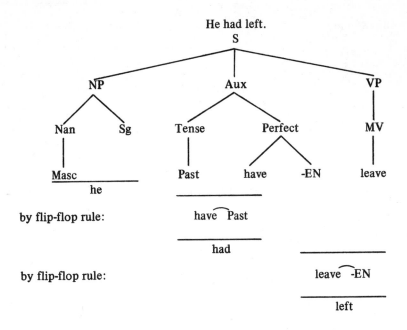

Notice that the flip-flop rules must apply twice: once to tense and once to *-en*. If *have* does not directly follow tense because of an intervening modal, tense is attached to the modal, and not to *have*. In that case, *have* is not inflected at all; that is, *have* is neither present nor past, but in the infinitive form. For example,

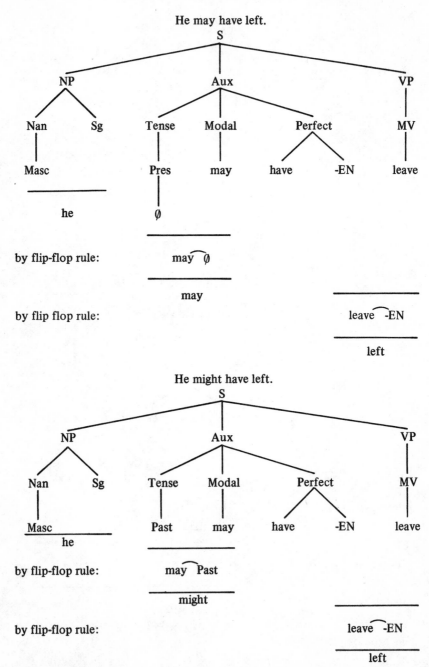

EXERCISE 2.6   **Perfect**

Draw phrase structure trees and apply the flip-flop rule(s) to the following
sentences:
1. John has won.
2. My ships had sunk.
3. The answer may have come.
4. A cook had quit.
5. Mary could have finished.
6. Somebody must have noticed.
7. The children should have written.

PROGRESSIVE

Like the perfect, the progressive consists of two parts: the helping verb *be*
and the present participle ending *-ing*, which is always attached to the verb
following *be*. This attachment is governed by the third version of the flip-flop
rule:

-ING verb ⟹ verb -ING

Here are some examples of the application of this rule:

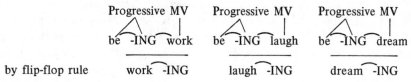

When a sentence is generated with no other optional elements in the auxiliary
besides the progressive, tense is then attached to the helping verb *be*, making a
contrast between the present progressive and the past progressive. For example,

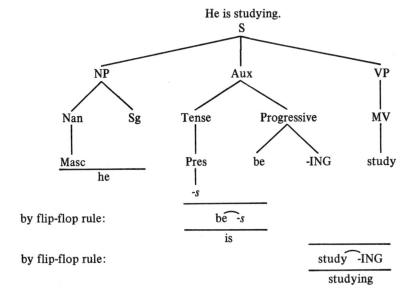

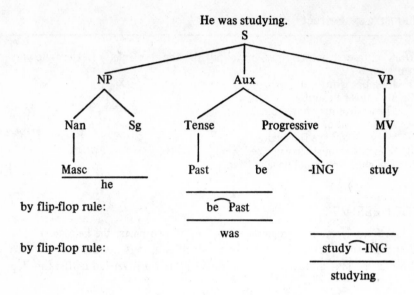

Final Version of the Flip-Flop Rule

The progressive is the last of the three optional elements in the auxiliary. If more than one optional element is selected, the relative position of the elements is fixed in this order: modal, perfect, progressive. Let us now generate a sentence employing all the auxiliary options:

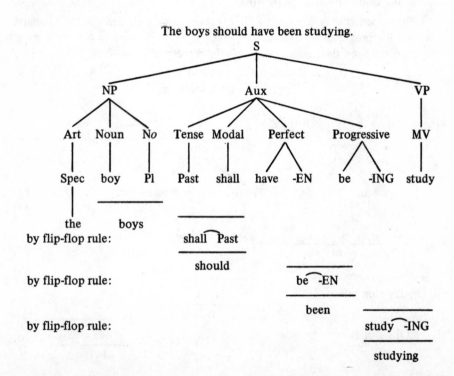

In order to make the operation of the flip-flop rules precise, we need to state that a flip-flop rule must apply to any ending only once. If you look at the sample derivation above, you will see that as a result of the first flip-flop, past is now to the left of *have*. We do not intend the rule to apply again to past because the result would produce the ungrammatical sequence:

*shall had been studying

We can simplify the expression of the flip-flop rules by combining all three rules into one. As the rules stand now, we have three separate but obviously related rules:

$$\text{Tense} \frown \text{verb} \Longrightarrow \text{verb} \frown \text{Tense}$$
$$\text{-EN} \frown \text{verb} \Longrightarrow \text{verb} \frown \text{-EN}$$
$$\text{-ING} \frown \text{verb} \Longrightarrow \text{verb} \frown \text{-ING}$$

All three flip-flop rules attach the verb endings to the following verb. By establishing one symbol to stand for all three verb endings, we can collapse the three rules into one. The symbol used for this purposes is *Af*, which stands for *affix*. We can now write the flip-flop rule this way:

Let Af = Tense, -EN, or -ING
$$\text{Af} \frown \text{verb} \Longrightarrow \text{verb} \frown \text{Af}$$

Since we now have only a single flip-flop rule, let us show the application of the flip-flop rule in a single line below the sentence rather than applying what is essentially the same rule in separate lines. Taking the derivation of the sentence above, *The boys should have been studying*, as an example, the application of the flip-flop rule would look like this:

by flip-flop rule:	shall ⌢ Past	be ⌢ -EN	study ⌢ -ING
	should	been	studying

EXERCISE 2.7 Progressive

Draw phrase structure trees and apply the flip-flop rule to the following sentences:
1. John is singing.
2. John was singing.
3. John has been singing.
4. John had been singing.
5. John may be singing.
6. John might be singing.
7. John may have been singing.
8. John might have been singing.

Time, Tense, Active and Stative Verbs

Tense occupies a special role in the auxiliary system because it is the only obligatory element. However, there are many complex restrictions about the use of tense with various verbs. Before beginning this discussion, though, it might be well to comment on some general characteristics of tense in English. The tense system of English is complex enough in its own right, but discussion of it is made even more complex by traditional terminology. Almost all of the traditional terminology for describing English is based on the terminology for describing Latin. Since English and Latin are related languages (albeit distantly), the terminology for Latin is applicable to English without too much difficulty. Unfortunately, the auxiliary system of English is profoundly different from the tense system of Latin. Consequently, the traditional terminology for talking about tense and time in English is very misleading.

In Latin it is perfectly reasonable to talk about past, present, and future tense because verbs have three separate forms corresponding to past, present, and future time. In English this is just not the case. First of all, English has no special form of the verb to mark future time. Obviously, however, English speakers are not prohibited from talking about the future because English has no future tense. English has a variety of ways for talking about the future. Perhaps the two most common ways are by means of the modal *will* and the construction *be going to:*

John will return tomorrow.
The tide will be in about 9 tonight.

John is going to return tomorrow.
The tide is going to be in about 9 tonight.

The greatest difference in function between tense in English and tense in Latin is seen in the use of the present tense. In the first place, present tense in English seldom means present time. The two most common uses of present tense are (1) indicating that something is universally true and (2) indicating that an action is habitual or repeated. Here are some examples of present tense to indicate universal truth:

Two and two is four.
Absence makes the heart grow fonder.
Too many cooks spoil the broth.
The sun rises in the east.

The use of present tense to mean habitual action is shown in the following sentence:

Every Sunday, Red Riding Hood takes a basket of goodies to her grandmother.

Here are some more examples of the habitual use of the present tense:

The swallows always return to Capistrano.
I usually eat lunch around 12:30.
Our vacation is in August.

The present tense can be used to mean present time, but it requires a special context to do so. Probably the most common situation is when the present tense is used as a commentary on something that is taking place at the present time. Some examples would be stage directions, for example, *Mrs. Anderson now crosses over to stage left*, or in describing an action such as a sports event, for example, *Johnson passes off to Smith in the forecourt*.

The normal way of describing action taking place at the present time is by means of the progressive, for example:

Bill is doing his homework now.
Captain Kidd is conducting diving practice on the main deck.
It's raining.
They are just finishing.

The use of the present tense and the progressive is greatly complicated by restrictions on which verbs can be used with the present and the progressive. There is a basic division of English verbs into two groups, which we'will call *active* and *stative*. This distinction appears not only in restrictions about present and progressive, but in many other areas of the grammar as well (as you will see later). As the name implies, active verbs are verbs in which some action or process takes place, for example, *jump, run, sing, read, change, die*. Stative verbs are harder to characterize. Very roughly, stative verbs describe states— states of mind or states of relations, for example, *know, love, be, have*.

Active and stative verbs have many formal differences. The two differences that are relevant to our concerns at the moment are their ability to be used with the present and progressive. Compare the following groups of verbs:

	Stative	Active
Present:	I know the answer.	*I learn the answer.
Progressive:	*I am knowing the answer.	I am learning the answer.
Present:	He sees them.	*He looks at them.
Progressive:	*He is seeing them.	He is looking at them.
Present:	I am ready.	*I get ready.
Progressive:	*I am being ready.	I am getting ready.
Present:	I need your help.	*I ask for your help.
Progressive:	*I am needing your help.	I am asking for your help.
Present:	They hear us.	*They listen to us.
Progressive:	*They are hearing us.	They are listening to us.

As you can see, stative verbs can be used in the present but not in the progressive, while active verbs can be used with the present tense only as a commentary (*He looks at them* is a perfectly grammatical stage direction) or with a change of meaning. For example, *listen to* can also mean something like "respect one's opinion." In this meaning, *They listen to us* becomes grammatical in the present tense. The progressive usually forces a clear-cut distinction between the two groups of verbs, although even here changes in the meaning or context can cause a verb to move from one group to another.

EXERCISE 2.8 **Stative and Active Verbs**

The following sentences are all in the past tense. Decide which verbs are stative and which are active by their ability to be used in the present tense and in the progressive. Do not assume any special intonation or situation.

1. I fixed myself a salami sandwich.
2. You remembered me.
3. I wished I were rich and famous.
4. He weighed about 190 pounds.
5. I thought about that.
6. It seemed silly.
7. The clerk overcharged me.
8. I wore my new shoes.
9. I thought so.
10. He owned a broken-down Buick.
11. It tasted too bland.
12. They visited their relatives in New Jersey.
13. John Wallis understood grammar.
14. The company developed a new process.
15. It sounded good to me.
16. John disliked custard pies.
17. I gave up smoking.
18. Seymour sliced the salami for me.
19. I warned you.
20. I believed that.
21. She belonged to a wealthy family.
22. We doubted their honesty.
23. They underwent considerable change.
24. He learned some Spanish.
25. He finished breakfast late today.

EXERCISE 2.9 **Review**

Draw phrase structure trees for the following sentences:
1. We would have lost.
2. John quit.
3. Some boys have been fighting.
4. It will be raining.
5. The President might be lying.

Answers to Exercise 2.1 PRESENT TENSE WITH SINGULAR NOUNS

IF Noun Sg Pres, THEN Pres $\longrightarrow$ -s/-es
IF Nprop Sg Pres, THEN Pres $\longrightarrow$ -s/-es
IF PPn Sg Pres, THEN Pres $\longrightarrow \emptyset$

The first two rules can be combined if we use the symbol *N* to stand for either common or proper noun as we did in the phrase structure tree for *they*:

IF N⌢Sg Pres, THEN Pres ⟶ *-s/-es*

Answers to Exercise 2.2   TENSE

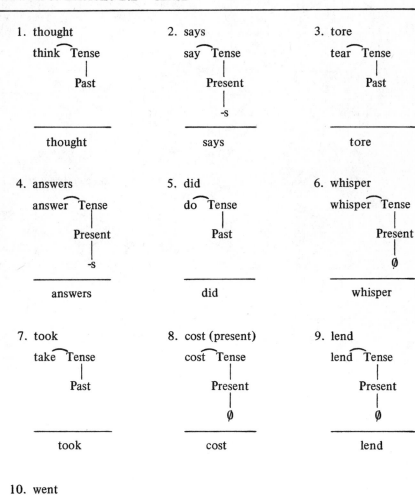

1. thought
   think⌢Tense
   |
   Past
   _____
   thought

2. says
   say⌢Tense
   |
   Present
   |
   -s
   _____
   says

3. tore
   tear⌢Tense
   |
   Past
   _____
   tore

4. answers
   answer⌢Tense
   |
   Present
   |
   -s
   _____
   answers

5. did
   do⌢Tense
   |
   Past
   _____
   did

6. whisper
   whisper⌢Tense
   |
   Present
   |
   ∅
   _____
   whisper

7. took
   take⌢Tense
   |
   Past
   _____
   took

8. cost (present)
   cost⌢Tense
   |
   Present
   |
   ∅
   _____
   cost

9. lend
   lend⌢Tense
   |
   Present
   |
   ∅
   _____
   lend

10. went
    go⌢Tense
    |
    Past
    _____
    went

Answers to Exercise 2.3   TENSE AND MAIN VERB

1.   The girl laughed.

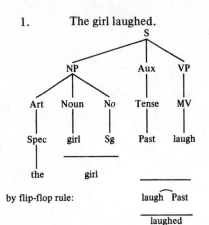

by flip-flop rule:

2.   The doorbells rang.

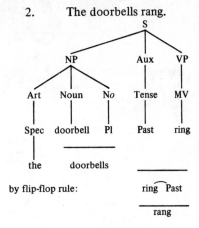

by flip-flop rule:

3.   My shoelace broke.

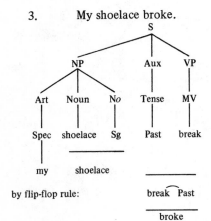

by flip-flop rule:

4.   Some children cried.

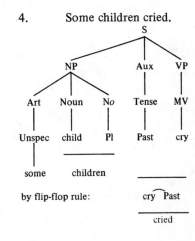

by flip-flop rule:

5.   John lisps.

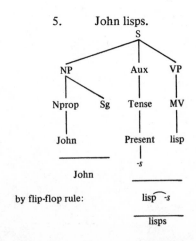

by flip-flop rule:

Answers to Exercise 2.4   PRESENT TENSE WITH MODAL AUXILIARIES

IF Pres⌢Modal, THEN Pres⟶∅

Why is it necessary to make this the first rule?

Answers to Exercise 2.5   TENSE AND MODAL AUXILIARIES

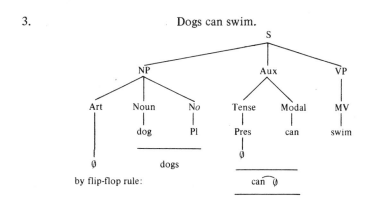

1.   **The day will come.**

2.   **She should resign.**

3.   **Dogs can swim.**

4.   You (plural) must leave.

                                          S
                  ┌───────────────────────┼───────────────────┐
                 NP   Aux   VP
            ┌─────┴─────┐   ┌─────┴─────┐   │
           PPn   No   Tense   Modal   MV
            │   │   │   │   │
           you   Pl   Pres   must   leave
            └─────┬──────┘   │
                 you   ∅

              by flip-flop rule: ‾‾‾‾‾‾‾‾‾‾‾‾‾‾
                                            must ⌒ ∅
                                          ‾‾‾‾‾‾‾‾‾‾‾‾‾‾
                                               must

5.   A dollar would help.

                                          S
               ┌──────────────────────────┼───────────────────┐
              NP   Aux   VP
        ┌──────┼───────┐   ┌──────┴─────┐   │
       Art   Noun   No   Tense   Modal   MV
        │   │   │   │   │   │
     Unspec dollar   Sg   Past   will   help
        │   └────┬───┘
        a   dollar
     by flip-flop rule: ‾‾‾‾‾‾‾‾‾‾‾‾‾‾‾
                                        will ⌒ Past
                                       ‾‾‾‾‾‾‾‾‾‾‾‾‾‾‾
                                           would

Answers to Exercise 2.6   PERFECT

───

1.   John has won.

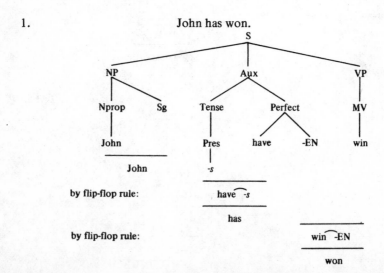

                                          S
         ┌────────────────────────────────┼────────────────────┐
        NP   Aux   VP
    ┌────┴────┐   ┌──────────┴────────┐   │
  Nprop   Sg   Tense   Perfect   MV
    │   │   ┌─────┴─────┐   │
   John   Pres   have   -EN   win
    │   │
  ‾‾‾‾‾‾   -s
   John
    by flip-flop rule: ‾‾‾‾‾‾‾‾‾‾‾
                                     have ⌒ -s
                                    ‾‾‾‾‾‾‾‾‾‾‾
                                        has

    by flip-flop rule: ‾‾‾‾‾‾‾‾‾‾‾
                                                     win ⌒ -EN
                                                    ‾‾‾‾‾‾‾‾‾‾‾
                                                        won

2.

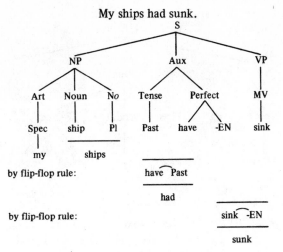

My ships had sunk.

3.

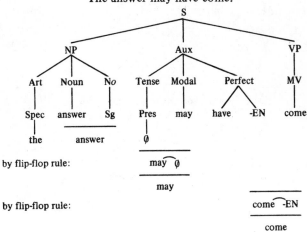

The answer may have come.

4.

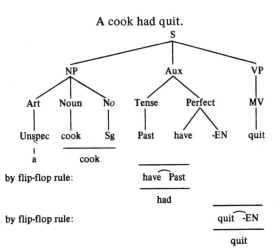

A cook had quit.

5.   Mary could have finished.

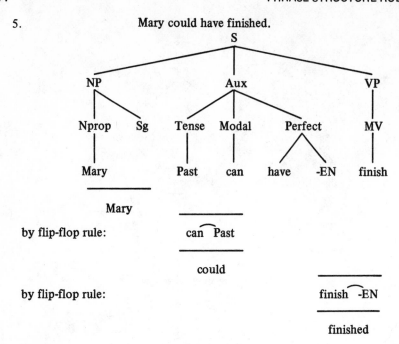

by flip-flop rule:

by flip-flop rule:

6.   Somebody must have noticed.

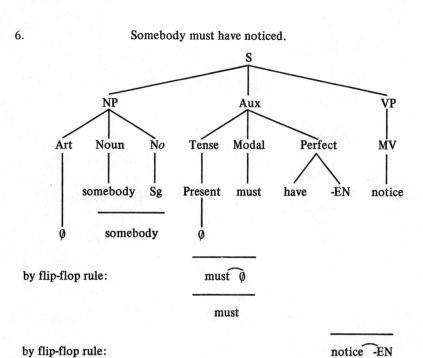

by flip-flop rule:

by flip-flop rule:

7.   The children should have written.

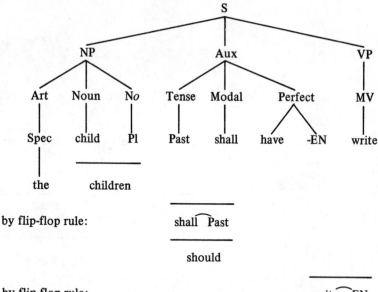

by flip-flop rule: shall⁀Past

                                                  should

by flip-flop rule: write⁀-EN

                                                                written

Answers to Exercise 2.7   PROGRESSIVE

1.   John is singing.

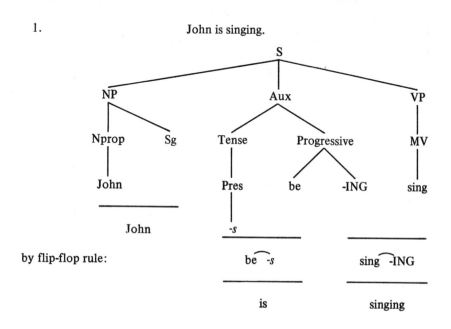

by flip-flop rule: be⁀-s   sing⁀-ING

                                                  is   singing

2.   John was singing.

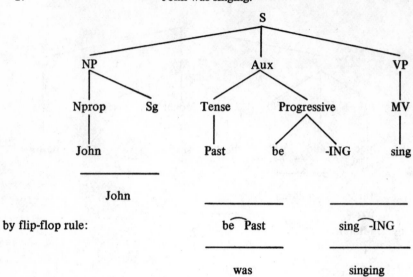

by flip-flop rule:

3.   John has been singing.

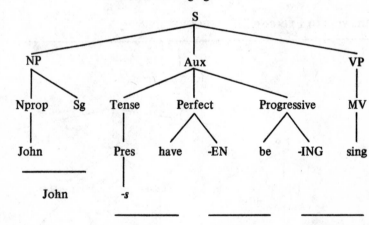

by flip-flop rule:

4.   John had been singing.

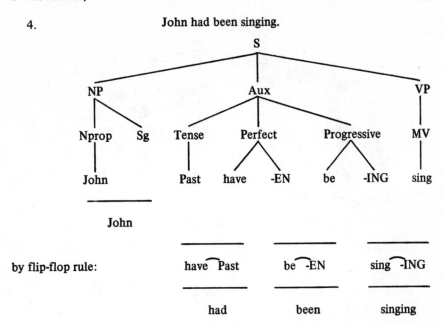

by flip-flop rule:

5.   John may be singing.

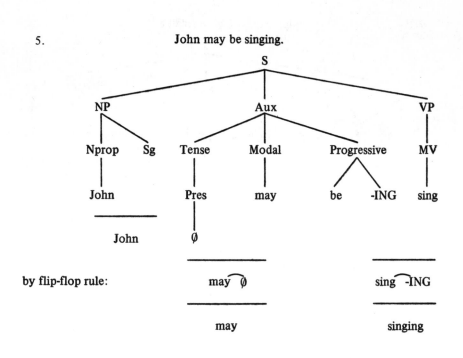

by flip-flop rule:

6.

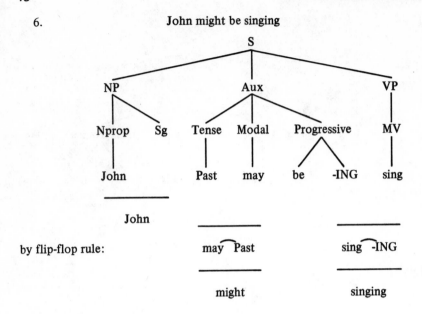

John might be singing

by flip-flop rule:

7.

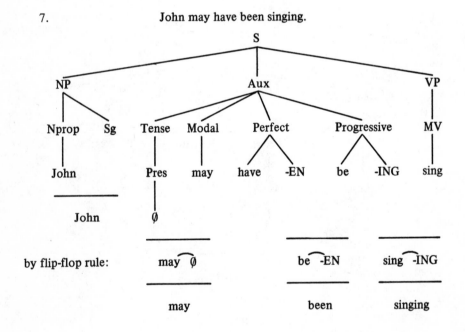

John may have been singing.

by flip-flop rule:

8. John might have been singing.

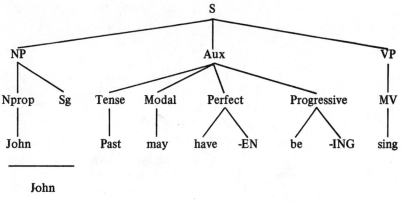

by flip-flop rule:

may Past	be -EN	sing -ING
might	been	singing

Answers to Exercise 2.8 STATIVE AND ACTIVE VERBS

1. fix—active
2. remember—stative
3. wish—stative
4. weigh—stative
5. think about—active
6. seem—stative
7. overcharge—active
8. wear—active
9. think—stative
10. own—stative
11. taste—stative
12. visit—active
13. understand—stative
14. develop—active
15. sound—stative
16. dislike—stative
17. give up—active
18. slice—active
19. warn—active
20. believe—stative
21. belong—stative
22. doubt—stative
23. undergo—active
24. learn—active
25. finish—active

Answers to Exercise 2.9   REVIEW

1.   We would have lost.

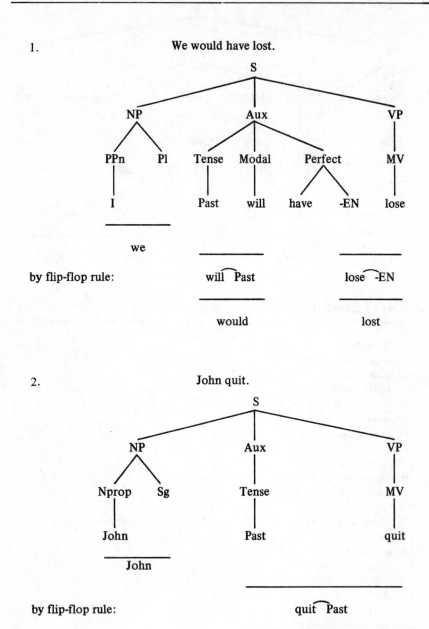

2.   John quit.

3.   Some boys have been fighting.

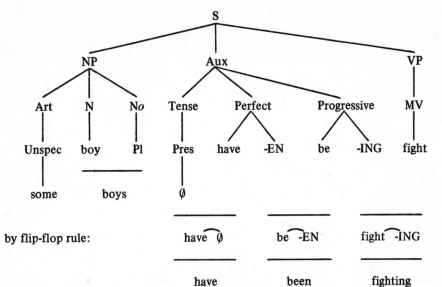

by flip-flop rule:

4.   It will be raining.

by flip-flop rule:

5.   The President might be lying.

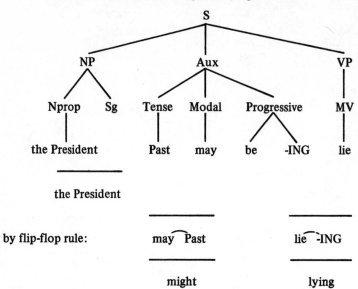

by flip-flop rule: may‿Past   lie‿-ING

                                 might   lying

CHAPTER 3

The Verb Phrase

OVERVIEW

The verb phrase consists of three elements in this order: the main verb, the complement, and an optional element called "adverbial." The main verb and the complement are closely interrelated. The traditional terms "transitive" and "intransitive" are ways of talking about this relation. In our terminology, a transitive verb is a main verb that takes a noun phrase complement. For example, in the sentence

She sells seashells.

sells is the main verb and *seashells* is the noun phrase complement. The main verb *sell*, at least in its common usage, requires an object noun phrase. All main verbs require a subject noun phrase, but only transitive main verbs require an object noun phrase. An intransitive verb, on the other hand, does not take an object noun phrase, for example,

Jesus wept.

In this grammar, we make the generalization that all main verbs must be followed by a complement. In the case of a transitive verb, the complement is obviously a noun phrase. In the case of an intransitive verb, the complement is the null set Ø. The complement, then, is a list of the elements that main verbs take. When we select a main verb we must also select one of the elements listed under complement, even if the element we select is Ø.

The major portion of this chapter is devoted to a discussion of eight different types of complements:

Ø
Noun Phrase
Adjective
(Noun Phrase) ⌒ Adverbial of Position
(Noun Phrase) ⌒ Adverbial of Direction
Adjective ⌒ Preposition ⌒ Noun Phrase
Noun Phrase ⌒ Noun Phrase
Noun Phrase ⌒ Preposition ⌒ Noun Phrase

The chapter concludes with a discussion of the way that English fuses verbs and prepositions to form new verbs. These new units are often called "two-word verbs" (for the obvious reason that they are made up of two words: a verb and a preposition). When a two-word verb is transitive, that is, when it takes a noun phrase complement, we must make a further distinction between separable and inseparable two-word verbs. Compare the following sentences:

John looked up the price.
John looked for the price.

In the first sentence the main verb is the two-word verb *look up*; in the second sentence it is *look for*. However, in one respect *look up* and *look for* behave quite differently. A *separable* two-word verb is one in which we may move the preposition after the object noun phrase. For example,

John looked up the price ⟹ John looked the price up.

An *inseparable* two-word verb is one in which we cannot move the preposition. For example,

John looked for the price ⟹*John looked the price for.

Thus, *look up* is a separable two-word verb, and *look for* is an inseparable two-word verb.

THE VERB PHRASE

Verb Phrase ⟶ Main Verb ⌒ Complement ⌒ (Adverbial)

The verb phrase in English consists of two obligatory elements and a third optional element. The first element, the main verb, is self-explanatory, at least for the moment. The second element, the complement, is not very well named. In this grammar, the term complement means anything following the main verb that is necessary to make the sentence grammatical. The final element, adverbial, is a loose term covering a multitude of different subclasses of adverbs. The crucial distinction between the second and third elements is that the complement is obligatory—without it the sentence is ungrammatical—while the third element, the adverbial, provides material not essential to the grammar of the sentence.

The Main Verb

With the exception of the "helping verbs" that were discussed in the chapter on the Auxiliary, the node *main verb* is the source for all verbs in English. Two of the helping verbs, *be* and *have*, can be used as main verbs:

Helping verb:	The tree *is* blooming.
Main verb:	The tree *is* full of flowers.
Helping verb:	The tree *has* bloomed.
Main verb:	The tree *has* flowers.

The phrase structure rule for Main Verb is very simple—the Main Verb is rewritten as all verbs in English (minus the modals):

Main Verb (MV) $\longrightarrow$ {*be, run, laugh, have, think...*}

(Note: We will have to revise this rule shortly.) An important thing to notice is that the rule for main verbs does not classify the verbs into types—for example, transitive and intransitive, to name two well-known (if not beloved) types. A transformational grammar has just as much need to classify verbs into types as any other kind of grammar. However, in most transformational grammars of English, the classifying is done in terms of what *follows* the main verb. In other words, we will break down the element that must follow the main verb, the complement, into various types. The main verbs are then classified in terms of which complement type they can be used with. For example, in traditional grammar a transitive verb is defined as a verb that has an object; in transformational terms, those verbs that are followed by a noun phrase complement are called transitive verbs. The important point to remember is that every main verb must be followed by a complement or else the sentence is not complete.

The next element in the verb phrase is the complement. However, it will be easier to understand the complement if we first examine the optional third element, the adverbial.

Adverbial

The third element in the verb phrase, the optional adverbial, is the source for all "adverbs" that are not a necessary part of the sentence. Before going any further, we need to clarify the terms *adverbial* and *adverb*. When we think of adverbs we usually think of three groups: adverbs of time, for example, *then, now, later, earlier*; adverbs of place, for example, *here, there*; and adverbs of manner, for example, *gracefully, cheerfully, sadly*. All of these words belong to

the part of speech called *adverbs*. The difficulty is that other parts of speech
have exactly the same *function* as the adverbs listed above. In other words, we
need to distinguish between *adverb* as the name for a part of speech and
"adverb" as a grammatical function. Let us use *adverbial* to refer to the
functional meaning. It is more accurate to say that there are adverbials of time,
place, and manner because prepositional phrases, clauses (which we will treat
later as embedded sentences), and even some noun phrases can also function as
adverbials. Here are some examples:

Adverbial of time: John is coming *soon* (adverb)
                              in the afternoon (prepositional phrase)
                              when he feels better (clause)
                              next week (noun phrase)

Adverbial of place: John is *here* (adverb)
                              in the garden (prepositional phrase)
                              where Mary is (clause)
                              next door (noun phrase)

Adverbial of manner: John behaved *badly* (adverb)
                                with great dignity
                                (prepositional phrase)
                                as he should (clause)

The classification of adverbials has long been the bane of English grammarians
because they seem to defy any simple classification or description. For example,
in Quirk, Greenbaum, Leech, and Svartvik's large reference work, *A Grammar of
Contemporary English,*[1] the authors find it necessary to recognize no less than 41
different classes of adverbials, and even then the classes are riddled with
exceptions and special restrictions. In this grammar we will deal only with the
three types of adverbials mentioned above. However, it will be necessary to
separate adverbials of place into two subclasses: adverbials of position and
adverbials of direction. Adverbials of position indicate the place where
something is, while adverbials of direction indicate motion to or from some
place. Here are some examples:

Adverbials of position: David found the cat *on the couch.*
                                  I saw Ms. Brown *over there.*
                                  They had dinner *at a restaurant.*
                                  They had coffee *outside.*

Adverbials of direction: David chased the cat *off of the couch.*
                                   Ms. Brown walked *into the store.*
                                   He hit the ball *out of the park.*
                                   They took their coffee *outside.*

The adverbials of direction obviously can be used only with verbs that imply

---

[1] Seminar Press, New York and London, 1972.

motion or movement of some kind; consequently, they cannot normally be used with stative verbs. For example,

*I saw Ms. Brown into the store.

(This sentence is grammatical in a completely different meaning of *see*. Can you think what that meaning is?) Notice that the prepositional phrases used as adverbials of direction have double prepositions, *off of, into, out of*. Notice also that adverbs can be used as adverbials of either direction or position depending on the rest of the sentence, for example, *outside* in the sentences given above

Since we have broken adverbials of place down into adverbials of position and adverbials of direction, we will not bother treating adverbials of place as a separate category. Thus, we have four types of adverbials in our limited grammar: time, position, direction, and manner. This categorization is stated by the following phrase structure rule:

$$\text{Adverbial} \longrightarrow \left\{ \begin{array}{l} \text{Adverbial of time} \\ \text{Adverbial of position} \\ \text{Adverbial of direction} \\ \text{Adverbial of manner} \end{array} \right\}$$

In turn, the adverbials of time, position, direction, and manner are rewritten as adverbs, prepositional phrases, or clauses (noun phrases functioning as adverbials are so rare that we will ignore them from now on). In a transformational grammar, adverbial clauses are derived from full sentences that are embedded into the main sentence. Consequently, we will postpone discussion of adverbial clauses until Part III.

For the time being, then, we will rewrite the four adverbials of time, position, direction, and manner as either adverbs or prepositional phrases. Prepositional phrases, in turn, will be rewritten as preposition plus a noun phrase. Here are the phrase structure rules:

$$\left\{ \begin{array}{l} \text{Adverbial of time (ADV time)} \\ \text{Adverbial of position (ADV position)} \\ \text{Adverbial of direction (ADV direction)} \\ \text{Adverbial of manner (ADV manner)} \end{array} \right\} \longrightarrow \left\{ \begin{array}{l} \text{Prepositional Phrase} \\ \text{Adverb} \end{array} \right\}$$

Prepositional Phrase (PP) $\longrightarrow$ Preposition NP

Preposition (Prep) $\longrightarrow$ *at, in, on, to, with. . .*

Adverb $\longrightarrow$ *away, have, soon, grandly. . .*

Obviously, a fuller grammer would specify which prepositions and which adverbs belong to which type of adverbial.

EXERCISE 3.1   Phrase Structure Rule for Adverbials

The rule that rewrites Time, Position, Direction, and Manner adverbials as either Prepositional Phrases or Adverbs is actually a shorthand for four different rules. Can you figure out what the four rules are?

Phrase Structure Trees with Optional Adverbials

Here are sample phrase structure trees for sentences containing adverbials. Remember, by definition, these adverbials are all optional—the sentences in which they occur are all grammatically complete without them:

John works in the afternoon.

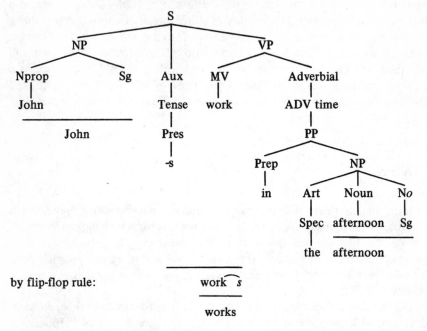

by flip-flop rule:

(Note that the ∅ complement is not yet shown in the MV)

They ate here.

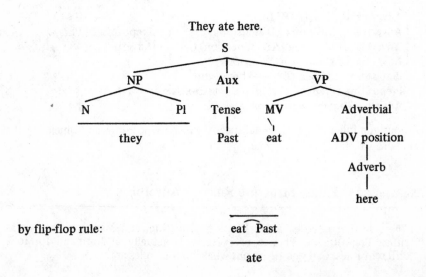

by flip-flop rule:

The water splashed onto a pedestrian.

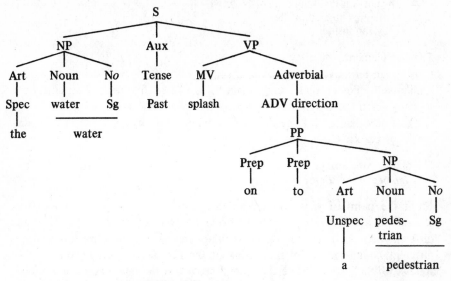

by flip-flop rule: splash ⌢ Past
                          ——————————
                              splashed

John laughed madly.

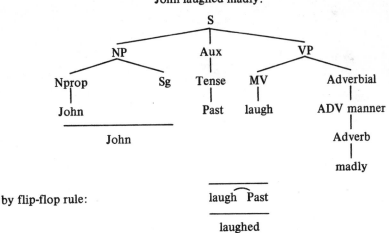

by flip-flop rule: laugh ⌢ Past
                              ——————————
                                  laughed

EXERCISE 3.2   **Adverbials**

Draw phrase structure trees for the following sentences:
1. It might be snowing in the mountains.
2. Ms. Brown had danced marvelously.

3. The boys slept in the yard.
4. The cat was drinking out of the bowl.
5. Someone coughed inside.
6. They ran inside.

The Complement

In rough terms, the complement is simply a list of things that can occur after a main verb. For example, some main verbs can be followed by an adjective, some by a noun phrase, others by an adverb of place, and so on.

One point that needs to be clarified is what is meant by a main verb. Compare the following sentences:

John became angry.
John became a doctor.

From the point of view adopted in this grammar, the *become* in the first sentence is a different verb from the *become* in the second sentence. They are different because they mean different things and because they are followed by different complements. We may think of the first *become* as the one that is followed by adjectives, while the second *become* is the one that is followed by noun phrases.

There are two different types of complements: simple complements that contain no embedded sentences, and complex complements that do. In this section, we will deal only with the simple complements. Complex complements will be dealt with in Part III. Here is a list of the simple complements that we will deal with:

$$\text{Complement (Comp)} \rightarrow \begin{cases} \emptyset \\ \text{NP} \\ \text{Adjective} \\ \text{(NP)} \frown \text{ADVposition} \\ \text{(NP)} \frown \text{ADVdirection} \\ \text{Adjective} \frown \text{Prep} \frown \text{NP} \\ \text{NP} \frown \text{NP} \\ \text{NP} \frown \text{Prep} \frown \text{NP} \end{cases}$$

THE ∅ COMPLEMENT

The minimal complement is the null set (∅). In traditional grammar, verbs that take a ∅ complement are called "intransitive" verbs. Here are a few examples of sentences with ∅ complements:

The baby slept.
She smiled.
They were working.
We laughed.

A tree diagram of the first sentence would look like this:

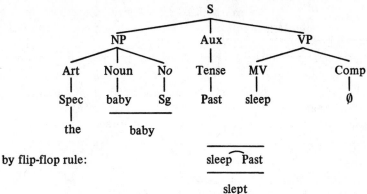

Many sentences that appear to have ∅ complement may be derived from sentences with noun phrase objects. For example,

John smokes.
We won.
She sang.

might be derived from

John smokes cigarettes.
We won the game.
She sang a song.

Nevertheless, at least some verbs have a true ∅ complement. Here is a famous sentence containing two clear-cut examples:

I *think*, therefore I *am*.

In this sentence, *think* means "to have the capacity for thought," and *be* means "to exist."

EXERCISE 3.3   ∅ **Complements**

Draw deep structures and apply the flip-flop rule to derive the following sentences:
1. The telephone rang.
2. Our roof leaks.
3. The baby was sleeping soundly.
4. She will laugh.
5. I have been working in the library.

THE NOUN PHRASE COMPLEMENT

The noun phrase is probably the most common of all complement types. There are several traditional terms used to describe it. The noun phrase is often called an *object*, while the main verb is called a *transitive* verb. In transformational grammar the term *transitive* is often used, but not the term *object*, at least in the formal rules. It is not necessary to single out this noun phrase with any special identifying term, since the phrase structure tree automatically gives a unique definition to every noun phrase. The object noun phrase is that noun phrase which comes from the complement node and is always to the immediate right of the main verb. Here are some examples of sentences with noun phrase complements, followed by a sample phrase structure tree:

Columbus discovered America.
The pitcher examined the ball.
The publisher reviewed the manuscript.
He snapped the twig.

The pitcher grabbed the ball.

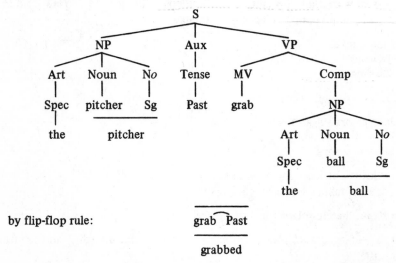

by flip-flop rule:

grab͡ Past

grabbed

It is necessary to distinguish between two different kinds of main verbs used with noun phrase complements. Most main verbs, those that we might call "normal" or "regular" transitive verbs, permit the sentence to be made passive. For example, all the example sentences given above contain "normal" transitive verbs, as shown by the following sentences:

Passive: America was discovered by Columbus.
The ball was examined by the pitcher.
The manuscript was reviewed by the publisher.
The twig was snapped by him.

There are a small number of verbs that do not permit a passive. In traditional terminology these verbs are called *linking* verbs, and the following noun phrase is sometimes called a *predicate nominal* rather than an object. Linking verbs are a special group of stative verbs (but note that there are many stative verbs that are "normal" transitive verbs) that describe the following noun phrase.

Here are two examples of sentences with linking verbs:

Columbus was a sailor.
He became a sailor.

If we attempt to put these sentences into the passive, the result is ungrammatical:

Passive: *A sailor was been by Columbus.
         *A sailor was became by him.

Since the inability to be put into the passive is an intrinsic characteristic of a small number of verbs, we will use the same phrase structure tree description for them as for the "normal" transitive verbs. That is, despite their differences, linking verbs are still followed by noun phrases.

EXERCISE 3.4   **Noun Phrase Complements**

Draw deep structures and apply the necessary transformational rules to produce the following sentences:
1. John broke the window.
2. I have a question.
3. The students passed the exam easily.
4. His father painted the picture.
5. Someone burned the toast.

THE ADJECTIVE COMPLEMENT

In the adjective complement, the main verb is followed by an adjective. There are relatively few verbs that can occur with this complement type; for example, *be* (by far the most common), *seem, taste, feel,* and *smell*:

Sally is silly.
The cook seems disorganized.
The salad tastes oily.
He felt angry.
The kitchen smells unpleasant.

The only difficult thing about this complement type is being able to recognize adjectives. We are concerned only with adjectives that occur after the main verb (adjectives used as noun modifiers will be dealt with later). (Almost) all adjectives meet the following tests: (1) they can have *very* in front of them, and (2) they can be compared, i.e., used in a comparative statement with *-er* or *more*. Not too surprisingly, these two tests show that the example sentences above all contain adjectives:

Sally is very silly.
Sally is sillier than Mary.

The cook seems very disorganized.
The cook seems more disorganized than usual.

The salad tastes very oily.
The salad tastes oilier than it should.

He felt very angry.
He felt angrier than he ever had before.

The kitchen smells very unpleasant.
The kitchen smells more unpleasant every day.

The tests are especially necessary with adjectives that end in *-ing*. Compare the following sentences:

The ladies are looking.
The ladies are interesting.

When we apply the two tests, we see that the two sentences are quite different:

*The ladies are very looking.
*The ladies are more looking than ever.

The ladies are very interesting.
The ladies are more interesting than ever.

The first sentence contains a ∅ complement with the progressive, while the second sentence contains an adjective complement with the present tense.

EXERCISE 3.5   Recognizing Adjectives

Which of the following sentences contain adjective complements and which contain ∅ complements?
1. The cup is cracking.
2. The movie was frightening.
3. The prisoners are escaping.
4. The sky is clearing.
5. His views are alarming.
6. The wine is overflowing.
7. Dawn is breaking.
8. The book is interesting.
9. The children are appealing.
10. He is retiring. [a trick question]

Active and Stative Adjectives

In the previous chapter we saw that verbs can be divided into two classes, active and stative, depending on their ability to be used in the progressive. The same is also true of adjectives. Active adjectives can be used in the progressive, while stative adjectives cannot. Here are some examples:

Active adjectives: He is being awkward.
                    He is being brave.
                    He is being rude.
                    He is being troublesome.

Stative adjectives: *He is being tall.
                        *He is being hungry.
                        *He is being suitable.
                        *He is being wide.

It is hard to characterize the difference between the two groups. Basically, though, active adjectives seem to refer to changeable qualities, while stative adjectives seem to refer to inherent qualities that cannot be changed. That is, whether or not I am awkward is up to me, but whether or not I am tall is completely beyond my control.

EXERCISE 3.6   Active and Stative Adjectives

Which of the adjectives in the following sentences are active and which are stative?
1. He is nervous.
2. He is kind.
3. He is lenient.
4. He is excellent.
5. He is dull.
6. He is young.
7. He is gray.
8. He is sad.
9. He is careful.
10. He is unreasonable.

Phrase Structure Rule for Adjectives

As with verbs, our phrase structure rules will not reflect the distinction between stative and active types. Here is the phrase structure rule for deriving adjectives:

Adjective ⟶ {*brave, cheerful, thrifty, courteous, interesting, worried...*}

Here is a sample derivation of an adjective complement sentence:

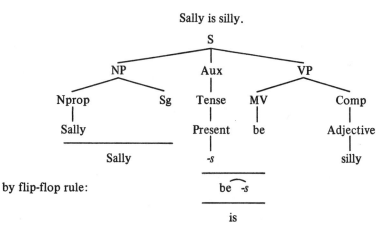

Sally is silly.

by flip-flop rule:

EXERCISE 3.7   **Adjective Complements**

Draw deep structures and apply the necessary transformational rules to produce the following sentences:
1. I am happy.
2. The girl turned pale.
3. We kept quiet.
4. The man became famous.

THE (NOUN PHRASE) ADVERBIAL OF POSITION COMPLEMENT

Adverbials of position function in two completely different ways: (1) as optional adverbials added on after the complement, or (2) as part of the complement itself. Virtually any verb can be used with an optional adverbial of position, but only a few can be used with an adverbial of position complement, *be* being by far the most common one:

Your coffee is on the table.
John is at school.
The money is here.

A sentence containing an adverbial of position complement can also have an optional adverbial of position, for example,

Your coffee is on the table in the kitchen.
John is at school back east.
The money is here in the drawer.

Adverbials of position have the same internal structure—adverb, prepositional phrase, clause—no matter what their function, so it is not necessary to have any new phrase structure rules for adverbial of position complements. However, it is very important to understand that an adverbial of position that is derived from the node labeled *Complement* has a completely different function from the adverbial of position that is derived from the node labeled *Adverbial*.

Here are some sentences with other verbs that are used with adverbial of position complements:

The picture hung on the wall.
The clock rested on the mantel.
I shop at Safeway.
He stood in the corner.
He stayed away.

As was mentioned before, adverbials in the complement can be confused with optional adverbials from the adverbial element. The proof that the adverbials in these sentences come from the complement is that they cannot be deleted without making the sentences ungrammatical in their original meaning; for example,

*The picture hung.
*The clock rested.
*I shop.
*He stood.
*He stayed.

Here is a sample derivation of a sentence with an adverbial of position complement:

The picture hung on the wall.

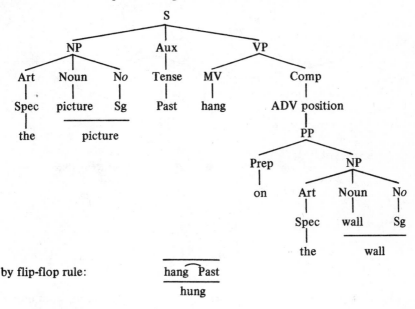

by flip-flop rule: hang Past
hung

The Noun Phrase Adverbial of Position Complement

The adverbial of position complements we have looked at so far have immediately followed the main verb. It is also possible to have a noun phrase in the complement before the adverbial of position. Here are some sentences with a Noun Phrase Adverbial of Position Complement:

John leaned the shovel against the door.
John rested his elbows on the mantel.
He stood the broom in the corner.

The evidence that these adverbials of position are part of the complement is the fact that they cannot be deleted without leaving an ungrammatical sentence fragment in the intended meaning:

*John leaned the shovel.
*John rested his elbows.
*He stood the broom.

The distinction between adverbials of position and noun phrase adverbial of position complements is found in a pair of verbs that are often confused: *lie* (*lay, lain*) and *lay* (*laid, laid*). *Lie* takes an adverbial of position complement, while *lay* takes a noun phrase adverbial of position complement:

lie: The baby lay in the crib.
lay: They laid the baby in the crib.

Here is a sample phrase structure tree for a sentence containing a noun phrase adverbial of position complement:

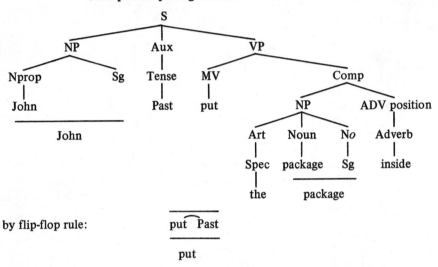

by flip-flop rule:

EXERCISE 3.8   **(Noun Phrase) Adverbial of Position Complements**

Draw phrase structure trees and apply the necessary transformational rules to produce the following sentences:
1. The dictionary is on the shelf.
2. Mr. Smith is on his farm upstate.
3. He is here.
4. You could live in Philadelphia.
5. The baby lay in the crib.
6. They laid the baby in the crib.

THE (NOUN PHRASE) ADVERBIAL OF DIRECTION COMPLEMENT

Like (NP) adverbial of position complements, the (NP) adverbial of direction complement consists of two closely related subtypes: a complement containing an adverbial of direction and a complement containing a noun phrase followed by an adverbial of direction. You might think of the first subtype as being used with certain "intransitive" verbs and the second with certain "transitive" verbs. Let us deal with the "intransitive" subtype first.

As you recall, adverbials of direction imply motion or direction and typically have double prepositions. They can be used only with active verbs that also imply motion or movement of some kind. Here are some sentences with adverbial of motion complements.

The train pulled into the station.
The train chugged out of the station.
The kids sneaked out of the classroom.
She reached into the dishwasher.

If the adverbial of direction complements are deleted, the sentences are no longer grammatical in their original meaning:

*The train pulled.
*The train chugged.
*The kids sneaked.
*She reached.

Here is a phrase structure tree for the first example sentence:

ADVERBIAL OF DIRECTION COMPLEMENT

The train pulled into the station.

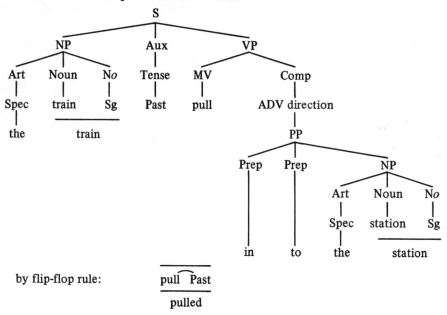

One of the most important characteristics of adverbial of direction complements is that the second preposition and the noun phrase can be deleted from the complement; for example,

The train pulled into the station ⟹ The train pulled in.
The train chugged out of the station ⟹ The train chugged out.
The kids sneaked out of the classroom ⟹ The kids sneaked out.
She reached into the dishwasher ⟹ She reached in.

We can easily write a transformational rule which formalizes the deletion of the second preposition and the noun phrase:

$$\overset{\frown}{MV} \overset{\frown}{Prep_1} \overset{\frown}{Prep_2} NP \Longrightarrow \overset{\frown}{MV} Prep_1$$

We will call this rule the *adverbial of direction deletion rule*. Notice how the rule is written. The rule includes the main verb because, if it did not, the rule would also apply to adverbials of direction that come from the optional adverbial node. The rule mentions nothing about adverbials of direction because only adverbials of direction can have double prepositions. Here is a question for you: why was it necessary to number the prepositions?

Here is a derivation of a sentence with the optional adverbial of direction deletion applied:

The car pulled away (*from the curb* understood).

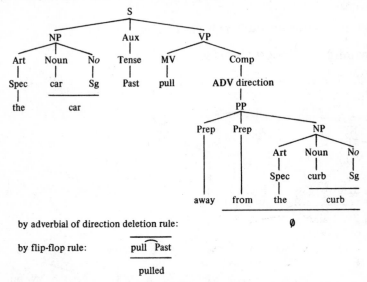

Notice that the area of the phrase structure tree that the deletion rule applies to has been underlined. The ∅ indicates that the material above the line has been deleted. Notice also that the adverbial of direction deletion rule applies before the flip-flop rule.

EXERCISE 3.9   **Adverbials of Direction**

Draw the phrase structure trees and apply the necessary transformational rules to produce the following sentences:
1. The truck turned into the driveway.
2. Ms. Brown walked out of the store.
3. The batter stepped up to the plate.
4. The boys dove in (*to the water* understood).

The Noun Phrase͡ Adverbial of Direction Complement

The other subtype of adverbial of direction complements occurs with a noun phrase. Since this subtype often resembles a noun phrase complement plus an optional adverbial of position, it might be well to compare the two different types:

We put the steak on the grill.
We cooked the steak on the grill.

The first sentence contains a noun phrase͡ adverbial of direction complement, while the second contains a noun phrase complement followed by an optional adverbial of position derived from the adverbial node. There are two formal differences between the two sentences. We can add a second preposition to the first sentence, but not to the second:

We put the steak onto the grill.
*We cooked the steak onto the grill.

However, the most important difference is that we can delete the noun phrase from the prepositional phrase in the first sentence, but not from the second sentence:

We put the steak on.
*We cooked the steak on.

Here are some sentences containing noun phrase͡ adverbial of direction complements.

I drove my car into the garage.
The crane lifted the cement up to the top floor.
The truck pushed the car over to the side.
The catcher threw the ball back to the pitcher.

The phrase structure tree for the first sentence looks like this:

I drove my car into the garage.

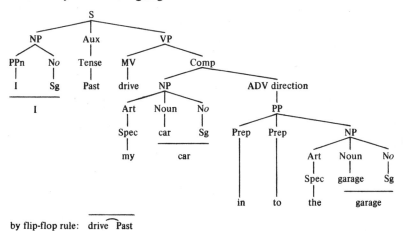

The second preposition and the noun phrase can be deleted from the adverbial of direction in all these sentences:

I drove my car into the garage $\Longrightarrow$ I drove my car in.

The crane lifted the cement up to the top floor $\Longrightarrow$ The crane lifted the cement up.

The truck pushed the car over to the side $\Longrightarrow$ The truck pushed the car over.

The catcher threw the ball back to the pitcher $\Longrightarrow$ The catcher threw the ball back.

We need to rewrite the adverbial of direction deletion rule so that it can deal with noun phrase adverbial of direction complements as well as complements that contain only adverbials of direction. Also, we can make the rule flexible enough to deal with sentences such as *We put the steak on the grill*, which contain only a single surface preposition.

EXERCISE 3.10   **Adverbial of Direction Deletion Rule**

Can you rewrite the adverbial of direction deletion rule so that it can (1) accommodate noun phrase adverbial of direction complements and (2) accommodate sentences that have only one preposition in the adverbial of direction?

EXERCISE 3.11   **(Noun Phrase) Adverbial of Direction Complements**

Draw phrase structure trees and apply the necessary transformational rules to produce the following sentences:
1. The truck pulled the car out of the mud.
2. The team threw the coach into the pool.
3. The coach will send Johnson in (*to the game* understood).
4. The division turned back (*from the front* understood).

THE ADJECTIVE PREPOSITION NOUN PHRASE COMPLEMENT

Despite the fact that there is no traditional name for the adjective preposition noun phrase complement, it is quite common. The adjective can be either a "true" adjective or one derived from the past participle form of the verb. In either case, the adjective in this complement type can have *very* in front of it and can be made into a comparative statement (the two tests for adjectives).

The most common prepositions are *about, at, in, of, on, to,* and *with* (*by* poses special problems, which will be dealt with in Chapter 4). Here are some examples for each preposition:

I am happy about your grades.
He was worried about you.

She is good at chess.
They were delighted at the gift.

He is fortunate in his choice.
He is justified in his opinion.

I am afraid of the dark.
I am scared of the dark.

She is hard on them.
The plan is based on them.

He is answerable to no one.
He is reconciled to his defeat.

They are impatient with her.
The children flushed with success.

EXERCISE 3.12   **Adjective Preposition Noun Phrase Complements**

Without the benefit of a model to follow, can you draw the phrase structure
tree and apply the necessary transformational rules to produce the following
sentence?
I am happy about your grades.

THE NOUN PHRASE NOUN PHRASE COMPLEMENT

A certain number of verbs can be used with two objects. In traditional terms,
the first object is called the *indirect object* and the second object is called the
direct object. Here are some sentences with this complement type.

The wizard granted the knight a wish.
The boss promised me the job.
I found Gene a house.
He made me a sandwich.
The catcher gave the pitcher the ball.

The phrase structure tree is as you would expect:

The wizard granted the knight a wish.

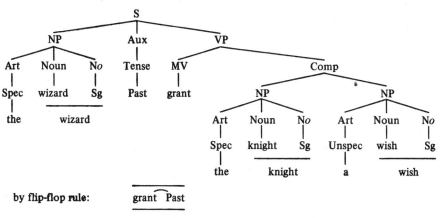

by flip-flop rule: grant Past

                               granted

An important characteristic of this complement type is that the two noun phrases can undergo an optional transformation that reverses the order of the two noun phrases and puts either *to* or *for* (depending on the main verb) between the reversed noun phrases, for example:

The wizard granted the knight a wish. ⟹ The wizard granted a wish to the knight.

The boss promised me the job. ⟹ The boss promised the job to me.

I found Gene a house. ⟹ I found a house for Gene.

He made me a sandwich. ⟹ He made a sandwich for me.

The catcher gave the pitcher the ball. ⟹ The catcher gave the ball to the pitcher.

Although this transformation is optional, it is nearly obligatory for speakers of American (but not British) English when the objects are pronouns. That is, most Americans would strongly prefer

The wizard granted it to him.

over the untransformed version

The wizard granted him it.

EXERCISE 3.13   Noun Phrase ⁀ Noun Phrase Switch Rule

Can you formalize the transformational rule (which we will call the *noun phrase ⁀ noun phrase switch rule*) that reverses the order of the two noun phrases and inserts either *to* or *for* between the noun phrases? Hint: the rule will not indicate which verbs take *to* and which take *for*.

EXERCISE 3.14   Noun Phrase ⁀ Noun Phrase Complements

Draw phrase structure trees and apply the necessary transformational rules to produce the following sentences:
1. I asked John his opinion.
2. He drew Ann a picture.
3. She read a story to the children.
4. He will leave it for you.

THE NOUN PHRASE ⁀ PREPOSITION ⁀ NOUN PHRASE COMPLEMENT

Compare the following three sentences:

He took some candy out of his pocket.   *NP Adv. of direct*
He took some candy to the baby.   *NP ⁀ NP*
He took some candy from the baby.

On the surface, these three sentences have nearly identical structures: the main verb is followed by a noun phrase, a preposition (in the case of the first sentence, two prepositions) and a second noun phrase. In fact, the three different sentences come from three different complement types. The first sentence contains a noun phrase adverbial of direction complement, the second sentence contains a noun phrase noun phrase complement that has had the noun phrase noun phrase switch rule applied to it, and the third contains a noun phrase preposition noun phrase complement. How do we know this? There are several ways we can tell. First of all, notice the prepositions. In the first sentence we have a double preposition, which, as you know, is characteristic of an adverbial of direction complement. There are only single prepositions in the other two sentences. The preposition in the third sentence is *from*. Since the noun phrase noun phrase switch rule generates only *to* and *for*, we know that the third sentence cannot be an instance of the noun phrase noun phrase complement.

However, a second and more important way of telling the three sentences apart is based on our ability to recognize the essential identity of the transformed and untransformed versions of the same deep structure sentence. In the case of the first sentence, we can establish that it indeed contains a noun phrase adverbial of direction complement because only sentences containing an adverbial of direction can undergo the adverbial of direction deletion rule. In other words, we can transform

He took some candy out of his pocket.

into

He took some candy out.

but we cannot transform the other two sentences by the same rule:

*He took some candy to.
*He took some candy from.

In a similar manner, we know that every sentence that has had the noun phrase noun phrase switch rule applied to it is derived from a deep structure that also produces an untransformed counterpart. That is, for the transformed version of the sentence

He took some candy to the baby.

there exists an untransformed counterpart

He took the baby some candy.

No such untransformed counterpart exists for the first sentence:

*He took his pocket some candy.

The third sentence does not have an untransformed counterpart either, although at first glance it may look as though it does:

*He took the baby some candy.

This sentence is grammatical *only* if we take it to be the transformed counterpart of

He took some candy *to* the baby.

Put another way, the sentence

He took the baby some candy.

can only mean *to the baby* and not *from the baby*.

Consequently, our definition of noun phrase preposition noun phrase complements is basically negative: they do not contain double prepositions, they cannot undergo the adverbial of direction deletion rule, and they do not have any counterpart sentence with the noun phrases reversed and the preposition deleted.

Noun phrase preposition noun phrase complements occur with a variety of prepositions, *about, of, for, on, to,* and *with* being the most common. Here are some examples:

I told him about my plan.
They informed him of the outcome.
I thanked him for his gift.
We congratulated her on her victory.
John introduced Bill to Mary.
We supplied him with paper towels.

As you can see from these sentences, there is not much danger of confusing noun phrase preposition noun phrase complements with noun phrase adverbial of direction complements. However, it is easy to confuse noun phrase preposition noun phrase complements with transformed noun phrase noun phrase complements, especially if the noun phrase preposition noun phrase complement contains the preposition *to* or *for*. The only reliable way to tell these two complement types apart is to check whether there is an untransformed counterpart sentence. If there is, then, by definition, the complement is a noun phrase noun phrase type. The lack of any untransformed counterpart establishes that the six sample sentences above have noun phrase preposition noun phrase complements:

*I told my plan him.
*They informed the outcome him.
*I thanked his gift him.
*We congratulated her victory her.
*John introduced Mary Bill.
*We supplied paper towels him.

EXERCISE 3.15   **Noun Phrase Preposition Noun Phrase Complements**

Draw phrase structure trees and apply the necessary transformational rules to produce the following sentences:
1. He took some candy out of his pocket.
2. He took some candy to the baby.
3. He took some candy from the baby.

WAYS OF MAKING NEW VERBS

Every language has a continual need to make up new verbs. One of the most common ways of making up new verbs in the Indo-European languages has been to fuse together a verb stem and preposition to make a new verb. In Latin, the preposition was attached to the beginning of the verb. Here are some examples of verbs made this way that have come into English:

compel Lat *com* "with, together" + *pellō* "drive, force"
comprehend Lat *com* "with, together" + *prehendō* "grasp" (*pre* is also itself a preposition)
devour Lat *de* "down, from" + *vorō* "swallow"
detain Lat *de* "down, from" + *tencō* "hold"
exceed Lat *ex* "out" + *cedō* "Go away, withdraw"

Many English verbs are made with prepositions prefixed in the Latin manner, for example:

bypass	overestimate
downplay	overlook
forget	understand
forgive	upset
offset	withdraw
outlast	withstand
overcome	

However, most English preposition–verb combinations are made with the preposition used as a suffix rather than a prefix. This deviation from the Latin model has turned the English way of suffixing prepositions into something of a second-class citizen (and in its own native land, too), even though the English way is as ancient as the Latin. On the other hand, much of the stigma of the verb plus preposition combination is due to the very fact that these forms are new; that is, they appear first as slang or part of a specialized technical jargon. If the combination withstands the passage of time, it becomes an unobjectionable part of the English vocabulary.

BEETLE BAILEY by Mort Walker

New Intransitive Verbs

Here are some examples of new intransitive verbs (verbs with a ∅ complement) made by adding a preposition to the verb stem:

I *give up*.
The fire *went out*.
The battery has *run down*.
The firecrackers *went off*.
His promotion finally *came through*.
The ship *came about*.
We finally *gave in*.
Christmas will soon *come around*.
Something will *turn up*.
The batter *struck out*.
She *passed out*.
Stop in sometime.

Even the verb *be* can be used as an intransitive verb if it has a suffixed preposition:

The batter *is up*.
The batter *is out*.
The game *is over*.

Here is a sample derivation of a sentence with an intransitive verb plus preposition construction:

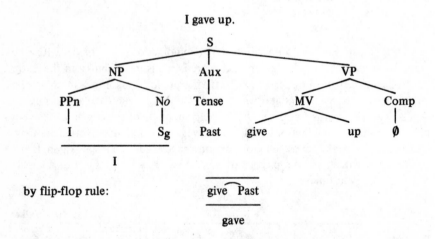

Notice that the preposition *up* is not included in the application of the flip-flop rule in the derivation of *I gave up*. From the standpoint of meaning, *give up* is a unit, but from the standpoint of word formation, it is two units: a verb and a preposition.

New Transitive Verbs

Transitive verbs are verbs with a NP complement. The only difficult thing about them is distinguishing them from sentences that also have a preposition and a noun phrase following the verb, for example:

The reporter walked into the doorway.
The reporter watched from the doorway.
The reporter looked at the doorway.

The first sentence contains an adverbial of direction complement, as evidenced by its ability to undergo the adverbial of direction deletion rule:

The reporter walked in.

If we apply this same transformational rule to the other sentences, the results are ungrammatical, showing that they do not contain adverbial of direction complements:

*The reporter watched from.
*The reporter looked at.

The second sentence contains an intransitive verb with a $\emptyset$ complement followed by an optional adverbial of position. Since the adverbial is optional, we can delete it without affecting the grammaticality of the rest of the sentence:

The reporter watched.

We cannot do this to the third sentence without producing a strange-sounding sentence:

*The reporter looked.

However, the key test for a transitive verb made from a verb plus a preposition is that the sentence can undergo the passive transformation:

The doorway was looked at by the reporter.

If we apply this transformation to the sentence containing the adverbial of position, the result is borderline grammatical at best:

?*The doorway was watched by the reporter.

Often (but not always) the transitive verb plus preposition unit can be replaced by a single-word verb with a nearly identical meaning. For example, we can replace *look at* by *examine* without substantially changing the meaning:

The reporter examined the doorway.

There is no such single-word replacement possible for *watch from* because *watch from* is not a single unit either grammatically or semantically.

Here are some more examples of transitive verbs made with verb plus preposition units:

We *depended on* him.
The board *approved of* the idea.
I have never *heard of* him.
I will *look after* him.
She will *stand by* him.

There are even a substantial number of transitive verbs made with not one but two prepositions:

The children *talked back to* their parents.
We *put up with* that nonsense.
They *found out about* it.
John *came up with* an idea.
He *faced up to* the problem.
Everyone *looked down on* them.
They *walked out on* us.

It seems clear that when we add a preposition (or two) to a verb, we create a new verb. These new verbs function semantically as a single unit, and with one group of exceptions, function grammatically as a single unit as well. However, there are a number of transitive verbs made from a verb plus a single preposition that have the special property of permitting the preposition to be separated from the verb itself. This separation is a purely formal matter, with no effect on meaning. Here are some examples:

She *called up* her parents.
I *took back* the pump.
He *made up* the story.
Johnson *knocked out* Smith.
The company *turned down* his offer.
They *blew up* the factory.

All of these permit the preposition to be moved to a position after the noun phrase without any change in meaning:

She *called* her parents *up*.
I *took* the pump *back*.
He *made* the story *up*.
Johnson *knocked* Smith *out*.
The company *turned* his offer *down*.
They *blew* the factory *up*.

Since there is a formal difference between the two groups of verbs, the phrase structure must also make a distinction between them. There are many ways to do this. The chief advantage of the way proposed here is simplicity. Let us use the symbol V to be the source node for all verb and verb plus preposition combinations *except* those verb plus preposition combinations that permit the preposition to be separated from the verb. We will indicate verbs with separable prepositions by a separate node dominated by the main verb node. Thus, our new rule for the development of main verb looks like this:

$$MV \longrightarrow \left\{ \begin{matrix} V \\ V \ Prep \end{matrix} \right\}$$
$$V \longrightarrow \left\{ be, \ have, \ talk, \ depend \ on, \ talk \ back \ to. . . \right\}$$

Only those verbs that can occur with a separable preposition will appear in the second line of the main verb rule. Thus, *call on* will appear in the first line, while the *call* that is part of the combination *call up* will appear in the second line.

EXERCISE 3.16   Separable Preposition Switch Rule

You now have enough information to understand the transformational rule which switches the positions of the preposition and the noun phrase. Can you now write the rule?

Two-Word Verbs

Here are some sample derivations of transitive verbs made from verb + preposition combinations:

We depended on his help.

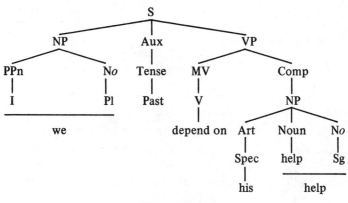

by flip-flop rule: depend ⌢ Past

                                        depended

She called her family up.

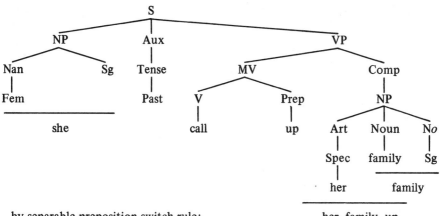

by separable preposition switch rule: her family up

by flip-flop rule: call ⌢ Past

                                called

He tried out for the team.

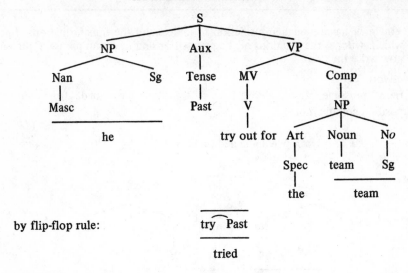

by flip-flop rule: try Past

                                              tried

Verb plus preposition combinations are often called two-word verbs (I do not think anybody calls the verb plus two preposition combinations three-word verbs, however). When the preposition in a two-word verb can have the separable preposition switch rule applied to it, it is called a *separable* two-word verb. It will come as no surprise that the two-word verbs that are not separable are called *inseparable* two-word verbs.

EXERCISE 3.17   **Two-Word Verbs**

Draw phrase structure trees and apply the necessary transformational rules to produce the following sentences:
1. You must allow for delays.
2. She broke off our engagement.
3. The general looked the situation over.
4. We looked forward to the party.
5. She called her parents up yesterday.

EXERCISE 3.18   **Review**

For the following sentences, indicate the complement type, the type of optional adverbial (if any), and any optional transformational rule, i.e., not the flip-flop rule, that has been applied.
1. The children caught up on their work.
2. He seems bright.
3. I am tired of his schemes.
4. John did me a favor.
5. The grand jury indicted them for bribery.
6. John set the stool on the porch.

7. The ball is on the roof.
8. The roses have died.
9. Mother cared for Aunt Sally.
10. We have run out of soap.
11. He reminded me of someone.
12. The lawyer got him out of jail.
13. They offered the job to Ruth.
14. We took him in (*to town* understood).
15. The plant laid the workers off.
16. The scouts returned.
17. He laid his cards on the table.
18. The pilot brought the plane down safely.
19. We saved a place for them.
20. Felix put a napkin under the glass.
21. They crept away from the sentry.
22. The wind is blowing today.
23. They were making a fuss about nothing.
24. Ms. Brown has resided at that address for several years.
25. Mays slid in (*to third base* understood).
26. I am fond of pickles.
27. The gardener tossed the trash into the can.
28. They are being tactful.
29. Sally answered the phone quickly.
30. We had been concerned about it.

SUMMARY OF PHRASE STRUCTURE RULES

The following is a summary of the phrase structure rules introduced in the first three chapters. The rules are not presented in the same order as they occurred in the text. For those rules that have been given in several forms, only the final form is presented here. Although it will be necessary to add a few new elements to the ones presented here (mostly embedded sentences), the general framework of rules presented here will not be altered.

Sentence (S) ⟶ Noun Phrase ⏜ Auxiliary ⏜ Verb Phrase

Noun Phrase (NP) ⟶ $\left\{ \begin{array}{l} \text{Article} \frown \text{Noun} \frown \text{Number} \\ \text{Proper Noun } \left\{ \begin{array}{l} \text{Singular} \\ \text{Plural} \end{array} \right\} \\ \text{Personal Pronoun} \frown \text{Number} \end{array} \right\}$

Article (Art) ⟶ $\left\{ \begin{array}{l} \text{Specified} \\ \text{Unspecified} \\ \emptyset \end{array} \right\}$

Specified (Spec) ⟶ $\left\{ \begin{array}{l} \textit{the, this, that, these, those}\text{; possessive} \\ \text{nouns and possessive pronouns; numbers...} \end{array} \right\}$

Unspecified (Unspec) ⟶ $\left\{ \begin{array}{l} \textit{a/an, some, a few, a couple, several,} \\ \textit{much, many...} \end{array} \right\}$

Noun ⟶ $\{ \textit{boy, tree, idea, elephant...} \}$

Proper Noun (Nprop) ⟶ $\{ \textit{Mr. Brown, Mary, America, the Alps...} \}$

Personal Pronoun (PPn) $\longrightarrow$ $\{I, you\}$

Number (No) $\longrightarrow$ $\left\{\begin{array}{l}\text{Singular}\\\text{Plural}\end{array}\right\}$

Auxiliary (Aux) $\longrightarrow$ Tense (Modal) (Perfect) (Progressive)

Tense $\longrightarrow$ $\left\{\begin{array}{l}\text{Present}\\\text{Past}\end{array}\right\}$

Present (Pres)
1. IF Pres Modal, THEN Pres $\longrightarrow \emptyset$
2. IF N Sg Pres, THEN Pres $\longrightarrow$ -s/-es
3. IF PPn Sg Pres, THEN Pres $\longrightarrow \emptyset$
4. IF Pl Pres, THEN Pres $\longrightarrow \emptyset$

Modal $\longrightarrow$ *can, may, must, shall, will*

Perfect $\longrightarrow$ *have* -EN

Progressive $\longrightarrow$ *be* -ING

Verb Phrase (VP) $\longrightarrow$ Main Verb Complement (Adverbial)

Main Verb (MV) $\longrightarrow$ $\left\{\begin{array}{l}\text{V}\\\text{V Preposition}\end{array}\right\}$

V $\longrightarrow$ $\{be, have, talk, seem, depend on, talk back to...\}$

Preposition (Prep) $\longrightarrow$ $\{at, in, on, to, with...\}$

Complement (Comp) $\longrightarrow$ $\left\{\begin{array}{l}\emptyset\\\text{NP}\\\text{Adjective}\\\text{(NP) Adverbial of position}\\\text{(NP) Adverbial of direction}\\\text{Adjective Prep NP}\\\text{NP NP}\\\text{NP Prep NP}\end{array}\right\}$

Adjective $\longrightarrow$ $\{angry, unpleasant, interesting, worried...\}$

Adverbial $\longrightarrow$ $\left\{\begin{array}{l}\text{Adverbial of time}\\\text{Adverbial of position}\\\text{Adverbial of direction}\\\text{Adverbial of manner}\end{array}\right\}$

$\left\{\begin{array}{l}\text{Adverbial of time (ADVtime)}\\\text{Adverbial of position (ADVposition)}\\\text{Adverbial of direction (ADVdirection)}\\\text{Adverbial of manner (ADVmanner)}\end{array}\right\} \longrightarrow \left\{\begin{array}{l}\text{Prepositional Phrase}\\\text{Adverb}\end{array}\right\}$

Prepositional Phrase (PP) $\longrightarrow$ Prep NP

Adverb $\longrightarrow$ *now, here, soon, there, softly, quickly...*

Answers to Exercise 3.1   PHRASE STRUCTURE RULE FOR ADVERBIALS

ADVtime $\longrightarrow$ $\left\{\begin{array}{l}\text{Prepositional Phrase}\\ \text{Adverb}\end{array}\right\}$

ADVposition $\longrightarrow$ $\left\{\begin{array}{l}\text{Prepositional Phrase}\\ \text{Adverb}\end{array}\right\}$

ADVdirection $\longrightarrow$ $\left\{\begin{array}{l}\text{Prepositional Phrase}\\ \text{Adverb}\end{array}\right\}$

ADVmanner $\longrightarrow$ $\left\{\begin{array}{l}\text{Prepositional Phrase}\\ \text{Adverb}\end{array}\right\}$

Answers to Exercise 3.2   ADVERBIALS

1. **It might be snowing in the mountains.**

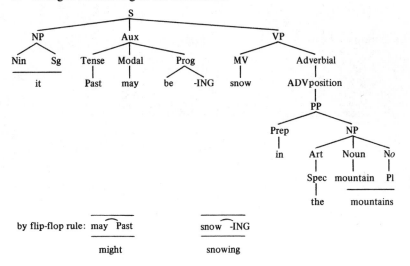

by flip-flop rule: $\overparen{\text{may \ Past}}$ = might $\overparen{\text{snow \ -ING}}$ = snowing

2.   **Ms. Brown had danced marvelously.**

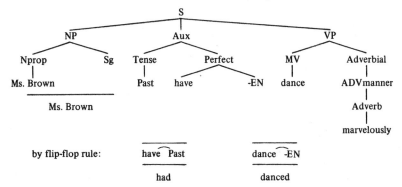

by flip-flop rule: $\overparen{\text{have \ Past}}$ = had $\overparen{\text{dance \ -EN}}$ = danced

3.   The boys slept in the yard.

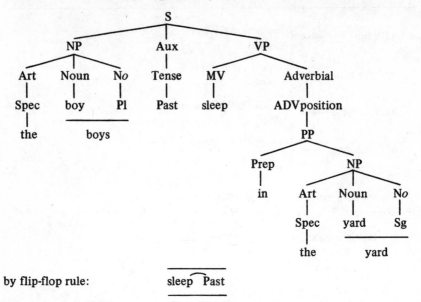

by flip-flop rule: sleep‿Past
                                            ———————
                                              slept

4.   The cat was drinking out of the bowl.

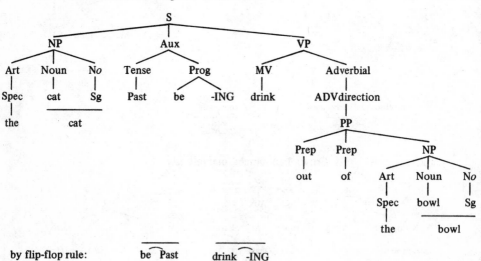

by flip-flop rule: be‿Past   drink‿-ING
                                ———————   —————————
                                  was   drinking

5. Someone coughed inside.

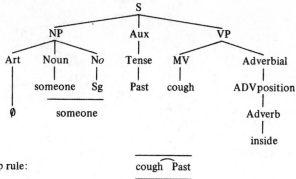

by flip-flop rule: cough͡ Past
_____
coughed

6. They ran inside.

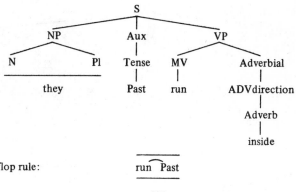

by flip-flop rule: run͡ Past
_____
ran

Answers to Exercise 3.3 ∅ COMPLEMENTS

1. The telephone rang.

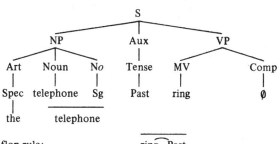

by flip-flop rule: ring͡ Past
_____
rang

2.   Our roof leaks.

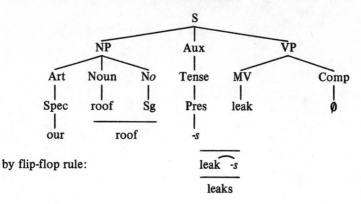

by flip-flop rule:

$$\frac{\text{leak} \frown \text{-s}}{\text{leaks}}$$

3.   The baby was sleeping soundly.

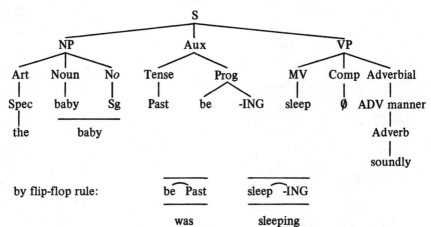

by flip-flop rule:

$$\frac{\text{be} \frown \text{Past}}{\text{was}} \qquad \frac{\text{sleep} \frown \text{-ING}}{\text{sleeping}}$$

4.   She will laugh.

by flip-flop rule:

$$\frac{\text{will} \frown \emptyset}{\text{will}}$$

5.   I have been working in the library.

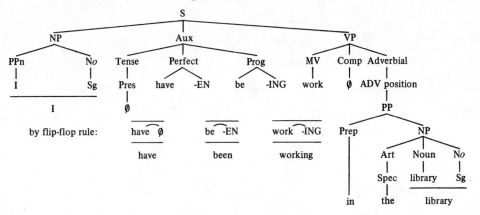

Answers to Exercise 3.4   NOUN PHRASE COMPLEMENTS

1.   John broke the window.

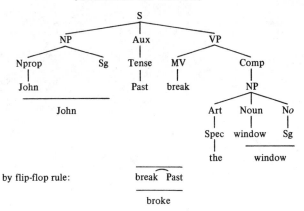

2.   I have a question.

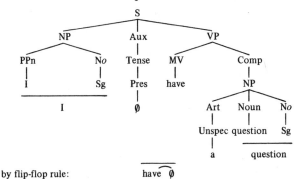

3.   The students passed the exam easily.

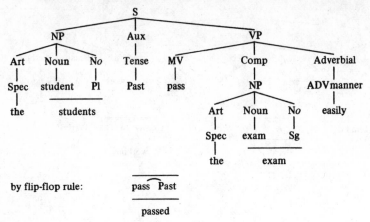

by flip-flop rule: pass ⌢ Past
                          ————————
                              passed

4.   His father painted the picture.

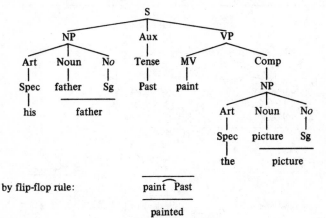

by flip-flop rule: paint ⌢ Past
                          ————————
                              painted

5.   Someone burned the toast.

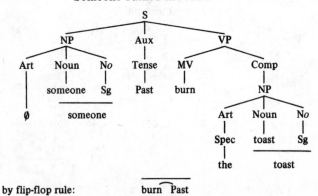

by flip-flop rule: burn ⌢ Past
                          ————————
                              burned

Answers to Exercise 3.5 RECOGNIZING ADJECTIVES

1. The cup is cracking. ∅ complement
2. The movie was frightening. Adjective complement
3. The prisoners are escaping. ∅ complement
4. The sky is clearing. ∅ complement
5. His views are alarming. Adjective complement
6. The wine is overflowing. ∅ complement
7. Dawn is breaking. ∅ complement
8. The book is interesting. Adjective complement
9. The children are appealing. Adjective complement
10. He is retiring. Both answers are correct, but with different meanings. In the meaning of "no longer working," *retiring* is used with a ∅ complement. In the meaning of "shy," *retiring* is an adjective.

Answers to Exercise 3.6 ACTIVE AND STATIVE ADJECTIVES

1. He is nervous. Stative
2. He is kind. Active
3. He is lenient. Active
4. He is excellent. Stative
5. He is dull. Stative
6. He is young. Stative
7. He is gray. Stative
8. He is sad. Stative
9. He is careful. Active
10. He is unreasonable. Active

Answers to Exercise 3.7 ADJECTIVE COMPLEMENTS

1.

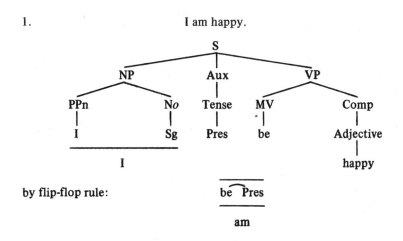

2.   The girl turned pale.

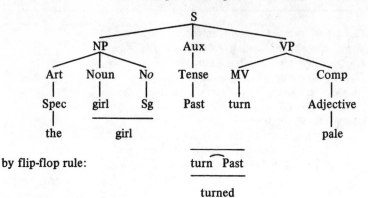

by flip-flop rule:

3.   We kept quiet.

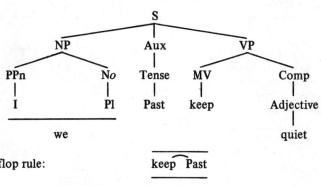

by flip-flop rule:

4.   The man became famous.

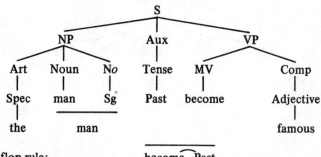

by flip-flop rule:

Answers to Exercise 3.8   NOUN PHRASE⁀ADVERBIAL OF POSITION
COMPLEMENTS

1.   The dictionary is on the shelf.

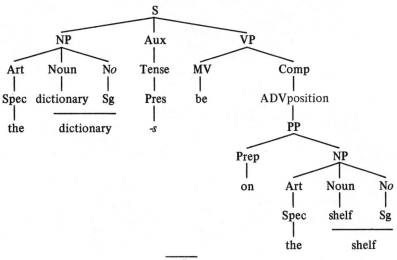

by flip-flop rule: be⁀-s
                                       ───
                                        is

2.   Mr. Smith is on his farm upstate.

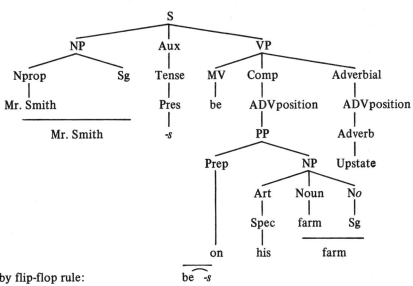

by flip-flop rule: be⁀-s
                                       ───
                                        is

·3   He is here.

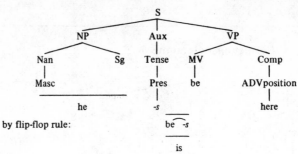

by flip-flop rule:

4.   You could live in Philadelphia.

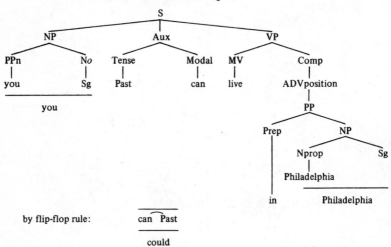

by flip-flop rule:

5.   The baby lay in the crib.

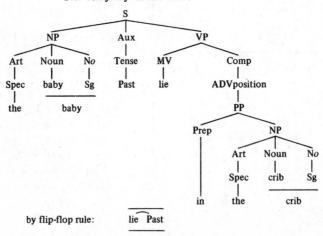

by flip-flop rule:

6.   They laid the baby in the crib.

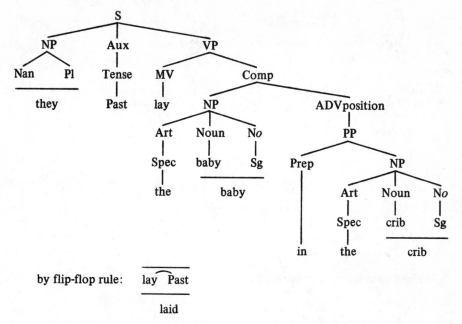

by flip-flop rule: lay͡ Past

                      laid

Answers to Exercise 3.9   ADVERBIALS OF DIRECTION

1.   The truck turned into the driveway.

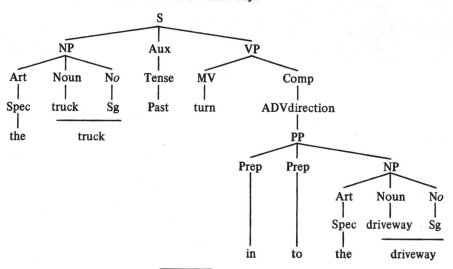

by flip-flop rule: turn͡ Past

                      turned

2.   Ms. Brown walked out of the store.

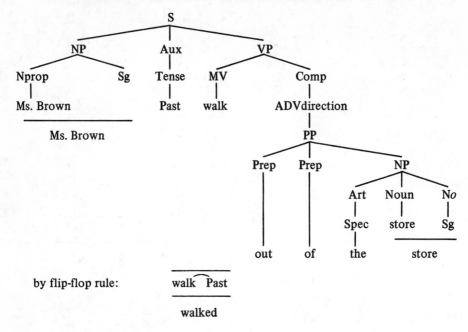

by flip-flop rule: walk⌢Past
                                ─────────
                                  walked

3.   The batter stepped up to the plate.

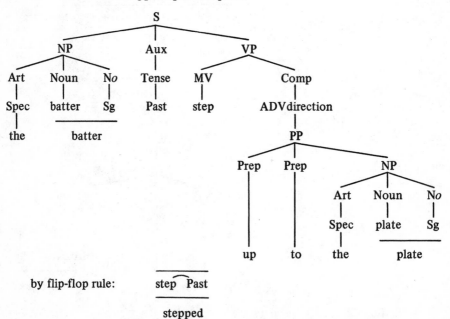

by flip-flop rule: step⌢Past
                                ─────────
                                 stepped

4.   The boys dove in (to the water).

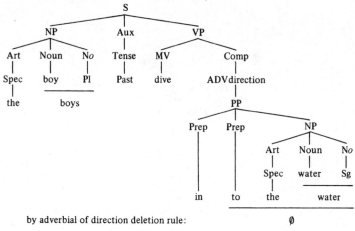

by adverbial of direction deletion rule: Ø

by flip-flop rule: dive͡ Past

                                dove

Answers to Exercise 3.10   ADVERBIAL OF DIRECTION DELETION RULE

MV͡ (NP₁)͡ Prep₁͡ (Prep₂)͡ NP₂ ⟹ MV͡ (NP₁)͡ Prep₁

Answers to Exercise 3.11   (NOUN PHRASE)͡ ADVERBIAL OF DIRECTION
                               COMPLEMENTS

1.   The truck pulled the car out of the mud.

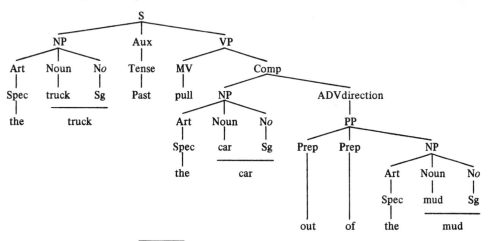

by flip-flop rule: pull͡ Past

                                pulled

2.   The team threw the coach into the pool.

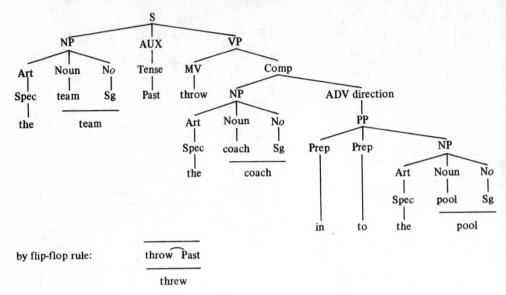

by flip-flop rule:

3.   The coach will send Johnson in (to the game).

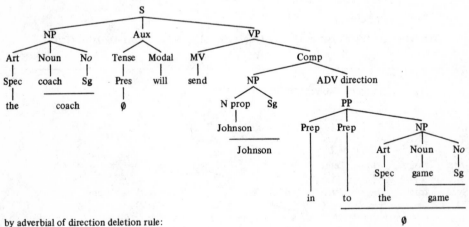

by adverbial of direction deletion rule:

by flip-flop rule:

4.   The division turned back (from the front).

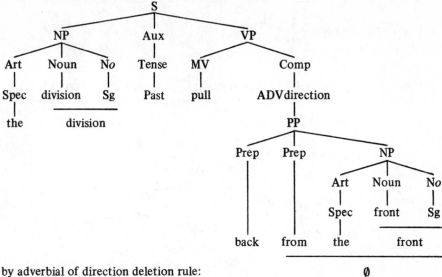

by adverbial of direction deletion rule: $\emptyset$

by flip-flop rule: turn͡ Past

                                      ─────────
                                      turned

Answers to Exercise 3.12   ADJECTIVE͡ PREPOSITION͡ NOUN PHRASE COMPLEMENTS

I am happy about your grades.

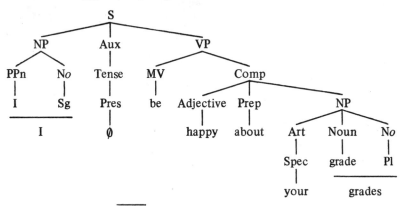

by flip-flop rule: be͡ ∅

                          ──────
                          am

Answers to Exercise 3.13   NOUN PHRASE⌒NOUN PHRASE SWITCH RULE

$$NP_1 \frown NP_2 \Longrightarrow NP_2 \frown \left\{ \begin{matrix} to \\ \overline{for} \end{matrix} \right\} NP_1$$

Answers to Exercise 3.14   NOUN PHRASE⌒NOUN PHRASE COMPLEMENTS

1.   I asked John his opinion.

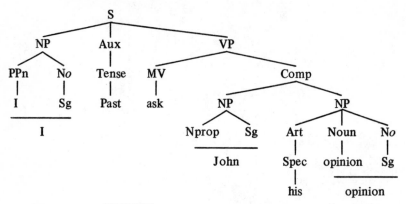

by flip-flop rule: ask⌒Past
                      ‾‾‾‾‾‾‾‾‾
                         asked

2.   He drew Ann a picture.

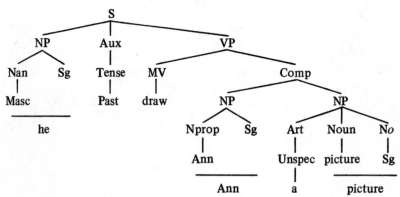

by flip-flop rule: draw⌒Past
                      ‾‾‾‾‾‾‾‾‾‾
                         drew

3. She read a story to the children.

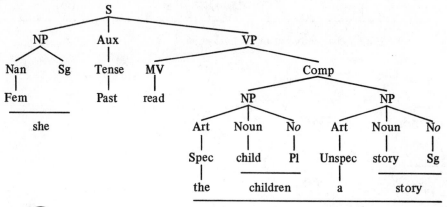

by NP NP switch rule: a story to the children

by flip-flop rule: read Past

                          read

4.   He will leave it for you.

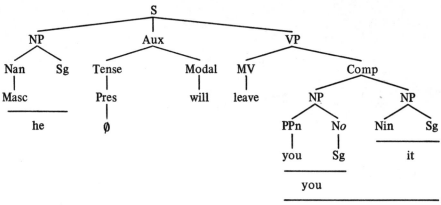

by NP NP switch rule: it for you

by flip-flop rule: will ∅

                                will

Answers to Exercise 3.15   NOUN PHRASE͡ PREPOSITION͡ NOUN PHRASE
                                COMPLEMENTS

1. He took some candy out of his pocket.

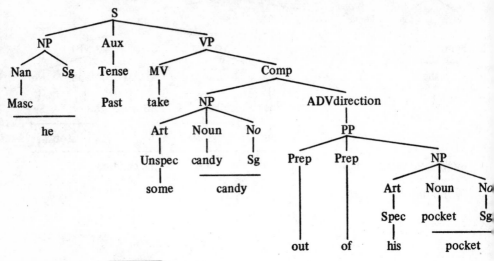

by flip-flop rule: take͡ Past
                      ——————
                         took

2.   He took some candy to the baby.

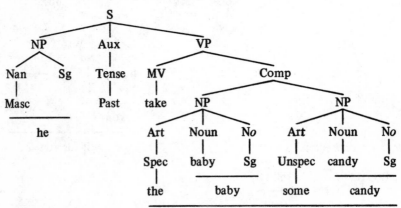

by NP͡ NP switch rule: some candy to the baby

by flip-flop rule: take͡ Past
                      ——————
                         took

3. He took some candy from the baby.

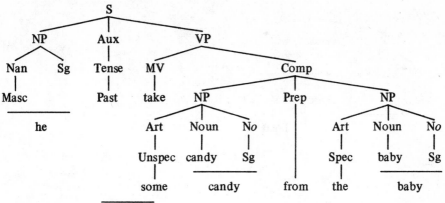

by flip-flop rule: take⌢Past

took

Answers to Exercise 3.16   SEPARABLE PREPOSITION SWITCH RULE

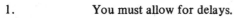

V⌢Prep⌢NP⟹V⌢NP⌢Prep

Answers to Exercise 3.17   TWO-WORD VERBS

1.   You must allow for delays.

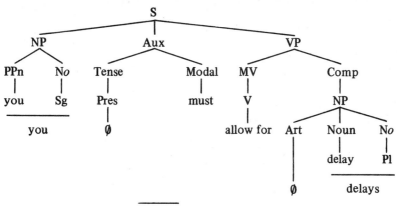

by flip-flop rule: must⌢∅

must

2.   She broke off our engagement.

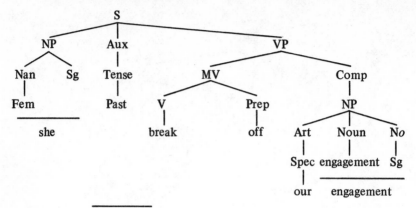

by flip-flop rule: break ⌢ Past
                    ─────────────
                         broke

3.   The general looked the situation over.

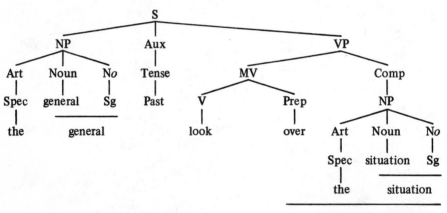

by separable preposition switch rule:

by flip-flop rule: look ⌢ Past
                           ──────────────
                               looked

4.   We looked forward to the party.

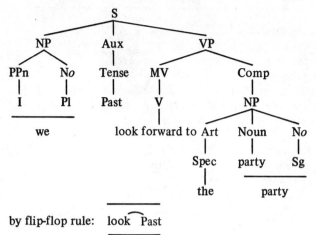

by flip-flop rule: look⌒Past
                      ‾‾‾‾‾‾‾‾‾‾
                         looked

5. She called her parents up yesterday.

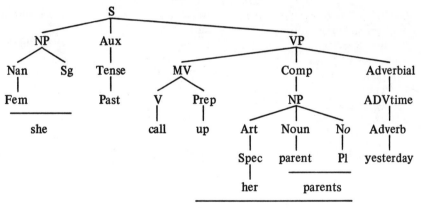

by separable preposition switch rule: her parents up

by flip-flop rule: call⌒Past
                                ‾‾‾‾‾‾‾‾‾
                                  called

Answers to Exercise 3.18   REVIEW

1. The children caught up on their work. ADVdirection
2. He seems bright. Adjective
3. I am tired of his schemes. Adjective Prep NP
4. John did me a favor. NP NP
5. The grand jury indicted them for bribery. NP Prep NP
6. John set the stool on the porch. NP ADVposition
7. The ball is on the roof. ADVposition
8. The roses have died. ∅
9. Mother cared for Aunt Sally. NP
10. We have run out of soap. ADVdirection
11. He reminded me of someone. NP Prep NP
12. The lawyer got him out of jail. NP ADVdirection
13. They offered the job to Ruth. NP NP; NP NP switch rule has been applied.
14. We took him in (to town). NP ADVdirection; ADVdirection deletion rule has been applied.
15. The plant laid the workers off. NP; separable preposition switch rule has been applied.
16. The scouts returned. ∅
17. He laid his cards on the table. NP ADVposition
18. The pilot brought the plane down safely. NP Comp plus ADVmanner; separable preposition switch rule has been applied.
19. We saved a place for them. NP NP; NP NP switch rule has been applied.
20. Felix put a napkin under the glass. NP ADVposition
21. They crept away from the sentry. ADVdirection
22. The wind is blowing today. ∅ Comp plus ADVtime
23. They were making a fuss about nothing. NP Prep NP
24. Ms. Brown has resided at that address for several years. ADVposition Comp plus ADVtime
25. Mays slid in (to third base). ADVdirection; ADVdirection deletion rule has been applied.
26. I am fond of pickles. Adjective Prep NP
27. The gardener tossed the trash into the can. NP ADVdirection
28. They are being tactful. Adjective
29. Sally answered the phone quickly. NP Comp plus ADVmanner
30. We had been concerned about it. Adjective Prep NP

PART II

Simple Transformational Rules

OVERVIEW

The grammar presented up to now produces the basic sentences that underlie the more complex sentences we actually use in speaking and writing. All of the basic sentences generated by the grammar of Part I are active (rather than passive), statements (rather than questions), affirmative (rather than negative), and neutral (rather than containing commands or any special emphasis). Obviously, passives, questions, negative statements, and emphatic sentences play a large role in actual language use. How, then, are these sentences generated by the grammar?

One theoretically possible way to produce these four different sentence types would be to have a separate set of basic rules for each. The grammar would then consist of at least five parts: the rules that generate active, affirmative, neutral statements; the rules that generate passive sentences; the rules that generate questions; the rules that generate negative statements; and the rules that generate commands and emphatic sentences. It is conceivable that some languages work that way. However, no one has ever found one that does, and it seems pretty unlikely that anyone ever will. Such enormous reduplication seems to go against the grain of human languages. All known languages use a quite different principle: they have just one basic set of rules that generate active, affirmative, neutral statements. These sentences can then be turned into passives, questions, negative statements, or commands by making some variation in the form of the underlying statement. This variation may be achieved by adding or deleting a word or phrase, or by rearranging some of the words in the basic sentence, or even by changing the way the sentence is pronounced. In transformational terms, passives, questions, negative statements, commands, and emphatic statements are produced by applying certain transformational operations to the basic underlying sentence. In this section, we will examine some of these transformations.

The following diagram may help clarify the relation of the different types of rule systems:

The phase structure rules produce the deep structure sentence, a simple, affirmative, active, statement. The optional simple transformational rules convert the deep structure sentence into a passive, question, negative, or emphatic sentence. The simple transformational rules are obviously optional, or else all sentences would be passive, questions, negatives, or emphatic. The obligatory "housekeeping" transformational rules are rules like the flip-flop rule that are necessary to form the surface sentence correctly. These rules do not affect the meaning of the sentence.

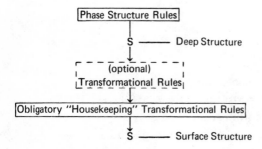

CHAPTER 4

The Passive

OVERVIEW

The phrase structure rules produce "active" sentences. "Passive" sentences are created from certain types of active sentences by an optional transformational rule. This rule reverses the subject and object noun phrases, inserts a *by* in front of the original subject noun phrase which now follows the main verb, and adds *be* -EN to the auxiliary. For example, the passive version of

John saw the accident.

is

The accident was seen by John.

A rule closely associated with the passive is the "agent deletion rule." This rule deletes the original subject noun phrase (and the *by* that precedes it). Applied to the passive sentence above, this rule would convert

The accident was seen by John.

to

The accident was seen.

The passive rule is formalized here as a sequence of three elementary (and unordered) rules: the noun phrase switch rule that reverses the subject and object noun phrases, the *by* insertion rule, and the be -EN insertion rule.

139

THE PASSIVE

The passive is an optional transformational operation that converts underlying active sentences into the passive. Here are some corresponding active and passive sentences:

Active: John hit the ball.
Passive: The ball was hit by John.

Active: The explosion injured several bystanders.
Passive: Several bystanders were injured by the explosion.

Active: An inexperienced reporter wrote the story.
Passive: The story was written by an inexperienced reporter.

The function of the passive is to shift the focus of attention away from the subject noun phrase and onto the object noun phrase. Sometimes the passive is employed because the subject noun phrase is unknown and irrelevant, and sometimes because the subject noun phrase is so obvious that it seems redundant to mention it. For example, compare the active and passive versions of these two sentences:

Someone made my camera in Japan.
My camera was made in Japan.

My mother bore me in Chicago.
I was born in Chicago.

Not every sentence that contains a noun phrase complement, however, can undergo the passive transformation. In the preceding chapter, it was pointed out that linking verbs, even with noun phrase complements, do not allow the passive transformation, for example:

John is a fool. ⟹ *A fool is become by John.
John resembles a horse. ⟹ *A horse is resembled by John.
John became a fool. ⟹ *A fool was become by John.

In addition to linking verbs, there are a number of stative verbs that do not permit a passive, for example, *cost, have* (the most common), *measure,* and *weigh*:

The book cost $5.95. ⟹ *$5.95 was cost by the book.
He has a book. ⟹ *A book was had by him.
The room measures 12 by 14. ⟹ *12 by 14 is measured by the room.
I weight 175 pounds. ⟹ *175 pounds is weighed by me.

There is a general restriction on the use of the passive if the subject noun and the object noun refer to the same person regardless of what verb is used. In the following pairs of sentences, the first sentence allows a passive whereas the second sentence, using the same verb, does not because the object and subject noun refer to the same person:

John hit Mary. $\Longrightarrow$ Mary was hit by John.
John hit himself. $\Longrightarrow$ *Himself was hit by John.

Mary saw John in the mirror. $\Longrightarrow$ John was seen in the mirror by Mary.
Mary saw herself in the mirror. $\Longrightarrow$ *Herself was seen in the mirror by Mary.

John cut her thumb. $\Longrightarrow$ Her thumb was cut by John.
John cut his thumb. $\Longrightarrow$ *His thumb was cut by John. (Grammatical if we
assume that *his* does not refer back to John.)

Before we try to formalize the passive, let us examine some corresponding active and passive sentences:

Active	Passive
John broke the glass.	$\Longrightarrow$ The glass was broken by John.
John may break the glass.	$\Longrightarrow$ The glass may be broken by John.
John is breaking the glass.	$\Longrightarrow$ The glass is being broken by John.
John has broken the glass.	$\Longrightarrow$ The glass has been broken by John.
John may have broken the glass.	$\Longrightarrow$ The glass may have been broken by John.
John has been breaking the glass.	$\Longrightarrow$ The glass has been being broken by John. (?)
John may be breaking the glass.	$\Longrightarrow$ The glass may be being broken by John. (?)
John may have been breaking the glass.	$\Longrightarrow$ The glass may have been being broken by John. (?)

The last three passives may not be fully grammatical for all people. Many people avoid using the passive when the auxiliary contains the progressive plus another optional element.

As you can see from these examples, there are three main characteristics of the passive transformation: (1) the subject and object noun phrases have reversed places—the subject noun phrase is placed after the main verb and the object noun phrase is placed before the main verb. (2) The original subject noun phrase (now following the main verb) has a *by* in front of it. (3) There are two, obviously related, changes in the verbs: *be* is inserted between the last element of the auxiliary and the main verb, and the main verb changes to the past participle form.

The first change, the reversal of the two noun phrases, is a clear illustration of the relative sequencing of rules in a transformational grammar. This need for sequencing appears quite clearly in the following pair of sentences:

John loves them.
They are loved by John.

In the first sentence, the present tense is in the -s form, that is, the third person singular form. In the passive version of the active sentence, however, the present tense form of *be* is *are*, that is, the form used with a plural subject. In other words, the three conditional rules for determining the form of the present tense do *not* apply only to the subject noun phrase in the deep structure, but to *any* noun phrase that occurs in front of the tense node. Thus, by the passive transformation, what was the object noun phrase has become the new subject noun phrase, at least in terms of agreement with the tense marker. If we applied the three conditional rules that determine the form of the present tense before we applied the passive, the passive version of the active sentence

John loves them.

would be

*They is loved by John.

If we assigned the subject and object forms directly in the deep structure, the passive version of the active sentence

John loves them.

would be

*Them are loved by John.

The three conditional rules for present tense require information contained in the noun phrase to their left, but the rules do not need to know if the noun phrase came from the S node or from the operation of the passive transformation. In the same way, the rule for pronoun form puts every pronoun into the object form if it follows the main verb (unless the main verb is a linking verb). The rule is indifferent to the source of the pronoun, whether it comes from a noun phrase in the complement or from a preposition phrase from the adverbial node or from the reversed noun phrases in a passive sentence. After we have dealt with the formalization of the passive rule, we will return to the placement of the rules for the present tense and pronoun form.

The second change involved in the passive is the insertion of *by* in front of the original subject noun phrase, which now follows the main verb. The *by* is often the easiest way to recognize a passive. There are two problems, however. The first problem is relatively minor. *By* is a preposition and can be used in prepositional phrases that can function in any number of ways. For example, here is a well-known sentence from Chomsky's *Syntactic Structures*:

John was drunk by midnight.

The *by* in this sentence is a perfectly respectable part of an optional adverbial of time, having nothing to do with the passive whatsoever.

The second problem is much more troublesome. Often, in fact, according to Quirk, Greenbaum, Leech, and Svartvik, 80 per cent of the time, the *by* and the following noun phrase are deleted from the sentence. It is very easy to recognize

They are loved by John.

as a passive, but it is not so easy to recognize

They are loved.

as a passive.

The third change involved in the passive is the insertion of the helping verb *be* in front of the main verb and the change of the main verb to the past participle form (it would be more accurate to say adding the past participle marker to the main verb). This is usually the only way to recognize a passive if the *by* and the original subject noun phrase have been deleted (as they usually have been). For example, let us take the following pair of sentences:

John was drunk.
The wine was drunk.

In both cases we have *be* followed by what appears to be the past participle form of the verb. The first sentence is not a passive, but the second one is. How can we tell? The main way is that we can make up an active sentence that corresponds to the passive; for example, we can say that

Somebody drank the wine.

is the active equivalent of the passive

The wine was drunk (by somebody).

However, the corresponding active to the first sentence is nonexistent:

*Somebody drank John.

The first sentence contains the verb *be* as a main verb, not as a helping verb. *Drunk* (even though it may have been derived from the verb *drink*) is an adjective. Remember that there are two tests for adjectives: (1) you can put *very* in front of them, and (2) they can form comparative sentences. *Drunk* in the first sentence passes both tests for adjectives:

John was very drunk.
John was drunker than a skunk.

Often, of course, the past participle in the passive has no corresponding adjective, so it is relatively easy to identify the sentence as a passive; for example, in the sentence

John was bitten.

bitten can only be a past participle since *bitten* fails the adjective tests:

*John was very bitten.
*John was more bitten than ever.

(Also, there exists a corresponding active sentence: *Something bit John.*)

However, there are a large number of past participles that are identical with adjectives. In fact, these past participles pose a classification problem since they are both verbs (i.e., main verbs with -EN added to them by the operation of the passive transformation) and adjectives *at the same time*. Here are some examples:

Active	Passive
The gift pleased John.	John was pleased (by the gift).
The suggestion offended John.	John was offended (by the suggestion).
The idea excited John.	John was excited (by the idea).
We amused John.	John was amused (by us).

All of the past participles in the passive sentences also meet the two tests for adjectives:

John was very pleased.
John was more pleased than ever.

John was very offended.
John was more offended than ever.

John was very excited.
John was more excited than ever.

John was very amused.
John was more amused than ever.

So what are *pleased, offended, excited,* and *amused*—adjectives or verbs? The only defendable answer is that they are both. One of the differences between traditional grammar and transformational grammar is that transformational grammar puts less emphasis on part of speech identification and more emphasis on the connection of words to underlying deep structure relations. These words merely point up the fact that there is a big difference between attaching part of speech labels and providing an analysis of how words function within sentences. Thus, from the standpoint of transformational grammar there is nothing particularly alarming about words belonging to more than one part of speech class at the same time. Nevertheless, it would be convenient to have a label to apply to these hybrids (crypto-adjectives? closet-passives?). Perhaps *hybrids* is as good a name as any.

EXERCISE 4.1   **Adjectives, Verbs, and Hybrids**

Decide which of the following sentences contain adjectives, which contain passive verbs, and which contain hybrids:
1. John was frightened.
2. The window was broken.
3. The team was downhearted.
4. The team was discouraged.
5. The team was destroyed.
6. John was hurt.
7. The outcome was unexpected.

8. The tests were completed.
9. John was caught.
10. They were alarmed.

Formalization of Passive Rules

The passive transformation can be broken down into a group of elementary transformational operations. The order in which these are presented is solely a matter of convenience, since there is no compelling evidence to indicate that the operations are relatively ordered. They are as follows:

1. NP switch rule: the subject NP and object NP change places.
2. *by* insertion rule: *by* is inserted between the main verb and the following NP (which was the original subject).
3. *be* -EN insertion rule: *be* -EN is inserted between the last element of the auxiliary and the main verb.

EXERCISE 4.2   **Formalization of Passive Rules**

We have described the three elementary rules necessary to produce passive sentences. Can you now write the actual rules?

Generation of Passive Sentences

Let us go through the generation of several passives in slow motion:

The glass was broken by John.

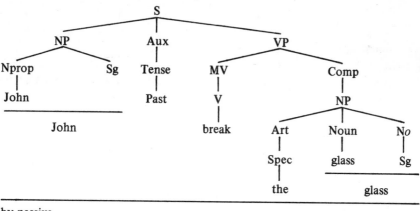

by passive
1. NP switch rule: the glass Past   break   John

2. *by* insertion rule: by

3. *be* -EN insertion rule: be   -EN

by flip-flop rule: be   Past break   -EN

                                          was   broken

The glass might have been broken by John.

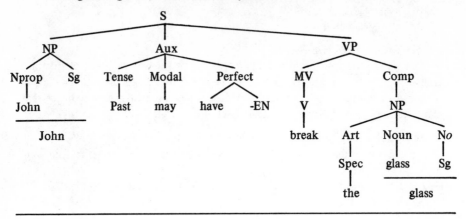

by passive
 1. NP switch rule   The glass Past may have -EN   break   John

 2. *by* insertion rule: by

 3. *be* -EN insertion rule: be -EN

by flip-flop rule: may Past   be -EN break -EN

                                            might   been   broken

When we were discussing the reversal of the subject and object noun phrases, we pointed out that the selection of the proper forms for pronouns and the present tense could be determined only after the passive rules had been applied. Let us agree to represent these changes in the following way: when we apply the passive, we will not rewrite the Pres node in the phrase structure tree, but will rewrite it after the passive has been applied. For the determination of pronoun form (or *case*, as it is usually called), we will merely change subject case to object case by drawing a line under the pronoun and putting in the correct object form without further comment. If we were constructing a full grammar we would treat both present tense and the pronoun case in somewhat different ways, but what is proposed here is adequate to give the reader an idea of the problems involved in the passive. Here is a sample phrase structure tree involving both present tense and pronouns:

They are understood by him.

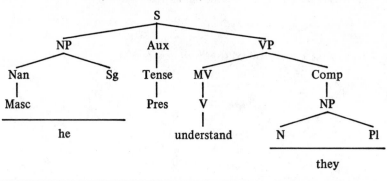

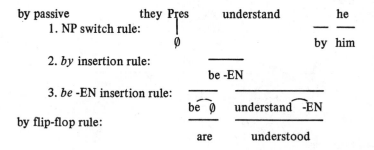

by passive   they Pres   understand   he

1. NP switch rule:

2. *by* insertion rule:

3. *be* -EN insertion rule:

by flip-flop rule:

A passive sentence can either retain the original subject noun phrase (and the *by* that is put in front of it) or the noun phrase can be deleted from the sentence. In fact, as we pointed out earlier, the original noun phrase is usually deleted. The original subject noun phrase is often called the *agent*. The rule that deletes the agent (and the *by*) is called the *agent deletion rule*. There are many ways that we can formalize this rule. The easiest way is to treat it as an optional part of the passive rule. That is, the agent deletion rule can be applied only if the passive has been applied. As part of the passive rule, it is simplicity itself:

$$by \frown NP_1 \Longrightarrow \emptyset$$

The rule works only because NP_1 is defined by the first elementary rule in the passive. Otherwise we would have to describe exactly which *by* NP the rule applied to or else we would go around deleting prepositional phrases that have nothing to do with the passive, for example:

The ashtray was by John.   *The ashtray was.

Here is the agent deletion rule applied in the derivation of a sentence:

The message was received (*by John* understood).

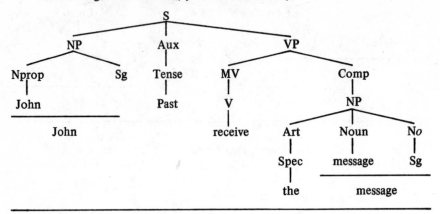

by passive   the message Past   receive John
    1. NP switch rule: ————————
                                                                       by

    2. *by* insertion rule: ————
                                                 be -EN

    3. *be* -EN insertion rule: ————————
                                                                       Ø

by agent deletion rule: ————   ————————
by flip-flop rule: be Past   receive -EN

                                         was   received

EXERCISE 4.3 **Passive**

Draw phrase structure trees and apply the necessary transformational rules
to produce the following sentences:
1. He is respected by everybody.
2. The school was being evaluated by the board.
3. My day was ruined (*by it* understood).
4. Jones must have been hit by the pitch.
5. The accident was reported (*by a witness* understood).

The Passive with Complex Complements

So far we have examined the passive transformation only as it applies to
noun phrase complements. However, there are four other complement types that
also contain noun phrases. The passive transformation applies to these as well.
(Actually there are five, but one of them, the adjective preposition noun
phrase complement is automatically ruled out because it can be used only with

linking verbs which do not permit the passive transformation.) The four complement types are

NP͡ ADVposition
NP͡ ADVdirection
NP͡ NP
NP͡ Prep͡ NP

We will consider the first two types together since they behave identically as far as the passive is concerned. Corresponding to the active sentences

John stood the broom in the corner. (NP͡ ADVposition)
John threw the broom into the corner. (NP͡ ADVdirection)

there exist the following passives:

The broom was stood in the corner by John.
The broom was thrown into the corner by John.

The only thing remarkable about these passives is the placement of the agent— it must be placed after the adverbial. If we place it immediately after the main verb as we did with the noun phrase complements, the result, while perhaps not completely ungrammatical, is quite unnatural sounding:

?*The broom was stood by John in the corner.
?*The broom was thrown by John into the corner.

If we wanted the grammar to produce sentences like these, it would seem much more satisfactory to treat them as optional variants of the more normal placement of the agent. In other words, the normal place for the agent is after the complement and in front of optional adverbial (if any). Thus, we need to adjust the first elementary transformational rule (the NP switch rule) for the passive in the following way:

$$NP_1 \widehat{\ }Aux\widehat{\ }MV\widehat{\ }NP_2\widehat{\ }ADV \begin{Bmatrix} \text{direction} \\ \text{position} \end{Bmatrix}\widehat{\ }(\text{Adverbial}) \Longrightarrow$$

$$NP_2\widehat{\ }Aux\widehat{\ }MV\widehat{\ }ADV \begin{Bmatrix} \text{direction} \\ \text{position} \end{Bmatrix}\widehat{\ }NP_1\widehat{\ }(\text{Adverbial})$$

The NP͡ NP complements have two kinds of passives, one with the indirect object moved in front of the main verb and one with the direct object moved in front. There is nothing special about the passive made with the indirect object (the first noun phrase in the complement) turned into the new subject:

The wizard granted the knight a wish. $\Longrightarrow$ The knight was granted a wish
                                                                 by the wizard.
I sold Gene a house. $\Longrightarrow$ Gene was sold a house by me.

Notice that the generalization we made above about the placement of the agent *after* the rest of the complement holds true here also. In order to formalize this rule, we will need to distinguish between the three noun phrases:

$$NP_1\widehat{\ }Aux\widehat{\ }MV\widehat{\ }NP_2\widehat{\ }NP_3 \Longrightarrow NP_2\widehat{\ }Aux\widehat{\ }MV\widehat{\ }NP_3\widehat{\ }NP_1$$

The other two rules of the passive (*by* insertion and *be* -EN insertion) will still automatically apply. Here is an example:

$$\underbrace{\textit{The wizard}}_{\text{NP}_1} \text{ Past grant } \underbrace{\textit{the knight}}_{\text{NP}_2} \underbrace{\textit{a wish.}}_{\text{NP}_3} \Longrightarrow$$

$$\underbrace{\textit{The knight}}_{\text{NP}_2} \text{ Past grant } \underbrace{\textit{a wish}}_{\text{NP}_3} \underbrace{\textit{the wizard.}}_{\text{NP}_1}$$

The *by* insertion rule will put a *by* in front of *the wizard*, and the *be* -EN insertion rule and the flip-flop rule will produce the right sequence of helping verbs and affixes:

The knight was granted a wish by the wizard.

When the direct object (the second noun phrase in the complement) is moved in front of the verb, there are two possible versions:

The wizard granted the knight a wish.
    (a) A wish was granted the knight by the wizard.
    (b) A wish was granted to the knight by the wizard.

I found Gene a house.
    (a) A house was found Gene by me.
    (b) A house was found for Gene by me.

Although apparently both versions are grammatical for some people, for this writer, at any rate, (a) sounds very strained, especially with sentences that drop the *for*.

The formalization of the (a) version requires that the second noun phrase in the complement (the direct object) be moved into the front position and the original subject be moved to a position following the first noun phrase in the complement (the indirect object):

$$\text{NP}_1 \frown \text{Aux} \frown \text{MV} \frown \text{NP}_2 \frown \text{NP}_3 \Longrightarrow \text{NP}_3 \frown \text{Aux} \frown \text{MV} \frown \text{NP}_2 \frown \text{NP}_1$$

Here is an example:

$$\underbrace{\textit{The wizard}}_{\text{NP}_1} \text{ Past grant } \underbrace{\textit{the knight}}_{\text{NP}_2} \underbrace{\textit{a wish.}}_{\text{NP}_3} \Longrightarrow$$

$$\underbrace{\textit{A wish}}_{\text{NP}_3} \text{ Past grant } \underbrace{\textit{the knight}}_{\text{NP}_2} \underbrace{\textit{the wizard.}}_{\text{NP}_1}$$

The two remaining elementary passive rules and the flip-flop rules will then produce:

A wish was granted the knight by the wizard.

The formalization of the (b) version also requires a new version of the NP switch rule. However, in order to produce the (b) version, we must first apply the $\overset{\frown}{NP \; NP}$ switch rule which, you will recall, reverses the order of the two noun phrases in the complements and puts either *to* or *for* between them. Here is an example:

The wizard Past grant the knight a wish. $\Longrightarrow$
The wizard Past grant a wish to the knight.

Our new NP switch rule will move the noun phrase following the main verb (the direct object) to the position in front of the verb, while the subject noun phrase will move to a position following the indirect object:

$$NP_1 \; Aux \; MV \; NP_2 \begin{Bmatrix} to \\ for \end{Bmatrix} NP_3 \Longrightarrow NP_2 \; Aux \; MV \begin{Bmatrix} to \\ for \end{Bmatrix} NP_3 \; NP_1$$

Here is an example:

$\underline{\text{The wizard}}$ Past grant $\underline{\text{a wish}}$ to $\underline{\text{the knight.}}$ $\Longrightarrow$
$\quad NP_1 \qquad\quad$ Aux MV $\;\; NP_2 \;$ to $\;\;\; NP_3$

$\underline{\text{A wish}}$ Past grant to $\underline{\text{the knight}} \; \underline{\text{the wizard.}}$
$\;\; NP_2 \;$ Aux MV to $\;\;\; NP_3 \qquad\quad NP_1$

The two remaining elementary passive rules and the flip-flop rule convert this into

A wish was granted to the knight by the wizard.

The final complement type that contains a noun phrase is the noun phrase $\overset{\frown}{\text{preposition}}$ noun phrase complement. As you can see, this complement type contains two noun phrases, one in front of the preposition and one after it. The one in front of the preposition can be used as a new subject in a passive sentence, for example:

They informed him of the outcome. $\Longrightarrow$ He was informed of the outcome by them.

However, the noun phrase following the preposition cannot be used as a new subject in a passive sentence, for example:

They informed him of the outcome. $\Longrightarrow$ *The outcome was informed him of by them.

Again, we need another form of the NP switch rule to deal with the first noun phrase:

$$NP_1 \; Aux \; MV \; NP_2 \; Prep \; NP_3 \Longrightarrow NP_2 \; Aux \; MV \; Prep \; NP_3 \; NP_1$$

Here is an example:

They Past inform him of $\underline{\text{the outcome.}}$ $\Longrightarrow$
NP_1 Aux $\;$ MV $\;\; NP_2$ Prep $\;\;\; NP_3$

He Past inform of *the outcome* them.
NP$_2$ Aux MV Prep   NP$_3$ NP$_1$

The two remaining elementary passive rules and the flip-flop rule convert this into

He was informed of the outcome by them.

We have now encountered no less than six different versions of the first elementary rule (the NP switch rule) of the passive:

(a) NP$_1$ Aux MV NP$_2$ $\Longrightarrow$ NP$_2$ Aux MV NP$_1$ (with NP complements)

(b) NP$_1$ Aux MV NP$_2$ ADV $\begin{bmatrix}\text{direction}\\\text{position}\end{bmatrix}$ (Adverbial) $\Longrightarrow$

       NP$_2$ Aux MV ADV $\begin{bmatrix}\text{direction}\\\text{position}\end{bmatrix}$ NP$_1$ (Adverbial)

     (with NP ADV $\begin{bmatrix}\text{direction}\\\text{position}\end{bmatrix}$ complements)

(c) NP$_1$ Aux MV NP$_2$ NP$_3$ $\Longrightarrow$ NP$_2$ Aux MV NP$_3$ NP$_1$
     (with NP NP complements; indirect object as new subject)

(d) NP$_1$ Aux MV NP$_2$ NP$_3$ $\Longrightarrow$ NP$_3$ Aux MV NP$_2$ NP$_1$
     (with NP NP complements; direct object as new subject)

(e) NP$_1$ Aux MV NP$_2$ $\begin{bmatrix}to\\for\end{bmatrix}$ NP$_3$ $\Longrightarrow$ NP$_2$ Aux MV $\begin{bmatrix}to\\for\end{bmatrix}$ NP$_3$ NP$_1$
     (with NP NP complements; NP NP switch rule applied)

(f) NP$_1$ Aux MV NP$_2$ Prep NP$_3$ $\Longrightarrow$ NP$_2$ Aux MV Prep NP$_3$ NP$_1$
     (with NP Prep NP complements)

Despite the apparent diversity in these six rules, they all work basically the same way: a noun phrase from the complement is moved into the position in front of the verb, while the original subject noun phrase is moved to the first position after the complement. The six different rules are necessary only because each of the complements has a different make-up.

EXERCISE 4.4   **NP Switch Rule**

For each of the following sentences, indicate which version of the NP switch rule must be applied to produce the passive sentences. Identify the version by letter as above, i.e., type (a), type (b). . . .

1. The answer was given John by the committee.
2. The injured were placed near the fire by the survivors.
3. Aunt Sally was confined to her bed by the doctor.
4. John was called out of the meeting by the director.
5. The table was reserved for us by Aunt Sally.
6. The incident was passed over by the board.
7. The children were left the house by Aunt Sally.
8. John was blamed for everything by everybody.
9. Aunt Sally was read the book by Mary.
10. The phone was answered by John.
11. The dog was brought into the clinic by Mr. Brown.
12. The money was given to the agency by Congress.
13. Aunt Sally was robbed of her afghan by a heartless crook.
14. The job was offered John by an eccentric millionaire.
15. The bicycle was put under the house by the children.

EXERCISE 4.5 **Review**

Draw phrase structure trees and apply the necessary transformational rules to produce the following sentences:
1. He was convicted of murder (*by the jury* understood).
2. She must have lost her glasses.
3. An agreement was entered into by the company.
4. Aunt Sally is opposed to snakes.
5. They were taught croquet by Mr. Brown.

Answers to Exercise 4.1   ADJECTIVES, VERBS, AND HYBRIDS

1. John was frightened. Hybrid
2. The window was broken. Verb
3. The team was downhearted. Adjective
4. The team was discouraged. Hybrid
5. The team was destroyed. Verb
6. John was hurt. Hybrid
7. The outcome was unexpected. Adjective
8. The tests were completed. Verb
9. John was caught. Verb
10. They were alarmed. Hybrid

Answers to Exercise 4.2   FORMALIZATION OF PASSIVE RULES

1. $NP_1 \frown Aux \frown MV \frown NP_2 \Longrightarrow NP_2 \frown Aux \frown MV \frown NP_1$

2. $NP_1 \Longrightarrow by \frown NP_1$

3. $Aux \frown MV \Longrightarrow Aux \frown be \frown \text{-}EN \frown MV$

Answers to Exercise 4.3   PASSIVE

1.   He is respected by everybody.

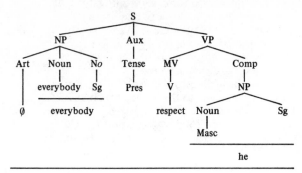

by passive

    1. NP switch rule: he Pres   respect   everybody

    2. *by* insertion rule: by

    3. *be* -EN insertion rule: be -EN

by flip-flop rule: be -s respect -EN

                       is   respected

2.   The school was being evaluated by the board.

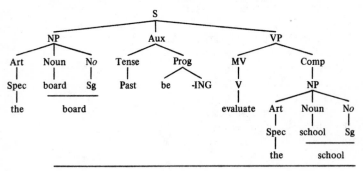

by passive

    1. NP switch rule: the school   Past be-ING   evaluate   the board

    2. *by* insertion rule: by

    3. *be* -*EN* insertion rule: be-EN

by flip-flop rule: be Past be -ING evaluate -EN

                     was   being   evaluated

3.   My day was ruined (*by it*).

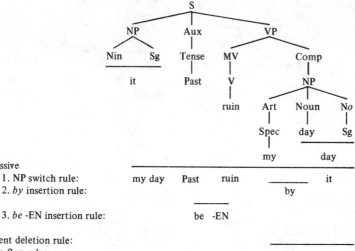

by passive
   1. NP switch rule: my day   Past   ruin   _____   it
   2. *by* insertion rule: by

   3. *be* -EN insertion rule: be -EN

by agent deletion rule: _____
by flip-flop rule: ∅

                                         be Past   ruin -EN

                                         was   ruined

4.   Jones must have been hit by the pitch.

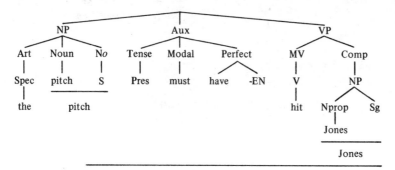

by passive
   1. NP-switch rule: Jones Pres   must   have-EN   hit   the   pitch

   2. *by*-insertion rule: ∅   by

   3. *be* -EN insertion rule: be -EN

by flip-flop rule: must ∅   be -EN hit -EN

                                         must   been   hit

5.   The accident was reported (*by a witness*).

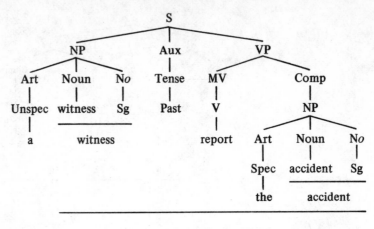

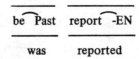

by passive
    1. NP switch rule: the accident Past   report   a witness
    2. *by* insertion rule: by
    3. *be* -EN insertion rule: be -EN

by agent deletion rule: ∅

by flip-flop rule: be Past   report -EN

                                    was   reported

Answers to Exercise 4.4   NP SWITCH RULE

    1. The answer was given John by the committee. (d)
    2. The injured were placed near the fire by the survivors. (b)
    3. Aunt Sally was confined to her bed by the doctor. (f)
    4. John was called out of the meeting by the director. (b)
    5. The table was reserved for us by Aunt Sally. (e)
    6. The incident was passed over by the board. (a)
    7. The children were left the house by Aunt Sally. (c)
    8. John was blamed for everything by everybody. (f)
    9. Aunt Sally was read the book by Mary. (c)
  10. The phone was answered by John. (a)
  11. The dog was brought into the clinic by Mr. Brown. (b)
  12. The money was given to the agency by Congress. (e)
  13. Aunt Sally was robbed of her afghan by a heartless crook. (f)
  14. The job was offered John by an eccentric millionaire. (d)
  15. The bicycle was put under the house by the children. (b)

Answers to Exercise 4.5 REVIEW

1. He was convicted of murder (*by the jury*).

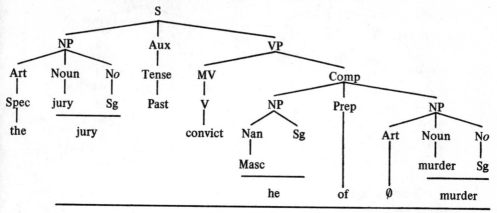

by passive

1. NP switch rule (f):   he Past   convict   of murder ____ the jury
2. *by* insertion rule: ____   by
3. *be* -EN insertion rule: be -EN

by agent deletion rule: ____
by flip-flop rule: ∅

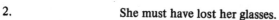

2.   She must have lost her glasses.

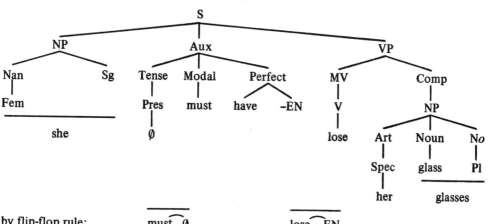

3.   An agreement was entered into by the company.

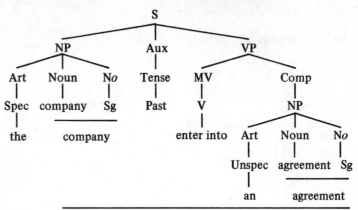

by passive
   1. NP switch rule (a):   an agreement Past   enter into___the company
   2. *by* insertion rule: —————   by
   3. *be* -EN insertion rule: be -EN

by flip-flop rule: be͡ Past enter͡ -EN

                                          was   entered

4.   Aunt Sally is opposed to snakes.

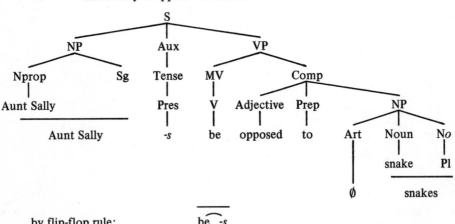

5.   They were taught croquet by Mr. Brown.

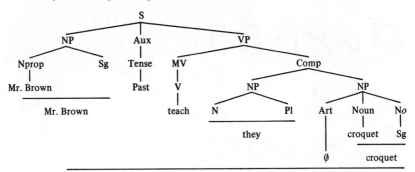

by passive
    1. NP switch rule (c):   they   Past   teach croquet_____ Mr. Brown
    2. *by* insertion rule: by

    3. *be* -EN insertion rule: be -EN

by flip-flop rule: be Past   teach -EN

                                     were   taught

CHAPTER 5

Questions

OVERVIEW

This chapter deals with two types of questions: (1) *yes-no* questions that expect a "yes" or "no" answer, for example, *Is it dinner time yet?* and (2) question-word questions that begin with a question word (*who, what, why*, and so on) and which ask for specific information, for example, *What is for dinner?*

The basic assumption of this chapter is that both types of questions are derived from underlying statements by transformational rules. It turns out that the rules which are necessary to convert underlying statements into questions are also quite closely connected with the rules that make underlying statements negative (Chapter 6) and give them special emphasis (Chapter 7).

There are two transformational rules necessary to convert underlying statements into *yes-no* questions. The first rule is called the "yes-no question switch rule." A switch rule changes the relative position of two or more elements in the underlying statement. This particular switch rule reverses the order of the subject noun phrase and some parts of the auxiliary. If the auxiliary contains any optional helping verb (recall that tense, the leftmost constituent of auxiliary, is obligatory), the tense plus the first helping verb move in front of the subject noun phrase. Thus, we have the following statement-question pairs formed by the operation of the *yes-no* question switch rule:

Statement: John may come. (Modal)
Question: May John come?

Statement: John has gone. (Perfect)
Question: Has John gone?

Statement: John is going. (Progressive)
Question: Is John going?

This version of the *yes-no* question switch rule is also used in one other situation: when the main verb is *be*:

Statement: John is crazy. (Main Verb *be*)
Question: Is John crazy?

However, when no optional element has been picked from the auxiliary and the main verb is not *be*, we must use a slightly different version of the *yes-no* question switch rule. In this version, the only thing that is moved to the first position in the sentence is the tense, for example:

Statement: John stubbed his toe.
Question: *Past* John stub his toe?

We now need to invoke the second transformational rule: the "*do* insertion rule." This is a very general rule that applies any time that the tense (either past or present) has been separated from a verb. *Do* is a verb substitute that unconnected tenses are attached to, but that has no particular meaning of its own. For this reason it is often called a "dummy" verb. Applying the *do* insertion rule to the question above, we produce a much more normal looking sentence:

Did John stub his toe?

As was mentioned above, these rules are necessary for other parts of the grammar as well. For instance, in the production of question-word questions we need only add one more rule to the two discussed above: the "question-word switch rule." A question-word question is derived from an underlying statement that has something missing. More accurately, it has an element with grammatical function but no lexical content. For instance, the question

Where is my toothbrush?

is presumed to be derived from an underlying statement

My toothbrush is ADVposition.

The first step in the question-word switch rule is to replace the element that has grammatical function but no lexical content with the appropriate question word (*where* in the case of adverbials of position). The question-word switch rule than moves the question word to the first position in the sentence (after the prior operation of the *yes-no* question switch rule). For example, we would first apply the *yes-no* question switch rule to the underlying statement

My toothbrush is ADVposition.

producing

Is my toothbrush ADVposition?

By the question-word switch rule the ADVposition would be replaced by that appropriate question word and then moved to the first position in the sentence, producing

Where is my toothbrush?

QUESTIONS

The various ways that English changes a statement into a question by changing only the intonation will not be discussed here. Rather, we will concern ourselves with questions that are formed by some change in the grammar of the underlying sentence.

YES-NO QUESTIONS

The basic type of question in English is the *yes-no* question. As you might guess, a *yes-no* question is a question that anticipates "yes" or "no" as the answer, for example:

Is your name John?
Will he be able to go?
Have they been here before?
Is he living there now?
Can you come?

These *yes-no* questions are formed from the underlying statement by moving the first verb to the front position in the sentence (in more technical language, it is moved in front of the subject noun phrase):

NP		NP
Your name is John	$\Longrightarrow$	*Is your name* John?

NP		NP
He will be able to go	$\Longrightarrow$	*Will he* be able to go?

NP   NP
They have been here before $\Longrightarrow$ *Have they* been here before?

NP   NP
He is living there now $\Longrightarrow$ *Is he* living there now?

NP   NP
You can come $\Longrightarrow$ *Can you* come?

For earlier stages of the language this generalization would have been very powerful indeed. For example, here are some *yes-no* questions from Shakespeare's play *As You Like It*:

Know you where you are?
Called your worship?
Looks he as freshly as he did?
Change you color?
Speak you so gently?
Begin you to grow upon me?

In Modern English, these *yes-no* questions would be said this way:

Do you know where you are?
Did your worship call?
Does he look as fresh as he did?
Do you change color?
Do you speak so gently?
Do you begin to grow upon me?

For Shakespeare, the first verb in any sentence could be moved to the first position in order to transform the underlying statement into a *yes-no* question. Obviously, as the examples above show, the case is a little more complicated in Modern English.

To understand the Modern English way of transforming the underlying statement into a *yes-no* question, we must first look at the verb *following* tense (assuming that the flip-flop rule has *not* yet been applied). In gross terms, tense can be followed by one of two types of verbs: (1) a modal or helping verb from one of the optional elements in the auxiliary, or (2) if no verb from the auxiliary is used, the main verb. As our first approximation of the *yes-no* question rule, we may make this generalization: if the tense is followed by a verb generated from any of the optional elements of the auxiliary, *both the tense and the auxiliary verb move to the front part of the sentence as a unit*. For example, these underlying statements are transformed by the *yes-no* rule into questions (with the subsequent application of the flip-flop rule assumed):

WITH MODALS

John *Past can* come $\Longrightarrow$ *Past can* John come?
                          could

He $\emptyset$ *will* be ready soon $\Longrightarrow$ $\emptyset$ *will* he be ready soon?
                               will

I *Past* *may* be surprised ⟹ *Past* *may* I be surprised?
                                           might

We Ø *may* go ⟹ Ø *may* we go?
                        may

WITH THE PERFECT

John *Past* *have* -EN come ⟹ *Past* *have* John -*EN* *come*?
                                        had   come

He -*s* *have* -EN be ready ⟹ -*s* *have* he -*EN* *be* ready?
                                      has   been

I Ø *have* -EN be surprised ⟹ Ø *have* I -*EN* *be* surprised?
                                     have   been

They Ø *have* -EN go ⟹ Ø *have* they -EN *go*?
                              have   gone

WITH THE PROGRESSIVE

John *Past* *be* -ING come ⟹ *Past* *be* John -*ING* *come*?
                                     was   coming

He -*s* *be* -ING be good about it ⟹ -*s* *be* he -ING *be* good about
  it?   is   being

We Ø *be* -ING go ⟹ Ø *be* we -*ING* *go*?
                          are   going

When the tense is followed by the main verb directly, the *yes-no* rule takes this form: *move just the tense by itself to the first position in the sentence*. The following sentences do not contain any optional verbs from the auxiliary, and consequently, the tense is next to the main verb in the underlying sentence:

John *Past* come ⟹ *Past* John come?
The phone *Past* ring ⟹ *Past* the phone ring?
The fish Ø seem to be biting ⟹ Ø the fish seem to be biting?
He -*s* have a headache ⟹ -*s* he have a headache?

As the sentences now stand, they are not only ungrammatical but unpronounceable. We now need to invoke a very powerful transformational rule: whenever tense (either present or past) is *not* followed immediately by a verb *for whatever reason*, put in a *do* directly after the tense. As you will see later on, this rule, which we will call the "*do* insertion rule," is not confined just to the production of *yes-no* questions, but is used in many areas of the grammar. Applying the *do* insertion rule (and then the flip-flop rule) to the above sentences, we produce the following grammatical (and pronounceable) questions:

Past John come? ⟹ *Past* *do* John come?
                          do *Past*
                             did

Past the phone ring? ⟹ *Past do* the phone ring?

$$\frac{do\ Past}{did}$$

∅ the fish seem to be biting? ⟹ ∅ *do* the fish seem to be biting?

$$\frac{do\ ∅}{do}$$

-*s* he have a headache? ⟹ -*s do* he have a headache?

$$\frac{do\ \text{-}s}{does}$$

If we were to apply the *yes-no* rule as it stands to sentences in which the main verb is *be*, the results would be ungrammatical, for example:

*Do you be hungry?
*Does John be a policeman?
*Do we be near a drugstore?
*Did he be angry?

In order to prevent this ungrammatical application of the *yes-no* rule, the *yes-no* rule needs to be modified to permit *be* to be moved with tense to the first position of the sentence no matter what *be*'s grammatical function is. With this modification, the *yes-no* rule would apply this way to the example sentences above:

You ∅ be hungry ⟹ ∅ be you hungry?

$$\overset{}{\text{are}}$$

John -*s* be a policeman ⟹ -*s* be John a policeman?

$$\overset{}{\text{is}}$$

We ∅ be near a drugstore ⟹ ∅ be we near a drugstore?

$$\overset{}{\text{are}}$$

He *Past* be angry ⟹ *Past* be he angry?

$$\overset{}{\text{was}}$$

Let us attempt now to formalize the transformational rules that we have invoked for dealing with *yes-no* questions. These rules can be made very compact by requiring that the rules be applied in a definite relative order. The first rule we discussed converts the statement

Your name is John.

into the *yes-no* question

Is your name John?

This rule applies when the tense in the underlying statement is followed by any one of the following: a modal auxiliary, the helping verb *have*, the helping verb *be*, or if none of these optional elements have been selected, the main verb *be*. Let us call this rule the "*yes-no* question switch rule 1." We may write this rule this way:

Let V_{Aux} = the first optional element in the auxiliary *or*, if no optional element has been selected, the main verb *be*

Yes-no question switch rule 1: NP Tense V_{Aux} $\Longrightarrow$ Tense V_{Aux} NP

Here are some examples of this rule:

John *Past* may come $\Longrightarrow$ *Past* may John come?
　　　　　　　　　　　　　　might

John -*s* have -EN go $\Longrightarrow$ -*s* have John -*EN* go?
　　　　　　　　　　　　has　　　　　　gone

John -*s* be -ING to $\Longrightarrow$ -*s* be John -*ING* go?
　　　　　　　　　　　is　　　　　　going

John -*s* be crazy $\Longrightarrow$ -*s* be John crazy?
　　　　　　　　　　is

What happens when the rule 1 cannot apply? In other words, what happens when it is the case that no optional element has been selected from the auxiliary and the main verb is not *be*? In that case, the tense moves to the first position by itself. Let us call this rule the "*yes-no* question switch rule 2." We may write the rule this way:

Yes-no question switch rule 2: NP Tense $\Longrightarrow$ Tense NP

Notice that if a sentence undergoes rule 1, the resulting transformational sentence cannot also undergo rule 2 because rule 1 has already moved the tense in front of the noun phrase. For the same reasons, if a sentence undergoes rule 2, it cannot then undergo rule 1. These two rules are said to be "disjunctive." Disjunctive rules are rules that are mutually exclusive as far as their application to any one sentence is concerned. That is, we may apply either one or the other but not both. Furthermore, these rules are relatively ordered. That is, it makes a difference which order we apply them in. For example, if we applied rule 2 to this underlying statement,

John -*s* be sick.

we would produce this ungrammatical *yes-no* question (assuming further the application of the *do* insertion rule):

*Does John be sick?

Put another way, rule 2 is the general rule for making *yes-no* questions in English. Rule 1 deals with an important class of exceptions to rule 2. Rule 2 becomes a valid generalization for all sentences only if we first apply rule 1 to eliminate all the exceptions. This same pattern for rules is found throughout transformational grammars: first deal with the exceptions, then make the general rule.

Stated now in technical language, the *yes-no* question switch transformation is a pair of ordered disjunctive rules. In order to generate a *yes-no* question, we first see if we can apply rule 1 to the underlying statement. If we can, we must then skip rule 2 altogether. If we cannot apply rule 1, then we must apply rule 2. All *yes-no* questions, then, result from the application of either rule 1 or rule 2 (but never from the application of both).

The *do* insertion rule is applied *after* the operation of the *yes-no* question switch rule and before the flip-flop rule. The *do* insertion rule must be applied whenever the tense has been separated from a following verb. This separation may be brought about by a transformational rule which moves tense away from the verb (as the *yes-no* question switch rule 2 does), or by the placement of some element between the tense and its verb. The *do* is inserted into the sentence to "carry" the tense marker. Since it has no meaning of its own, *do* is sometimes called a "dummy" verb. Another way of looking at this rule is to consider that the flip-flop rule is obligatory for each occurrence of tense. In those cases where the flip-flop rule cannot apply because tense is not followed by a verb, then we must supply a *do* to make the flip-flop rule work. We may formalize the operation of the *do* insertion rule this way:

Let X = any element *except* a verb

do insertion rule: Tense $\overset{\frown}{\quad}$ X $\Longrightarrow$ Tense $\overset{\frown}{do}$ X

We can now restate the *yes-no* rule in its final version for American English: If tense is followed by a modal, the helping verb *have*, or the verb *be* (either as a helping verb or as a main verb), tense and the following verb move *as a unit* to the first position in the sentence. On the other hand, if the tense is followed by a main verb (except *be*), tense moves *by itself* to the first position in the sentence, and the *do* insertion rule must be applied.

For British English, the story is a little different. Compare the following sentences:

British: Have you been sick?
American: Have you been sick?

British: Have you the time?
American: Do you have the time?

British and American English treat the helping verb *have* the same way: it is moved to the first position of the question along with tense by the *yes-no* rule. However, British and American English differ in their treatment of *have* as a main verb. In American English *have* is just like any other main verb; when the *yes-no* rule is applied to sentences containing *have* as a main verb, tense is moved by itself to the first position in the sentence and then the *do* insertion rule must be applied. In British English, *have* is like *be*: it moves to the first position with tense whether it is a helping verb or a main verb. Thus, in American English, in order to use the *yes-no* rule correctly, we must sharply distinguish between *have* used as a main verb and *have* used as a helping verb (although, of course, Americans sometimes do it the British way). This is a clear illustration of the importance of the underlying structure of a sentence in the proper application of the transformational rules.

Here are some sample derivations of *yes-no* questions:

Is John sick?

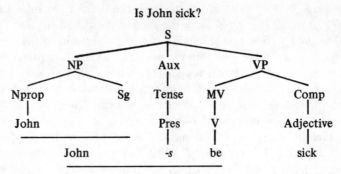

by *yes-no* question switch rule 1: -s   be   John

by flip-flop rule: be͡ -s

                                                     is

Did he bring the beer?

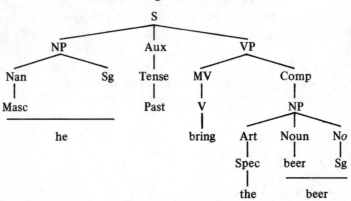

by *yes-no* question   Past   he
switch rule 2:
                             ─────────

by *do* insertion rule: do

by flip-flop rule: do͡ Past

                                 did

EXERCISE 5.1 Yes-No Questions

Draw the phrase structure and apply the necessary transformational rules to produce the following sentences:
1. Can John come?
2. Do you know Mr. Smith?
3. Has something hurt him?
4. Does he have the answer?
5. Did John call you up?

QUESTION-WORD QUESTIONS

The second major type of question is called a "question-word question" because the question begins with a question word, for example: *who, whom, which, what, where, when, why, how often, how much, how many*. Question-word questions ask for specific pieces of information, not just agreement or disagreement. For example, compare the following questions and answers:

Q. *What* is your major?   A. My major is *French.*
Q. *Who* are you?   A. I am *Mr. Phelps.*
Q. *Where* have you been?   A. I have been *out.*
Q. *When* can you come?   A. I can come *anytime you like.*
Q. *How much* money is missing?   A. *$50* is missing.
Q. *How often* will he call?   A. He will call *about once a day.*

The italicized word or phrase in the answer is the piece of information that the question was eliciting. It is perfectly grammatical to delete from the answer everything except the desired information, for example:

Q. *What* is your major?   A. *French.*
Q. *Who* are you?   A. *Mr. Phelps.*
Q. *Where* have you been?   A. *Out.*
Q. *When* can you come?   A. *Anytime you like.*
Q. *How much* money is missing?   A. *$50.*
Q. *How often* will he call?   A. *About once a day.*

How do we know that the appropriate answer to the first question is *French*, and not *Mr. Phelps* or *out*? Obviously the question words call forth certain kinds of answers. *What* is used with nonanimate noun phrases, *who* with animate or human noun phrases, *where* with adverbials of position and direction, *when* with adverbs of time, and so on.

Our basic assumption is that all questions are derived from corresponding underlying statements. What kind of statements underlie question-word questions? Let us take, for example, the question *Where have you been?* The minimal assumption about the underlying statement is that *you* is the subject noun phrase, $\emptyset\ \overbrace{have}\ \textit{-EN}$ is the auxiliary, and $be\ \overbrace{adverbial\ of\ position}$ is the verb phrase.

Where have you been?

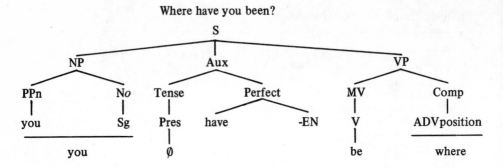

The underlying statement must contain one element that has grammatical function but no lexical content. In the sentence above, this element is the complement. When this element is replaced by the appropriate question word (*where* in this case), the hearer or reader knows that the question is asking him to supply one specific piece of information: an adverbial of position. In order for a question-word question to exist, it must contain one grammatical element that can be replaced by a question word. The first step in the generation of the surface form of the question, then, is to replace that element with the appropriate question word.

It would appear that the next step in the process of transforming the underlying statement into a question would be to move the question word to the first position in the sentence, that is, changing the underlying

you ∅ have -EN be *where*

into

where you ∅ have -EN be.

This solution creates a new problem, since the *yes-no* rule would then move tense and the following helping verb to the first position in the sentence, producing

*<u>∅ have</u> where you <u>-EN</u> be.
    have   been

We could correct the operation of the *yes-no* rule by setting up a condition, for example, that the tense goes to the first position in the sentence except when the first element in the underlying sentence is a question word. With a little tinkering, the *yes-no* rule could be made to produce the proper results.

However, if we reorder the two transformations so that the *yes-no* switch rule comes first, and then we move the question word to the first position, we can always get the proper results without having to complicate the *yes-no* rule with special conditions. For example, by the *yes-no* rule, the underlying statement

you ∅ have -EN be where

is transformed into

∅ have you -EN be where.

Next, by the rule that switches the question word to the first position in the sentence (let us call this the "question-word switch rule") the final form of the question is achieved:

∅ have you -EN be where ⟹ where ∅ $\overgroup{\text{have}}$ you -EN $\overgroup{\text{be}}$?
 have been

We may formalize the question word switch rule in the following way:

$$X_1 \frown X_2 \ldots \text{QWord} \ldots X_n \Longrightarrow \text{QWord} \frown X_1 \frown X_2 \ldots X_n$$

[Where QWord = *who/whom, what, where, when, why* . . .

X = any grammatical element (except QWord)]

The *yes-no* rule and the question-word switch rule show how the relative ordering of transformational rules can simplify the description of the generation of the surface form.

The interdependence of the *yes-no* and question-word switch rules is shown very clearly in the generation of these two questions *Whom did Bill see?* and *Who saw Bill?*

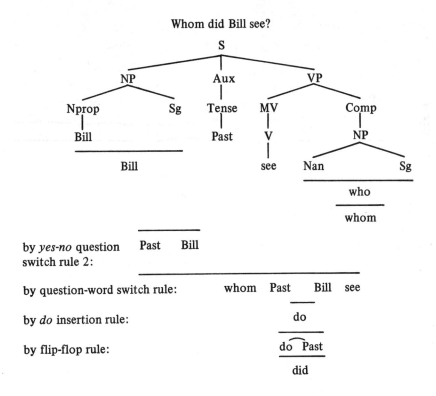

Whom did Bill see?

by *yes-no* question switch rule 2:

by question-word switch rule:

by *do* insertion rule:

by flip-flop rule:

Who saw Bill?

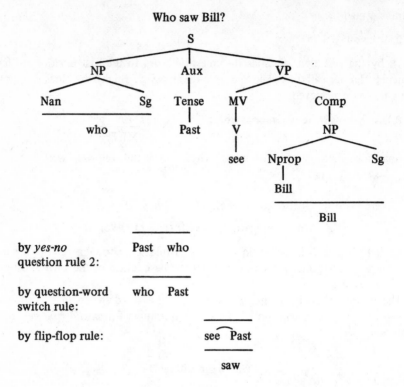

by *yes-no* question rule 2:	Past who
by question-word switch rule:	who Past
by flip-flop rule:	see Past

saw

Notice that in the derivation of *Whom did Bill see*? the subject form *who* was given in the phrase structure and then replaced by the object form *whom*. We will follow this same format for all words that have a contrast between subject and object form. The idea is that the phrase structure rules produce words only in the subject form, and then the transformational rules make the change from subject to object form where appropriate.

The question word in the first sentence comes from the underlying object, while in the second sentence it comes from the underlying subject. In the generation of the first question, *yes-no* question switch rule 2 separates the tense from the following main verb, so the *do* insertion rule is required. However, in the generation of the second sentence, the question-word switch reverses the operation of question switch rule 2 and leaves tense right back where it started from, next to the main verb. Thus, the *do* insertion rule cannot be employed.

We have already seen that in earlier stages of the language, *yes-no* questions were made by moving the tense to the first position of the sentence along with whatever verb followed, even a main verb, so that the *do* insertion rule was not necessary, for example:

Know you where you are?
Called your worship?

The same general pattern holds true for the formation of question-word questions. Here are some question-word questions from *As You Like It*:

How looked he?
What said he?
How like you this?
Where dwell you?
Where learned you that oath?

In Modern English, we would have to use *do*:

How did he look?
What did he say?
How do you like this?
Where do you dwell?
Where did you learn that oath?

As an exercise, the reader might work out the rules that govern the generation of question-word questions for Shakespeare.

EXERCISE 5.2   Question-Word Questions

Draw the phrase structure and apply the necessary transformational rules to produce the following sentences:
1. Who knows the answers?
2. Where is a telephone?
3. What did you see?
4. When does the program start?
5. Whom did you want?

EXERCISE 5.3   Review

Draw phrase structure trees and apply the necessary transformational rules to produce the following sentences:
1. Are you kidding me?
2. He came down with a cold.
3. What is John angry about?
4. John was reprimanded by Aunt Sally.
5. Who threw the overalls into Mrs. Murphy's chowder?

Answers to Exercise 5.1   *YES-NO* QUESTIONS

1.   Can John come?

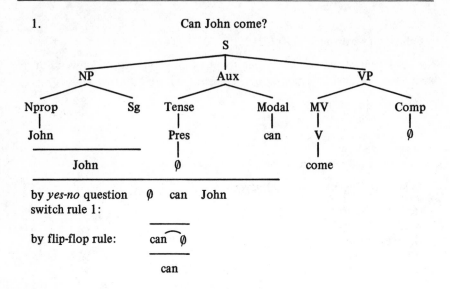

by *yes-no* question   ∅   can   John
switch rule 1:

by flip-flop rule: can͡ ∅

                          can

2.   Do you know Mr. Smith?

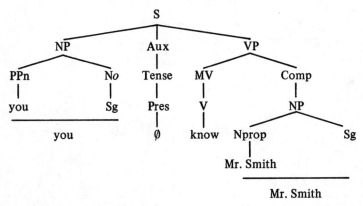

by *yes-no* question   ∅   you
switch rule 2:

by *do* insertion rule: do

by flip-flop rule: do͡ ∅

                          do

3.   Has something hurt him?

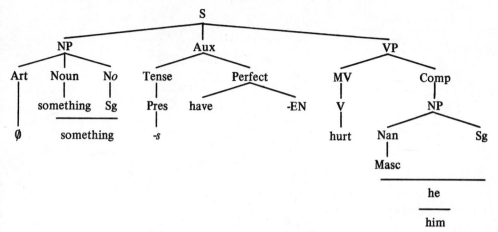

by *yes-no* question   -s   have   something
switch rule 1:
by flip-flop rule: have͜ -s   hurt͜ -EN

                           has   hurt

4.   Does he have the answer?

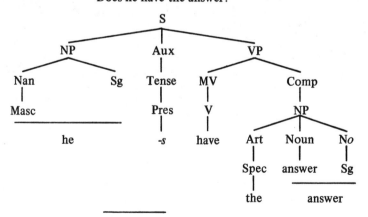

by *yes-no* question   -s   he
switch rule 2:

by *do* insertion rule: do

by flip-flop rule: do͜ -s

                           does

5.   Did John call you up?

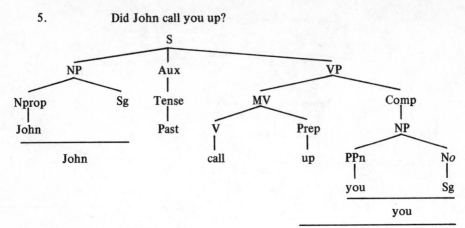

by separable preposition switch rule:

by *yes-no* question   Past   John
switch rule 2:
                          ‾‾‾‾
by *do* insertion rule: do
                              ‾‾‾
by flip-flop rule: do͡ Past

                              did

Answers to Exercise 5.2   QUESTION-WORD QUESTIONS

1.   Who knows the answers?

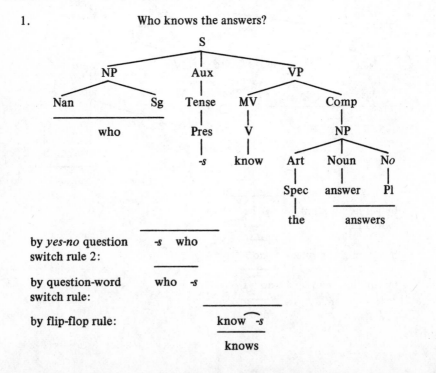

by *yes-no* question   -*s*   who
switch rule 2:

by question-word   who   -*s*
switch rule:

by flip-flop rule: know͡ -*s*

                                   knows

2.   Where is a telephone?

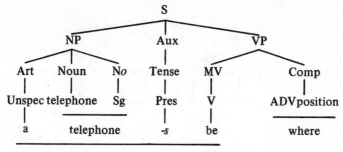

by *yes-no* question switch rule 1:   -s be a telephone

by question-word switch rule: where -s be a telephone

by flip-flop rule: be ⌒ -s

                                             is

3.   What did you see?

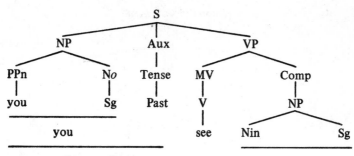

by *yes-no* question switch rule 2:   Past you   what

by question-word switch rule: what Past you see

by *do* insertion rule: do

by flip-flop rule: do ⌒ Past

                         did

4.   When does the program start?

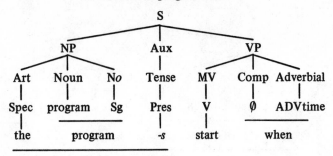

by *yes-no* question   -s   the   program
switch rule 2:   ————————————————————————————
by question-word switch rule: when -s   the   program   start
                                        ——
by *do* insertion rule: do
                                        ————————————————
by flip-flop rule: do‿-s
                                        ————————————————
                                             does

5.   Whom did you want?

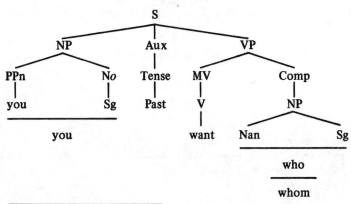

by *yes-no*   Past   you
question
switch rule 2:   ——————————————————————————————
by question-word   whom   Past   you   want
switch rule:
                         ——
by *do* insertion rule: do
                         ——————————————————————
by flip-flop rule: do‿Past
                         ——————————————————————
                                did

Answers to Exercise 5.3 REVIEW

1. Are you kidding me?

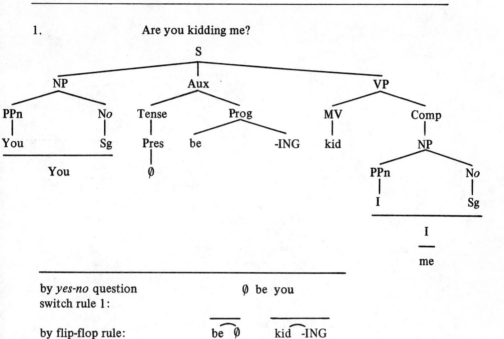

by *yes-no* question
switch rule 1:   ∅ be you

by flip-flop rule: be ∅   kid -ING
                                              ―――   ―――――
                                              are   kidding

2. He came down with a cold.

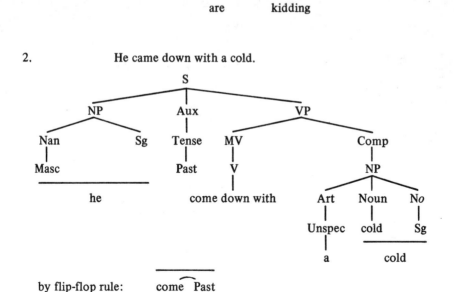

by flip-flop rule: come Past
                                ―――――
                                came

3.   What is John angry about?

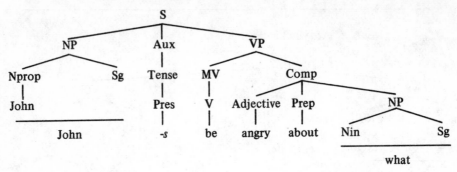

by *yes-no* question   -s be John
switch rule 1:
_____

by question word switch rule: what -s be John angry about

by flip-flop rule: be -s
                                         _____
                                              is

4.   John was reprimanded by Aunt Sally.

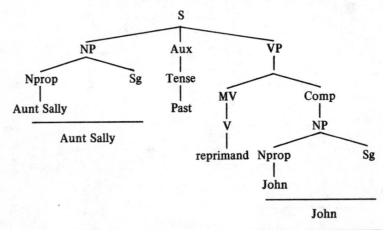

by passive:
    1. NP switch rule (a):   John Past   reprimand   Aunt Sally

    2. *by* insertion rule: by

    3. *be* -EN insertion rule: be -EN

by flip-flop rule: be Past   reprimand -EN
                                     _____   _____
                                        was   reprimanded

5.   Who threw the overalls into Mrs. Murphy's chowder?

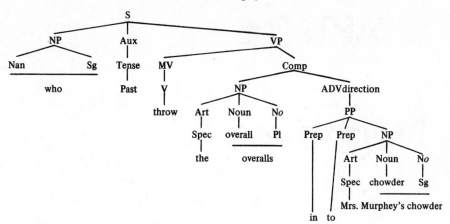

by *yes-no* question switch rule 2:	Past who
by question-word switch rule:	who Past
by flip-flop rule:	throw‿Past
	threw

CHAPTER 6

Negatives

OVERVIEW

This chapter deals with two separate but closely related areas of grammar: (1) sentences made negative by the use of *not*, and (2) the derivation of question tags. Question tags are tacked on to the end of statements in order to get a confirming response from the hearer. For example, the *isn't it* in the sentence *It is hot, isn't it?* is a question tag.

The placement of *not* is governed by the *"not* insertion rule." When the underlying statement contains a helping verb or the main verb *be, not* is inserted directly after the first verb. For example:

I will *not* be able to come. (Modal)
He has *not* been feeling well. (Perfect)
John is *not* going. (Progressive)
He is *not* ready yet. (Main Verb *be*)

However, when there are no helping verbs and the main verb is not *be*, the *not* is inserted between tense and the main verb; tense is thus separated from a following verb, and the *do* insertion rule must be used. For example, the negative of

He saw the steamroller.

is

He did not see the steamroller.

Notice that the placement of *not* is governed by the same conditions that govern the way in which questions are formed.

One of the most striking things about question tags is the negative-positive reversal. That is, if the main sentence is affirmative, the tag is negative; if the main sentence is negative, the tag is affirmative. For example,

Main Sentence	Tag
It is hot,	isn't it?
It isn't hot,	is it?
It rained,	didn't it?
It didn't rain	did it?

The form of the question tag is completely determined by the form of the main sentence. In other words, the tag consists of elements that are either copied from the main sentence (the tense and the subject noun phrase) or are determined by the nature of the main sentence (the positive-negative reversal). The last part of this chapter is devoted to a formalization of the *question tag rule*. The question tag rule operates under much the same conditions as the rules governing the production of questions and negative statements. In particular, if the tense in the main sentence is followed by a helping verb or *be* used as a main verb, both the tense and the verb following tense are copied in the question tag. However, if tense is followed directly by a main verb other than *be*, the tense alone is copied in the tag, thus requiring the use of the *do*-insertion rule (as in *It rained, didn't it?*).

NEGATIVES

There are many ways of negating a statement. We will confine our attention to the use of *not*. It would seem a simple matter to insert *not* after the verb, for example:

I will *not* be able to come.
He has *not* been feeling well.
John is *not* going.
He is *not* ready yet.

As you can see, *not* is placed after the first helping verb or the main verb *be*. What happens, however, when there is no optional element from the auxiliary, that is, when tense is next to the main verb (other than *be*)? Here are some examples of sentences of this sort with *not* inserted directly after tense:

*You ∅ not know what I mean.
*He *Past* not see the steamroller.

The sentences come out like an Indian talking in a grade-B movie. Obviously, in order to be grammatical these sentences must use the *do* insertion rule:

You do not know what I mean.
He did not see the steamroller.

Notice that the conditions governing the placement of the *not* are identical to the conditions for the operation of the *yes-no* question switch rule: the auxiliary verbs and the main verb *be* work one way, and all main verbs (except *be*) work the other way. We can even use the same cover symbol V_{Aux} to describe the first condition. If tense is followed by V_{Aux}, then the *not* is placed directly after the V_{Aux}; if tense is followed by a main verb other than *be*, the *not* is placed after tense and in front of the main verb. We may write this rule, which we will call the "*not* insertion rule," in the following manner:

NOT INSERTION RULE:

(Let V_{Aux} be defined as in the *yes-no* question switch rule)

1. Tense $\frown$ V_{Aux} $\Longrightarrow$ Tense $\frown$ V_{Aux} $\frown$ *not*
2. Tense $\Longrightarrow$ Tense $\frown$ *not*

1 and 2 are disjunctive and ordered. That is, we first try to apply 1. If the conditions for its application are met, we apply the rule and skip 2. If the conditions for its application are not met, then we must skip 1 and apply 2.

As an automatic consequence of the application of *not* insertion rule 2, the *do* insertion rule must also be applied, since tense is not followed by a verb. Here are some sample derivations of sentences with *not* in them (the rule that contracts *not* to *n't* would be given in the phonological component, the set of rules that govern the pronunciation of the surface structure):

Mary has not finished her paper.

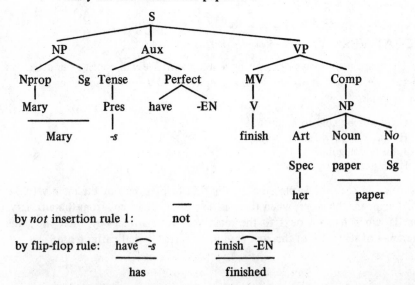

by *not* insertion rule 1:   not

by flip-flop rule: have $\frown$ *-s*   finish $\frown$ *-EN*

                                   has   finished

I didn't listen.

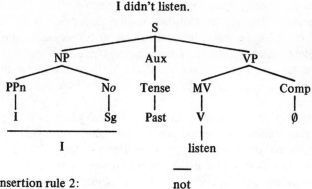

by *not* insertion rule 2:   not

by *do* insertion rule: do

by flip-flop rule: do⌢Past

                                         did

EXERCISE 6.1   **Negatives**

Draw the phrase structure and apply the necessary transformational rules to generate the following sentences:
1. We cannot win.
2. The class did not meet.
3. The plumbers are not coming.
4. The clock does not work.
5. I do not get it.

QUESTION TAGS

Question tags, as the name suggests, are elements tagged onto the sentence which turn the sentence from a statement into a question. They are included in this chapter in part because of their use of negatives, and in part because question tags do not always function as genuine questions. Often they request the hearer to react to or confirm the speaker's statement. Here are some samples of sentences containing question tags:

It is hot, *isn't it*?
It is not hot, *is it*?
It rained, *didn't it*?
It didn't rain, *did it*?
Mary can come, *can't she*?
The boys have finished, *haven't they*?
John didn't know the answer, *did he*?
I am winning, *aren't I*?

Perhaps the most striking characteristic of question tags is the negative-positive reversal: if the main sentence is positive the tag is negative (i.e., it contains *not*), while if the main sentence is negative (i.e., it contains *not*), the tag is positive. The tag itself always has the same tense as the main sentence. The tag contains the same optional helping verb that carries the tense marker if the main sentence has one. If the main sentence contains *be* as a main verb, then the tag will also contain *be*. If the main sentence contains no helping verb or *be* used as a main verb, then the tag must have a *do* to carry the tense marker.

Finally, the noun phrase in the tag is identical with the subject noun phrase in the main sentence if that subject is a third person pronoun (*he, she, it, they*). If the subject noun phrase in the main sentence is not a third person pronoun, then the tag will still have a third person pronoun, but in this case, it will be the third person pronoun that replaces the subject noun phrase.

Clearly, the question tag is completely determined by the nature of the main sentence. That is, given any statement, we can automatically predict what the question tag will be. The transformational rule that creates the question tag is basically a copying rule. It copies part of the main sentence and inserts it immediately after the end of the main sentence. We will call this rule the *question tag insertion rule*. The only thing that is different about this insertion rule is that what is inserted depends on what is in the main sentence. The other insertion rules that we have had—for example, the *do* insertion rule—always inserted the same things. Here is the question tag insertion rule:

$$\text{NP Tense V}_{\text{Aux}} \text{ X}_1 \text{ X}_2 \ldots \text{X}_n \Longrightarrow \text{NP Tense V}_{\text{Aux}} \text{ X}_1 \text{ X}_2 \ldots$$
$$\text{X}_n \text{ NP Tense V}_{\text{Aux}}$$

(where V_{Aux} may be null)

Here is the application of the question tag insertion rule on some sample sentences:

it	-s	be	hot	$\Longrightarrow$	it	-s	be	hot,	it	-s	be
NP	Tense	V$_{\text{Aux}}$	X$_1$		NP	Tense	V$_{\text{Aux}}$	X$_1$	NP	Tense	V$_{\text{Aux}}$

it	Past	rain	$\Longrightarrow$	it	Past	rain,	it	Past	
NP	Tense	X$_1$		NP	Tense	X$_1$	NP	Tense	(V$_{\text{Aux}}$ is null)

the boys	-s	have	-EN	finish	$\Longrightarrow$	the boys	-s	have	-EN	finish,
NP	Tense	V$_{\text{Aux}}$	X$_1$	X$_2$		NP	Tense	V$_{\text{Aux}}$	X$_1$	X$_2$

the boys	-s	have
NP	Tense	V$_{\text{Aux}}$

No other new rules are necessary to convert the output of the question tag insertion rule into the correct surface form. However, we do need to apply a number of old rules. We need to apply the *yes-no* switch rule to turn the tag into a question. We need to also apply the *not* insertion rule to either the main sentence or to the question tag, but not to both. (This treatment of question tags was suggested by Robert J. Geist.) Let us apply the *yes-no* switch rule to the tag in the three sample sentences above:

it -s be hot, it -s be $\Longrightarrow$ it -s be hot, -s be it

it Past rain, it Past $\Longrightarrow$ it Past rain, Past it

the boys -s have -EN finish, the boys -s have $\Longrightarrow$
             the boys -s have -EN finish, -s have the boys

Next we will apply the *not* insertion rule to either the main sentence or the question tag. If we apply it to the main sentence, the tag will remain unchanged; if we apply it to the question tag, the main sentence will remain unchanged. Let us apply the *not* insertion rule to the main sentence of the first sample sentence. After the flip-flop rule applies, this will produce

It isn't hot, is it?

If we apply the *not* insertion rule to the question tag, we will produce

It is hot, isn't it?

The second sample sentence is a little more complicated. If we apply the *not* insertion rule to the main sentence, we get this sequence of elements:

it Past *not* rain, Past it

Since neither tense marker is followed by a verb, we must now also apply the *do* insertion rule twice (and the flip-flop rule, of course), producing the following surface sentence:

It did not rain, did it?

If we apply the *not* insertion rule to the question tag, the tense marker in the main sentence is not separated from the main verb, so we need only apply the *do* insertion rule once:

It rained, didn't it?

The third sample sentence is essentially the same as the first one because they both contain V_{Aux}. If we apply the *not* insertion rule to the main sentence, we produce

The boys have not finished, have the boys?

Obviously, we must also replace the noun phrase in the question tag with the appropriate third person pronoun (which we will assume without further comment):

The boys have not finished, have they?

If we apply the *not* insertion rule to the question tag, we produce

The boys have finished, haven't they?

Here are some sample phrase structure trees for sentences with question tags:

It is raining, isn't it?

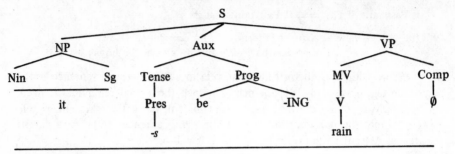

by question tag insertion rule:	it -s be -ING rain ∅ it -s be	
by *yes-no* switch rule 1:	-s be it	
by *not* insertion rule 1:	not	
by flip-flop rule:	be͡ -s rain͡ -ING be͡ -s	
	is raining is	

John didn't know the answer, did he?

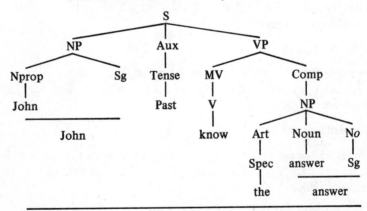

by question tag insertion rule:	John Past know the answer John Past
by *yes-no* switch rule 2:	Past John
	he
by *not* insertion rule 2:	not
by *do* insertion rule:	do do
by flip-flop rule:	do͡ Past do͡ Past
	did did

There is a stylistic variation possible with the question tag. Compare the following pairs of sentences:

It is hot, isn't it?   It is hot, is it not?
It rained, didn't it?   It rained, did it not?
Mary can come, can't she?   Mary can come, can she not?
The boys have finished, haven't they?   The boys have finished, have they not?
John knew the answer, didn't he?   John knew the answer, did he not?
I am winning, aren't I?   I am winning, am I not?

We can produce this variation on the question tag merely by reversing the order in which we apply the *yes-no* switch rule and the *not* insertion rule. The question tags on the left above can all be produced by applying the *yes-no* switch rule before the *not* insertion rule (as we have been doing up to now). However, if we apply the *not* insertion rule immediately after the question tag insertion rule and before the *yes-no* switch rule, we produce the question tag forms on the right. Here is the phrase structure tree and transformation for *it is raining, is it not*? Compare this with the derivation of *it is raining, isn't it*? given above:

It is raining, is it not?

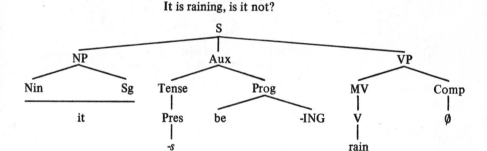

by question tag insertion rule:	it -*s* be -ING rain it -*s* be	
by *not* insertion rule 1:		not
by *yes-no* switch rule 1:	-*s* be	
by flip-flop rule:	be -*s* rain -ING be -*s*	
	is raining is	

EXERCISE 6.2 **Question Tags**

Draw phrase structure trees and apply the necessary transformational rules to produce the following sentences:
1. John has answered the letter, hasn't he?
2. He won't fail, will he?
3. The ships didn't sink, did they?

4. I finished the story, didn't I?
5. The shower doesn't leak, does it?
6. He will clean his room up, will he not?

EXERCISE 6.3   **Review**

Draw phrase structure trees and apply the necessary transformational rules to produce the following sentences:
1. Aunt Sally did not like the play.
2. What did they talk about?
3. We wanted them, did we not?
4. The police must have been called by the butler.
5. She is lively, isn't she?

Answers to Exercise 6.1   NEGATIVES

1.   We cannot win.

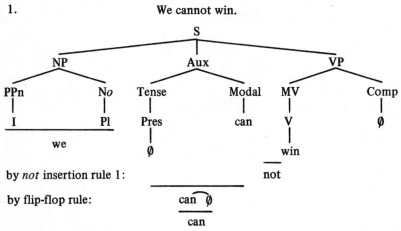

2.   The class did not meet.

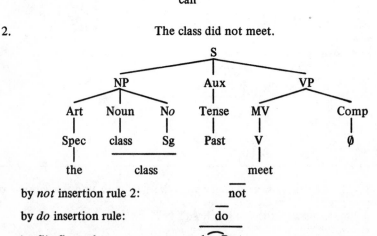

3.   The plumbers are not coming.

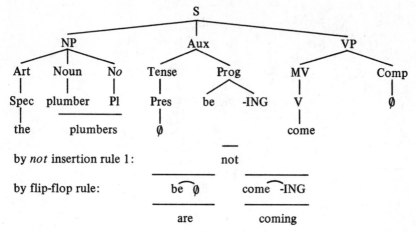

by *not* insertion rule 1:   not

by flip-flop rule: be͡ ∅   come͡ -ING

                                      are   coming

4.   The clock does not work.

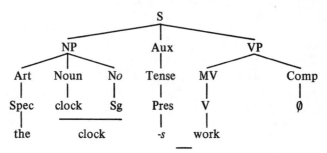

by *not* insertion rule 2:   not

by *do* insertion rule: do

by flip-flop rule: do͡ -s

                                               does

5.   I do not get it.

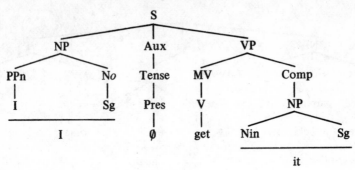

by *not* insertion rule 2:   not

by *do* insertion rule: do

by flip-flop rule: do ⌢ ∅

                                                  do

Answers to Exercise 6.2   QUESTION TAGS

1.   John has answered the letter, hasn't he?

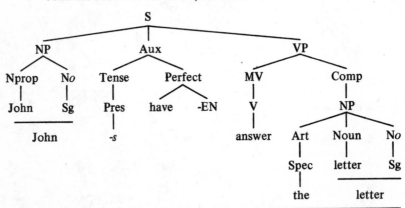

by question tag   John -*s* have -EN answer the letter John -*s* have
insertion rule:
by *yes-no* switch rule 1:   -*s* have John

                                                                      he

by *not* insertion rule 1:   not

by flip-flop rule: have ⌢ -*s* answer ⌢ -EN   have ⌢ -*s*

                                         has   answered   has

2. He won't fail, will he?

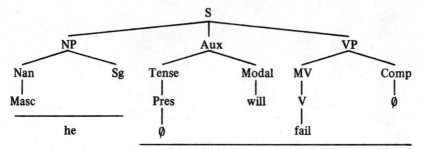

by question tag insertion rule:	he ∅ will fail he ∅ will	
by *yes-no* switch rule 1:	∅ will he	
by *not* insertion rule 1:	not	
by flip-flop rule:	will ∅	will ∅
	will	will

3. The ships didn't sink, did they?

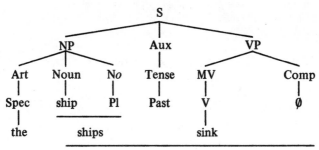

by question tag insertion rule:	the ships Past	sink the ships Past
by *yes-no* switch rule 2:		Past the ships
		they
by *not* insertion rule 2:	not	
by *do* insertion rule:	do	do
by flip-flop rule:	do Past	do Past
	did	did

4.   I finished the story, didn't I?

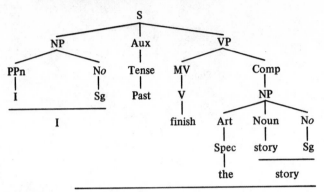

by question tag   I Past finish the story I Past
insertion rule: —————————
by *yes-no* switch rule 2:   Past   I
                                        ————

by *not* insertion rule 2:   not
                                                  ——

by *do* insertion rule: do
                                         ——

by flip-flop rule: finish͡ Past   do͡ Past
                       —————————   ————————

                         finished   did

5.   The shower doesn't leak, does it?

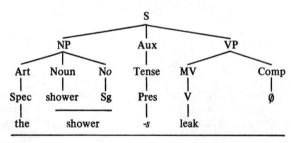

by question tag   the shower -s   leak the shower -s
insertion rule:
by *yes-no* switch rule 2:   -s   the shower
                                                —————————————

                                                     it

by *not* insertion rule 2:   not
                               ———

by *do* insertion rule: do   do
                               ——   ——

by flip-flop rule: do͡ -s   do͡ -s
                               ————   ————

                               does   does

6.   He will clean his room up, will he not?

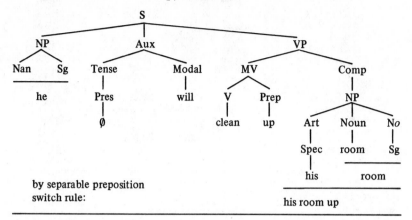

by separable preposition
switch rule: his room up

by question tag   he ∅ will clean his room up he ∅ will
insertion rule:
by *not* insertion rule 1:   not

by *yes-no* switch rule 1:   ∅ will he

by flip-flop rule: will ∅   will ∅

                          will   will

Answers to Exercise 6.3   REVIEW

1.   Aunt Sally did not like the play.

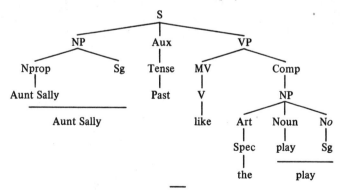

by *not* insertion rule 2:   not

by *do* insertion rule: do

by flip-flop rule: do Past

                          did

2.   What did they talk about?

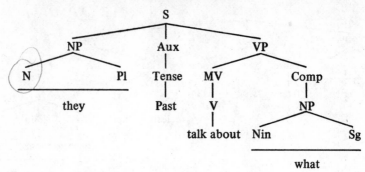

by *yes-no*	Past they
switch rule 2:	———————————
by question-word	what Past they talk about
switch rule:	—
by *do* insertion rule:	do
by flip-flop rule:	do͡ Past
	did

3.   We wanted them, did we not?

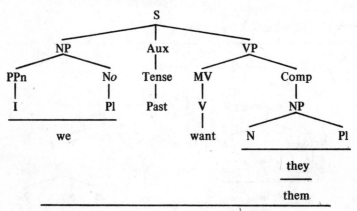

by question tag switch rule:	we Past want them we Past	
by *not* insertion rule 2:		not
by *yes-no* switch rule 2:	Past we	
by *do* insertion rule:	do	
by flip-flop rule:	want͡ Past	do͡ Past
	wanted	did

4.   The police must have been called by the butler.

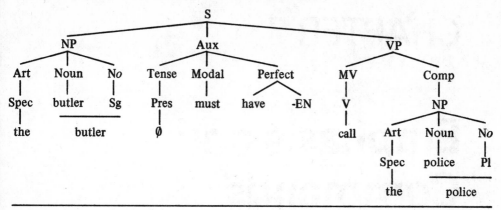

by passive
   1. NP switch rule (a):   the police ∅   must have -EN   call the butler
                                                                          ‾‾‾‾

   2. *by* insertion rule: by
                                                              ‾‾‾‾‾‾‾

   3. *be* -EN insertion rule: be -EN
                                                         ‾‾‾‾‾‾‾‾‾‾‾

by flip-flop rule:

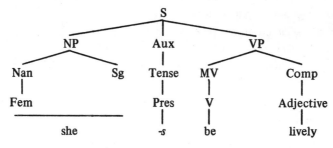

5.   She is lively, isn't she?

                              S
              ┌───────────────┼───────────────┐
             NP   Aux   VP
          ┌───┴───┐   │   ┌────┴────┐
         Nan   Sg   Tense MV   Comp
          │   │   │   │
         Fem   Pres   V   Adjective
          │   │   │   │
         she   -s   be   lively

   by question tag insertion rule: she -s be lively she -s be
                                                       ‾‾‾‾‾‾‾‾‾‾‾

   by *yes-no* switch rule 1:   -s be she
                                                     ‾‾‾‾‾‾

   by *not* insertion rule 1:   not

   by flip-flop rule: be ⌢-s   be ⌢-s
                                        ‾‾‾‾‾‾‾   ‾‾‾‾‾‾‾

                                          is   is

CHAPTER 7

Emphasis and Commands

OVERVIEW

In this chapter we deal with two different kinds of emphases: (1) whole sentence emphasis, in which the truth value of the whole sentence is asserted, and (2) element emphasis, in which a word or grammatical element is singled out for special attention. The chapter closes with a brief discussion of sentences that give commands.

The rules governing whole sentence emphasis are closely related to the rules governing questions and negative statements. When the underlying statement contains a helping verb or the main verb *be*, whole sentence emphasis is marked by extra heavy stress on the first verb following tense, for example:

He *could* win! (Modal)
I *have* seen a lawyer! (Perfect)
She *is* telling the truth! (Progressive)
John *was* sick after all! (Main Verb *be*)

However, when tense is followed directly by a main verb other than *be*, we must apply the *do* insertion rule. For example, the emphatic version of

I saw a lawyer.

is

I *did* see a lawyer!

We can account for this use of *do* by imagining that there is an abstract element called "EMP" (for emphasis) that represents the presence of extra heavy stress. EMP is inserted into the sentence by a rule exactly parallel to the *not* insertion rule. If tense is followed by a helping verb or by the main verb *be*, EMP is inserted after the verb following tense; however, if tense is followed directly by a main verb other than *be*, EMP is inserted between tense and the main verb, thus requiring the use of the *do* insertion rule.

There is a second kind of emphasis that stresses individual words or grammatical elements. Individual word emphasis is achieved by placing extra heavy stress on the word or element we wish to emphasize. This is called "contrastive stress" because it contrasts two words of the same type. For example, if we place contrastive stress on the word *small*, we are placing special emphasis on the contrast of *small* versus *big*, as, for example, in the following sentence:

John saw a *small* dog.

The contrastive stress singles out the dog's size as being of special importance.

In addition to giving special emphasis to individual words by means of contrastive stress, English can also place special emphasis on entire grammatical elements (which may consist of one or more words). In this chapter we deal informally with two families of transformational rules that do this: (1) the "cleft" family, and (2) the "predicate" family. Taking the sentence

The plane circled the field.

as our starting point, here are some of the ways that we can place special emphasis on certain grammatical elements by means of the two families of rules:

CLEFT:

Subject Noun Phrase:	What circled the field was *the plane*.
Object Noun Phrase:	What the plane circled was *the field*.
Verb Phrase:	What the plane did was to *circle the field*.

PREDICATE:

Subject Noun Phrase:	It was *the plane* that circled the field.
Object Noun Phrase:	It was *the field* that the plane circled.

The final part of the chapter deals with commands. The unequivocal form of command in English is the imperative sentence, a sentence with no overt subject noun phrase, for example,

Go away.
Stop that.
Bring me the file on Smith.

Traditional grammar assumed that there was an "understood" *you* subject in imperative sentences. The chapter discusses this claim and produces evidence from the form of tag questions to support the traditional analysis. The chapter closes by discussing the combination of passive, question, negative, and emphatic transformations.

THE EMPHATIC SENTENCE

We will include under this heading both sentences that have some special emphasis and sentences that have been transformed from statements into commands. In English, there seem to be two basically different kinds of emphasis. One kind of emphasis asserts the truth value of the whole sentence, while a second kind of emphasis singles out one particular element within the sentence for special emphasis. For the sake of convenience, let us call the first type of emphasis "whole sentence emphasis," and the second type "element emphasis."

Whole Sentence Emphasis

Whole sentence emphasis is achieved by placing extra heavy stress on the pronunciation of the first optional element from the auxiliary that follows tense, or on the main verb *be*, for example:

WITH A MODAL AUXILIARY:

> He *could* win, after all!
> You *must* be quiet!

WITH THE PERFECT:

> So he *had* been lying!
> I *have* seen a lawyer!

WITH THE PROGRESSIVE:

> She *is* telling the truth!
> They *were* hiding there!

WITH *BE* USED AS A MAIN VERB:

> But he *is* a Korean!
> John *was* sick after all!

However, as you might guess, when tense is followed directly by a main verb other than *be*, the *do* insertion rule is applied, for example:

He *did* win, after all!
I *did* see a lawyer!
She *does* know the answer!
We *do* have a new telephone!

If we imagine the presence of emphatic stress as being indicated in the grammar as an element, say, by the symbol EMP, we can then account for the placement of the stress and the use of the *do* insertion rule in exactly the same way as we did with *not*. If tense is followed by a helping verb or *be* as a main verb, *EMP* is placed *after* the first helping verb or *be*, for example:

He *Past* can EMP win, after all.
could

I ∅ have EMP *-EN* see a lawyer.
have seen

She *-s* be EMP *-ING* tell the truth.
is telling

John *Past* be EMP sick after all.
was

If tense is directly followed by a main verb other than *be*, EMP is placed directly after tense (and before the main verb), for example:

He *Past* EMP win, after all.
I *Past* EMP see a lawyer.
She *-s* EMP know the answer.
We *-s* EMP have a new telephone.

Since tense is not now followed directly by a verb, the *do* insertion rule automatically applies:

He *Past do* EMP win, after all.
did

I *Past do* EMP see a lawyer.
did

She *-s do* EMP know the answer.
does

We ∅ *do* EMP have a new telephone.
do

In the phonological part of the grammar, EMP will be realized as extra heavy stress on the preceding verb.

We may formalize the "EMP insertion rule" as follows (let V_{Aux} be defined as in the *yes-no* question switch rule):

1. $\text{Tense} \frown V_{Aux} \Longrightarrow \text{Tense} \frown V_{Aux} \frown \text{EMP}$
2. $\text{Tense} \frown \text{Main verb} \Longrightarrow \text{Tense} \frown \text{EMP} \frown \text{Main Verb}$

Rules 1 and 2 are disjunctive and ordered. If the conditions for rule 1 are not met, then rule 2 will automatically apply. Since rule 2 separates tense from a following verb by inserting EMP, the *do* insertion rule must also be applied. Here are several derivations of emphatic sentences:

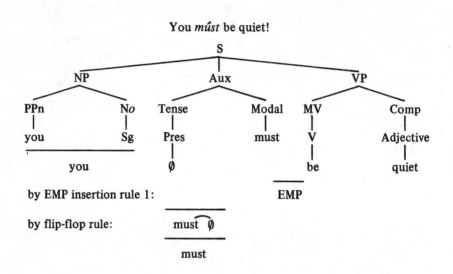

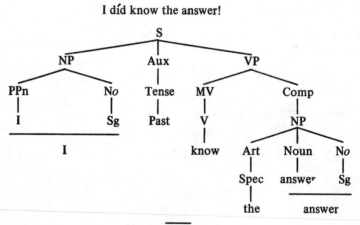

EXERCISE 7.1   **Whole Sentence Emphasis**

Draw the phrase structure trees and apply the necessary transformational rules to generate the following sentences:
1. She *might* be telling the truth!
2. I *am* coming!
3. He *did* have a car!
4. He *had* stolen a car!
5. The package *did* turn up!

Element Emphasis

Any word in a sentence can be given contrastive stress, for example:

John saw a small dog.
John *saw* a small dog.
John saw *a* small dog.
John saw a *small* dog.
John saw a small *dog*.

This kind of element emphasis is called "contrastive stress" because it contrasts two words of the same type. By giving contrastive stress to *John* we are asserting that it was *John* and not somebody else who saw a small dog. When we stress *saw*, we are not giving the whole sentence an emphasis (or else we would use *do*), but we are stressing that John did in fact *see*, not *hear* or *imagine*, the dog. By stressing the article *a*, we emphasize that it was just one dog, not several, and that the dog was not otherwise specified (or else we would have used *the*). Likewise, *small* is contrasted with *big* and *dog* with *cat* or whatever else John could conceivably have seen. From the standpoint of grammar, contrastive stress would be indicated by placing the extra heavy stress marker EMP after the word to be given contrastive stress. The phonological rules would govern its actual realization into sound.

English, like most other languages, has ways of giving special emphasis, not just to single words but to entire grammatical units. This emphasis is accomplished by a diverse group of transformational rules that invert the normal sentence order to give prominence to certain elements.

There are at least two different families of transformations that invert the underlying sentence in order to give emphasis to a particular grammatical element. One of these families of transformations is called the "cleft." For example, let us take this underlying sentence: *The plane circled the field*. The cleft transformation that emphasizes the subject noun phrase is

What circled the field was *the plane*.

The cleft that emphasizes the object noun phrase is

What the plane circled was *the field*.

The cleft that emphasizes the entire verb phrase is

What the plane did was *(to) circle the field*.

Here is another underlying sentence: *John saw Mary at the park yesterday*. The cleft that emphasizes the subject noun phrase is

(The person) who saw Mary at the park yesterday was *John*.

The cleft that emphasizes the object noun phrase is

(The person) whom John saw at the park yesterday was *Mary*.

The cleft that emphasizes the adverb of place is

(The place) where John saw Mary yesterday was *at the park*.

The cleft that emphasizes the adverb of time is

(The time) when John saw Mary at the park was *yesterday*.

The cleft can also emphasize predicate adjectives; for example, from the underlying sentence *John is hungry* we can generate the cleft

What John is is *hungry*.

The mechanism of the cleft transformation is quite complex. The grammatical element being emphasized is moved to the end of the sentence; the verb *be* is then put between the end of the original sentence and the element being emphasized. A relative pronoun appropriate to the element being emphasized is placed at the beginning of the sentence. If the element being emphasized is the verb phrase, then *do* must be inserted after the original subject noun phrase.

The second family of inversion transformations is less complex to describe because it employs a version of the question-word switch. For the sake of a label, we will call it the "predicate" family of transformational rules. Let us take as a sample underlying sentence *John saw Mary at the park yesterday*. If we choose to emphasize the subject noun phrase we get

It was *John* who saw Mary at the park yesterday.

If we emphasize the object noun phrase we get

It was *Mary* whom John saw at the park yesterday.

If we emphasize the adverb of place we get

It was *at the park* that John saw Mary yesterday.

If we emphasize the adverb of time we get

It was *yesterday* when John saw Mary at the park.

This type of inversion transformation moves the element being emphasized to the first position of the sentence, follows that element by the appropriate relative pronoun, and then places *It tense be* in front of the emphasized element, with the tense taken from the tense of the underlying sentence.

Commands

There are many ways of telling people to do things. For example, commands are often presented as questions:

Will you close the door?
Do you mind stopping that?

If the context is clear enough, even a statement can serve as a command. For instance, if a person in a room looks pointedly at another person near the door and says, "It sure is cold in here," the person near the door would have to be thickheaded not to realize that he has been asked to close the door.

However, the unequivocal form of a command in English is the imperative sentence:

Go away.
Stop that.
Bring me the file on Smith.

The obvious characteristic of the imperative sentence is that there is no overt subject. In traditional grammar, it was said that the subject of an imperative sentence was an understood *you*. Structural linguists tended to reject the "understood" subject on philosophical grounds. They did not approve of invoking imaginary elements to explain tangible data.

In this case, the transformational linguists side with the traditional grammarians. The chief piece of evidence that there is a *you* as the subject of the statement underlying the command is when we add a question tag to the commands:

Go away, *will you*? or *won't you*?
Stop that, *will you*? or *won't you*?
Bring me the file on Smith, *will you*? or *won't you*?

Since the form question tag is completely dependent upon the grammar of the underlying sentence, the underlying sentence must contain *you* as the subject noun phrase.

Combinations of Simple Transformational Rules

In the last four chapters we have examined a number of transformational rules that convert the underlying basic sentence represented by the phrase structure tree of the deep structure into a variety of different surface structures. These surface structures, despite their great difference in form and meaning, nevertheless have a basic family relationship to each other. That is, there is a single deep structure which underlies (1) an active, affirmative, neutral statement, (2) a passive, (3) a group of related questions, (4) a negative, and (5) an emphatic sentence. For example, from the deep structure

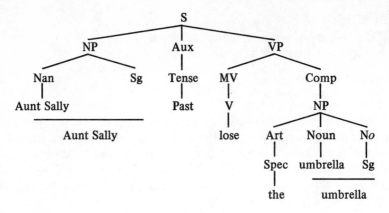

we can derive (at least) the following surface sentences.

1. Aunt Sally lost the umbrella. (active, affirmative, neutral statement)
2. The umbrella was lost by Aunt Sally. (passive)
3. The umbrella was lost. (passive plus agent deletion)
4. Did Aunt Sally lose the umbrella? (*yes-no* question)
5. Who lost the umbrella? (question-word question)
6. What did Aunt Sally lose? (question-word question)
7. Aunt Sally did not lose the umbrella. (negative)
8. Aunt Sally *did* lose the umbrella. (emphatic)

[handwritten: What was lost by Aunt Sally was...]
[handwritten: It was Aunt Sally who]

One of the assumptions of a transformational grammar is that the active, affirmative, neutral statement is automatically produced by applying the obligatory transformational rules to the deep structure, while the production of a passive, a question, or a negative sentence requires the operation of one or more optional transformations.

Following this reasoning, is there any reason why we could not apply more than one set of optional transformations on the same underlying sentence? In other words, can we have combinations of optional transformations, such as the passive and the negative, or a negative and a question, or an emphatic and a passive, and so on? The answer, of course, is that such combinations are both grammatical and quite common. Here is a theme-and-variations on *Aunt Sally lost the umbrella.*

PASSIVE + QUESTION:

Was the umbrella lost by Aunt Sally?

PASSIVE + NEGATIVE:

The umbrella was not lost by Aunt Sally.

PASSIVE + EMPHATIC:

The umbrella *wás* lost by Aunt Sally!

QUESTION + NEGATIVE:

Didn't Aunt Sally lose the umbrella? (*yes-no* question)
Who didn't lose the umbrella? (question-word question)
What didn't Aunt Sally lose? (question-word question)

QUESTION + EMPHASIS:

*Di*dn't Aunt Sally lose the umbrella?
Who *di*dn't lose the umbrella?
What *di*dn't Aunt Sally lose?

NEGATIVE + EMPHASIS:

Aunt Sally *di*dn't lose the umbrella!

We can also have three-way combinations, for example,

PASSIVE + QUESTION + NEGATIVE:

Wasn't the umbrella lost by Aunt Sally?

and even the ultimate four-way combination:

PASSIVE + QUESTION + NEGATIVE + EMPHASIS:

*Wa*sn't the umbrella lost by Aunt Sally?

The optional transformations that produce the passive, questions, negatives, and emphasis seem only partly ordered. The passive must be used before the question transformations because the NP switch rule for the passive requires a noun phrase in the first position. Otherwise, the order in which optional transformations are applied does not seem critical.

However, as we have seen with question tags, the relative ordering of the *yes-no* question switch rule and the *not* insertion rule give stylistically different results. That is, if we apply the *yes-no* question switch rule before the *not* insertion rule, we get the following sentences:

Didn't Aunt Sally lose the umbrella?
What didn't Aunt Sally lose?

If we apply the *not* insertion rule first, we get these sentences:

Did Aunt Sally not lose the umbrella?
What did Aunt Sally not lose?

(As an exercise, the reader might attempt to discover why the sentence *Who didn't lose the umbrella?* can come from either sequencing of the *yes-no* question switch and the *not* insertion rules.)

EXERCISE 7.2   **Review**

Draw phrase structure trees and apply the necessary transformational rules to produce the following sentences:
1. Didn't you hear me?
2. When did they call?
3. Queen Victoria was not amused by the incident.
4. Were they not ready?
5. Wasn't America discovered by Columbus?

Answers to Exercise 7.1   WHOLE SENTENCE EMPHASIS

   1.   She *might* be telling the truth!

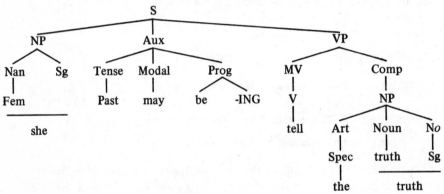

by EMP insertion rule 1:   EMP

by flip-flop rule: may ⌒ Past   tell ⌒ -ING
                       might   telling

   2.   I *am* coming!

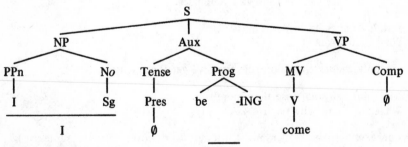

by EMP insertion rule 1:   EMP

by flip-flop rule: be ⌒ ∅   come ⌒ -ING
                            am   coming

3. He *díd* have a car!

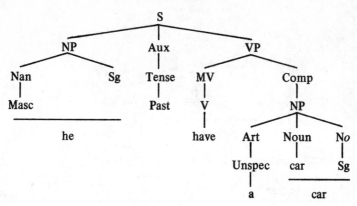

by EMP insertion rule 2: $\overline{\text{EMP}}$

by *do* insertion rule: $\overline{\text{do}}$

by flip-flop rule: $\overline{\text{do} \frown \text{Past}}$

                               did

4. He *hád* stolen a car!

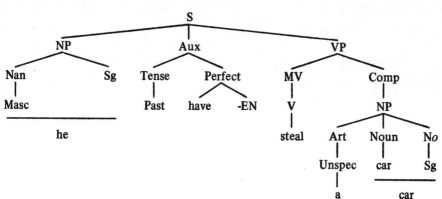

by EMP insertion rule 1: $\overline{\text{EMP}}$

by flip-flop rule: $\overline{\text{have} \frown \text{Past}}$ $\overline{\text{steal} \frown \text{-EN}}$

                               had   stolen

5.   The package *did* turn up!

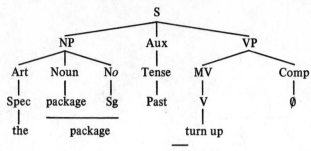

by EMP insertion rule 2:   EMP

by *do* insertion rule: do

by flip-flop rule: do Past

                                      did

Answers to Exercise 7.2   REVIEW

1.   Didn't you hear me?

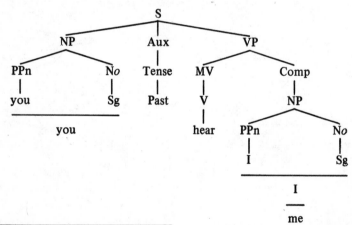

by *yes-no* question   Past   you
switch rule 2:
by *not* insertion rule   not

by *do* insertion rule: do

by flip-flop rule: do Past

                              did

2.   When did they call?

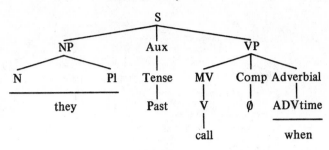

by *yes-no* question switch rule 2:	Past	they
by question word switch rule:	when past	they call
by *do* insertion rule:	do	
by flip-flop rule:	do͡ Past	
	did	

3.   Queen Victoria was not amused by the incident.

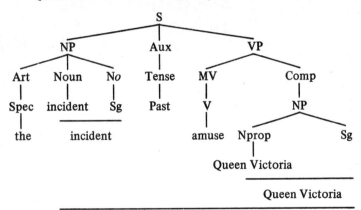

by passive	Past	amuse	the incident
1. NP switch rule (a): Queen Victoria		—	
			by
2. *by* insertion rule:		—	
		be -EN	
3. *be* -EN insertion rule:		—	
		not	
by *not* insertion rule 1:		—	—
		be͡ Past	amuse͡ -EN
by flip-flop rule:		was	amused

4.   Were they not ready?

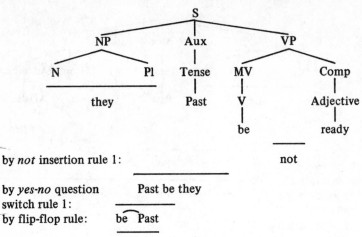

by *not* insertion rule 1:   not

by *yes-no* question   Past be they
switch rule 1:   _____
by flip-flop rule: be Past
                             _____
                               were

5.   Wasn't America discovered by Columbus?

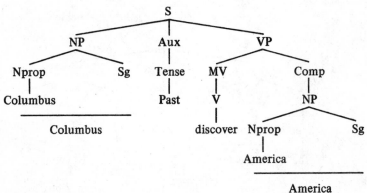

by passive   discover   Columbus
    1. NP switch rule (a):   America Past   —
                                               by
    2. *by* insertion rule: _____
                                         be -EN
    3. *be* -EN insertion rule: _____
                                 Past be America

by *yes-no* question   —
switch rule 1:   not
by *not* insertion rule: _____   _____
                             be Past   discover -EN
by flip-flop rule: _____   _____
                               was   discovered

PART III

Sentence-Combining Rules

OVERVIEW

The sentences we have dealt with up to now have been of a simplistic nature quite unlike the complex sentences that we encounter in real life. This is not a defect of the grammar. One of the key ideas of transformational grammar is that complex sentences are made up from groups of simple, elementary sentences. These simple, elementary sentences (deep structures) are produced by the phrase structure rules. The rules in Part III take the simple sentences produced by the phrase structure rules and combine them together to produce more complex surface sentences by means of sentence-combining transformational rules. We may represent the relation of the different kinds of rule systems by means of the follow-ing diagram (the reader should compare this diagram with the one in the Overview to Part II on page 138):

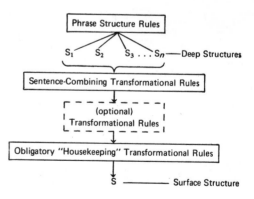

Part III deals with four ways in which sentences can be combined: (1) by embedding a sentence in the verb phrase complement of another sentence (Chapters 8 and 9), (2) by using a sentence to modify a noun

(Chapter 10), (3) by turning a sentence into a nominalized phrase and embedding it inside another sentence (Chapter 11), and (4) by joining two sentences together to form a new surface sentence by means of conjunction (Chapter 12).

Chapters 8 and 9 treat the process of putting a sentence inside the verb phrase complement of another sentence (in the terminology adopted in Part III, the sentence that is put inside is called the *embedded* sentence, while the sentence that it is put into is called the *main* sentence). Chapter 8 deals with embedded sentences that are kept intact as complete sentences; that is, they retain the three obligatory elements of the deep structure—the subject noun phrase, the auxiliary, and the verb phrase. Chapter 9 deals with embedded sentences that are reduced to less than full sentences.

Chapter 10 deals with the process of modification. In a transformational grammar, a noun is modified by an embedded sentence. This modifying sentence may come to the surface in a variety of ways, sometimes as an adjectival clause, sometimes as an adjectival phrase, and sometimes as a single word.

Chapter 11 deals with the process of nominalization. A nominalized sentence is a sentence that has been turned into a noun phrase, which in turn is embedded into another sentence. Put the other way around, certain sentences permit an embedded sentence to function as a noun phrase within the main sentence.

Chapter 12 deals with conjunction, the process of joining two sentences together with coordinating conjunctions, subordinating conjunctions, and conjunctive adverbs.

CHAPTER 8

Sentences Embedded in the Verb Phrase Complement: Clauses

OVERVIEW

In Chapter 3 we discussed various types of verb phrase complements. A complement, as you recall, is the obligatory element that follows the main verb. The complement types presented here and in the following chapter all contain embedded sentences. In this chapter we deal with the embedded sentences that come to the surface as clauses. A clause is a sentence that is a part of a larger sentence. By definition all clauses (and all sentences as well) must contain a subject noun phrase, tense, and a verb phrase—the obligatory elements from the three nodes that come directly from the sentence node.

Since we will now derive sentences within sentences, we need to adopt a terminology to keep straight which sentence we are talking about. Let us agree to use the term *main sentence* to refer to the sentence that is derived first, that is, the "larger" sentence that contains the embedded sentence within it. We will refer to the embedded sentence simply as the *embedded sentence*.

There are four different complement types that we will deal with in this chapter. In all four the embedded sentence is preceded by an optional *that*, which in turn is preceded by either a noun phrase (of one sort or another) or an adjective. The first complement type presented is the NP ⌒(that)⌒ S complement. An example is *I convinced John that he could ski*. The complement consists of *John⌒ that⌒ he could ski*, where the segment *he could ski* is the clause that comes from the embedded sentence.

215

The second complement type presented is the *it (that) S* complement. This type is not nearly so straightforward because the *it* is usually deleted from the surface unless the passive transformation is applied to the main sentence. For example, we would probably prefer the passive version

It was assumed (*by us* understood) that they would not be ready.

to the active version of the same basic sentence:

We assumed (it) that they would not be ready.

When the embedded sentence contains *be*, the tense of the embedded sentence may be deleted, turning the embedded sentence from a clause into a phrase. Thus we can have either of these sentences:

John believed they were lying.
John believed them to be lying.

The third complement type is the *it to NP (that) S* complement, as in

John explained (it) to me that they had been lost.

Many of the same optional transformational rules that can apply to *it (that) S* complements can also apply to this complement type.

The final complement type is the Adjective *(that) S* complement, as in

I am sure that you will be happy.

This is the first of two chapters that deal with sentences embedded into the verb phrase complement. As you know, an embedded sentence is a sentence contained inside another sentence. In this case, we will be dealing with sentences that come from the Complement node.

The difference between this chapter and the following chapter is that this chapter is concerned with those complement types in which the embedded sentence comes to the surface as a clause, while the following chapter deals with those complement types in which the embedded sentence comes to the surface as a phrase. Thus it is important that we distinguish clause from phrase. A clause is a complete sentence with a subject noun phrase, tense, and a verb phrase. All three elements, subject noun phrase, tense, and verb phrase, must be present. In a phrase, however, one or more of the three necessary elements is not present. We have already encountered many prepositional phrases, for example, *at home, in the house, at the beach.* These phrases contain a noun phrase, but neither tense nor a verb phrase.

In our earlier discussion of the verb phrase, all the complements were what we might call "simple" complements; that is, they did not contain embedded sentences. To the list of "simple" complement types, we will now add four new "complex" complement types, each containing an embedded sentence:

$$\text{Comp} \longrightarrow \left\{ \begin{array}{l} \text{NP } \textit{(that)} \text{ S} \\ \text{it } \textit{(that)} \text{ S} \\ \text{it to NP } \textit{(that)} \text{ S} \\ \text{Adjective } \textit{(that)} \text{ S} \end{array} \right\}$$

NP (THAT) S COMPLEMENT

Here are some examples of this complement type:

John persuaded him (that) Aunt Sally was trustworthy.
We warned them (that) the road was dangerous.
I assured Mr. Brown (that) I finished the job.
The class informed the teacher (that) they hated homework.

While the embedded sentences are grammatically complete, they are dependent in some ways on the main sentence. For example, if the tense in the main sentence is past, there is a tendency for the tense in the embedded sentence to be past also. Compare the following sentences:

I told him that I would finish the job.
(?)*I told him that I will finish the job.

The second sentence, while not completely ungrammatical, certainly looks strange as a written sentence, though it probably would not be so objectional as a spoken sentence. However, when the embedded sentence contains a "timeless" statement, that is, one that is presumed to be true for all time, it is not unusual to have past tense in the main sentence with present tense in the embedded sentence, for example:

I told him that Aunt Sally hates snakes.

We can apply many optional transformations to the embedded sentence. For example, corresponding to the sentence

I assured Mr. Brown that I finished the job.

there is a passive,

I assured Mr. Brown that the job was finished by me.

a negative,

I assured Mr. Brown that I didn't finish the job.

and an emphatic sentence,

I assured Mr. Brown that I *did* finish the job.

Here is a sample phrase structure tree for a sentence containing a NP (that) S complement:

I convinced John that he could ski.

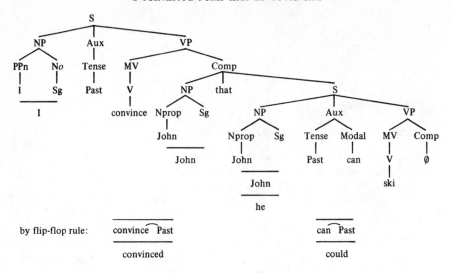

by flip-flop rule:

Notice that the flip-flop rule applies twice: once to the main sentence and once to the embedded sentence. Also note that the pronoun in the embedded sentence is in the subject form despite the fact that it follows the verb in the main sentence.

EXERCISE 8.1 NP⌢(that)⌢S Complements

Draw phrase structure trees and apply the necessary transformational rules to produce the following sentences:
1. I showed him that the house was a mess.
2. The company notified him that his bill was late.
3. We convinced Mary she should go.
4. She was advised by the mechanic that the tires should be replaced (*by the mechanic* understood).

IT⌢(THAT)⌢S COMPLEMENT

There are a number of verbs that can be used with this complement type. With many of them, however, there is a problem: the *it* does not come to the surface except when the passive is applied. First, though, here are some sample sentences of this complement type in which the *it* can appear in an active sentence (at least for me, but maybe not for you):

I regret it that you have been misinformed.
The salesman guaranteed it that the boat would sail.
We understood it that all parties would agree.
They doubted it that we would ever succeed.
The magazine reported it that the government had been overthrown.

All of these sentences have a counterpart passive:

It is regretted (by me) that you have been misinformed.
It was guaranteed (by the salesman) that the boat would sail.
It was understood (by us) that all parties would agree.
It was doubted (by them) that we would ever succeed.
It was reported (by the magazine) that the government had been overthrown.

There are many verbs taking this complement type which sound strange when used with the *it* in the active:

(?)We assumed it that they would not be ready.
(?)We discovered it that the data were incomplete.
(?)Columbus supposed it that the world was round.
(?)John expected it that you would come.

However, the passive counterparts of these sentences seem quite normal:

It was assumed (by us) that they would not be ready.
It was discovered (by us) that the data were incomplete.
It was supposed (by Columbus) that the world was round.
It was expected (by John) that you would come.

The group of sentences that do not normally occur with *it* in the active pose a problem. On the one hand, it seems incorrect to produce sentences with an element (the *it*) that must be deleted for the surface sentence to be grammatical. On the other hand, if we do not build the *it* in as part of the complement, we are at a loss to give a simple explanation of how all these sentences have passive counterparts with *it* as the new surface subject.

The approach adopted here is that the *it* is produced by a phrase structure rule. In the passive, the *it* comes to the surface as the new subject. In the active, the *it* may or may not be deleted depending on the main verb. With some main verbs, such as *understand*, the *it* deletion is optional. With other verbs, such as *suppose* (at least for some people), the *it* deletion rule will be obligatory—always assuming, of course, that the passive rule has not been applied. Here is the formalization of the *it deletion rule*:

$$it \; \overparen{(that)} \; S \Longrightarrow \overparen{(that)} \; S$$

EXERCISE 8.2   *It* Deletion Rule

Why won't the *it* deletion rule also apply to NP $\overparen{(that)}$ S complements?
(Hint· what kind of nouns are used in NP $\overparen{(that)}$ S complements? *animate*

Here are sample phrase structure trees and the necessary transformational rules for producing *He hoped that they would win* and *It was noticed (by us understood) that the phone was off the hook*:

He hoped that they would win.

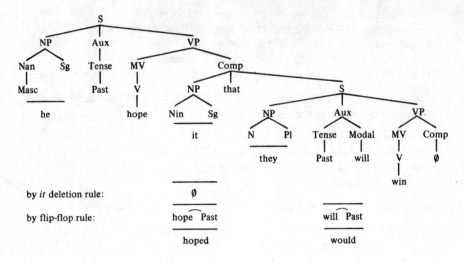

It was noticed *(by us)* that the phone was off the hook.

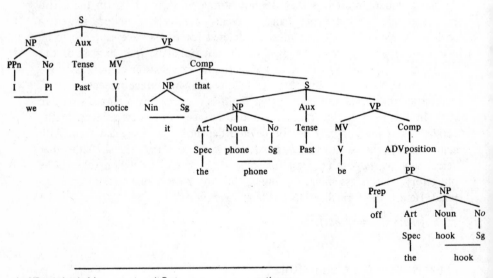

It (that) S complements can be reduced from a clause to a phrase by means of an optional transformational rule. This rule has three restrictions on its use: (1) the complement cannot contain the optional *that*; (2) the embedded sentence must contain *be* as either a main verb or a helping verb, and no other helping verbs are permitted; and (3) the *it* must be deleted. Here are some examples of this transformation:

He guaranteed the boat was sound. ⟹ He guaranteed the boat to be sound.
They did not notice he was a policeman. ⟹ They did not notice him to be a policeman.
We suspected the umbrella was damaged by Aunt Sally. ⟹ We suspected the umbrella to be damaged by Aunt Sally.
John believed they were lying. ⟹ John believed them to be lying.

The rule reduces the clause to a phrase by replacing the tense with *to*. We will call this rule the *to replacement rule*:

Tense ⟹ *to*

As you can see, the rule as it stands could be applied to any tense node. The only way the rule can be restricted to apply to the right tense node is by specifying in the grammar that the rule can be applied only to verbs in the embedded sentences of *it (that)* S complements and that the three restrictions above have been met.

When an embedded sentence comes to the surface as a clause, the pronouns in the clause are just like the ones in an independent sentence. For example, in the sentence

They did not notice he was a policeman.

he is in the subject form because *he* is the subject of the embedded sentence. However, when we apply the *to* replacement rule, the clause is reduced to a phrase, and *he* is no longer the subject of a sentence and thus falls under the rules that govern pronoun form in the main sentence. Since the *he* follows the verb in the main sentence, it is changed to *him*:

They did not notice him to be a policeman.

Here is a sample derivation employing the *to* replacement rule:

They did not notice him to be a policeman.

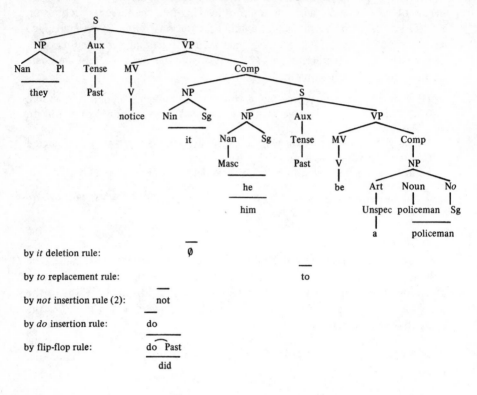

by *it* deletion rule: ∅

by *to* replacement rule: to

by *not* insertion rule (2):   not

by *do* insertion rule: do

by flip-flop rule: do⌢Past
                           ―――――
                               did

EXERCISE 8.3   *It (that) S* Complements

Draw phrase structure trees and apply the necessary transformational rules to produce the following sentences:
1. We understood it that you would cooperate with us.
2. Aunt Sally said that it had been nice.
3. The Captain discovered the ship to be sinking.
4. It was shown (*by the government* understood) that John had not paid his taxes.
5. She knew them to be alarmed by the accusations.

IT TO NP (THAT) S COMPLEMENT

This unlikely looking complement type is very similar to the previous type. Like the *it (that) S* complement, the *it* is often deleted from the surface sentence. Here are some sample sentences where the *it* does not seem unduly objectionable, although we would probably delete the *it* more often than not:

John explained it to me that they had been lost.
We mentioned it to Aunt Sally that the umbrella was in the hall.
They announced it to the crowd that the government had fallen.
He admitted it to everybody that he had misled them.

We may easily reformulate the *it* deletion rule to include this complement type:

$$it \overparen{(to \ NP)} \overparen{(that)} \ S \Longrightarrow \overparen{(to \ NP)} \overparen{(that)} \ S$$

John explained to me that they had been lost.
We mentioned to Aunt Sally that the umbrella was in the hall.
They announced to the crowd that the government had fallen.
He admitted to everybody that he had misled them.

Unlike the two previous complement types, *that* is normally used. Notice how odd the following sentences sound when the *that* is not used:

(?)John explained it to me they had been lost.
(?)John explained to me they had been lost.
(?)John explained it they had been lost.

However, when both the *it* and the *to NP* are deleted, apparently we may choose not to use *that:*

John explained they had been lost.

We will call the optional rule that deletes the *to NP* the *to⁀NP deletion rule.*

EXERCISE 8.4   *To⁀NP* Deletion Rule

Can you formalize this rule so that it will apply only when it is supposed to, and not, for example, to the sentence: *I gave the bone to Rover?* In which order are the *to⁀NP* deletion rule and the *it* deletion rule applied?

$$it \overparen{} to \overparen{} NP \overparen{} (that) \overparen{} S$$
$$\underline{\quad\quad\quad}$$
$$\text{delt}$$

Here is a sample derivation of a sentence containing this complement type:

Aunt Sally pointed out that we were lost.

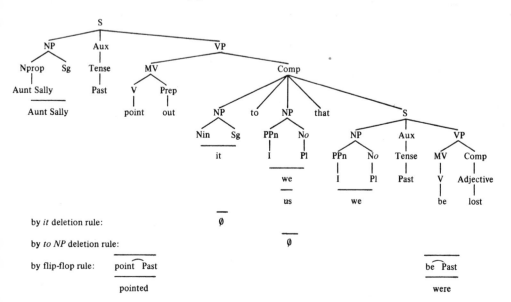

by *it* deletion rule: ∅

by *to NP* deletion rule: ∅

by flip-flop rule: point⁀Past   be⁀Past

                          pointed   were

Like *it (that)* S complements, we can turn the main sentence into a passive with *it* as the new subject. However, when we do this, we would usually apply either the agent deletion rule or the *to NP* deletion rule. If we do not, we have a grammatical but somewhat strange-sounding sentence, for example,

(?)It was explained by John to me that they had been lost.

Most of us would probably prefer either of the following versions:

It was explained to me that they had been lost.
It was explained by John that they had been lost.

Also, like *it (that)* S complements, we can apply the *to* replacement rule to *it to NP (that)* S complements with certain (but not all) verbs; for example, corresponding to the sentence

The Army declared it to us that we were fit.

we can produce the following sentence by applying the *it* deletion rule, the *to* NP deletion rule, and the *to* replacement rule:

The Army declared us to be fit.

EXERCISE 8.5 *It to NP (that)* S Complements

Draw phrase structure trees and apply the necessary transformational rules to produce the following sentences:
1. We suggested it to John that he might join the Army.
2. It was reported (*by them* understood) to the police that they had wrecked the car.
3. May I point out to you that your dog ruined my flowers?
4. Aunt Sally acknowledged (*to us* understood) the criticism to be fair.

ADJECTIVE *(THAT)* S COMPLEMENT

This complement type is used with two different groups of adjectives. Here are some examples of the first group:

I am sure that you will be happy.
John was grateful that you were able to come.
They seemed afraid that the trip would be postponed.
Aunt Sally was certain that you would come.

Adjectives derived from past participles (verb -EN) can also be used:

We were amazed that he would want to come.
Everyone was amused that John ignored the incident.
We were upset that they felt that way.

(Question: how can you show that *amazed, amused,* and *upset* are adjectives?)
The second group of adjectives, unlike the first group, does not take an animate subject. Instead, they are normally used with *it* as the subject:

It is true that John wrote a poem.
It is clear that we are lost.
It is probable that they will be defeated.
It is curious that they felt that way.
It is sad that they lost the game.
It is regrettable that they crashed the party.

Adjectives derived from present participles (verb -ING) can also be used:

It was surprising that the party ended early.
It is frightening that no one seems to care about it.
It is alarming that the investigation was halted.

(Question: how can you show that *surprising, frightening,* and *alarming* are adjectives?)

EXERCISE 8.6   Adjective *(that)* S Complements

Without the benefit of a model, can you draw phrase structure trees and apply the necessary transformational rules to produce the following sentences?
1. Aunt Sally was grateful that you came.
2. It is well known that John is afraid of the dark.
3. We were astonished that the computer knew the answer.
4. It was disappointing that we did not win.

EXERCISE 8.7   Review

For each of the following sentences, identify the complement type:
1. We complained to Aunt Sally that she was neglecting us.
2. I was disturbed that you would think that.
3. It was hoped (*by us* understood) that you would cooperate.
4. We informed him that his contract had been canceled (*by us* understood).
5. He is mistaken in his beliefs.
6. She expected the guests to be on time.
7. John confessed to us that he was ashamed of himself.
8. He warned them that the bridge was unsafe.
9. I introduced John to Mary.
10. It was proposed (*by them* understood) to me that we should sell out.
11. John persuaded Aunt Sally that she should leave her umbrella at home.
12. It is annoying that they did not finish the job.
13. We saw that we had been tricked by them.
14. He is adverse to criticism.
15. He declared to us that he would give up peanut butter.
16. We were not aware that the ship was sinking.
17. It was denied (*by everyone* understood) that the world was round.
18. They reminded us that we had promised to go.
19. We promised the job to John.
20. It is necessary that you leave as soon as possible.

Answers to Exercise 8.1 NP $\overparen{(THAT)}$ S COMPLEMENTS

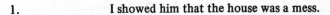

1.   I showed him that the house was a mess.

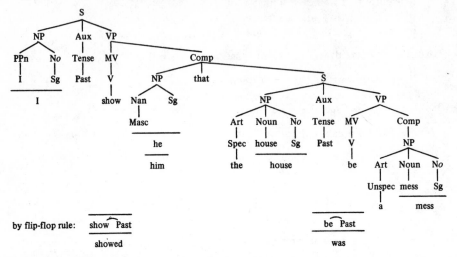

2.   The company notified him that his bill was late.

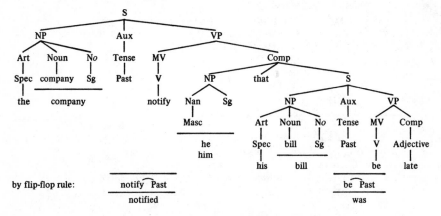

3.   We convinced Mary she should go.

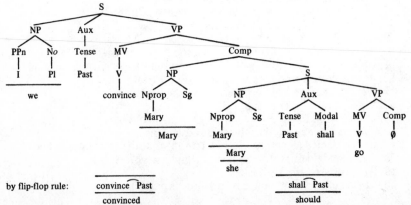

4. She was advised by the mechanic that the tires should be replaced (*by the mechanic* understood).

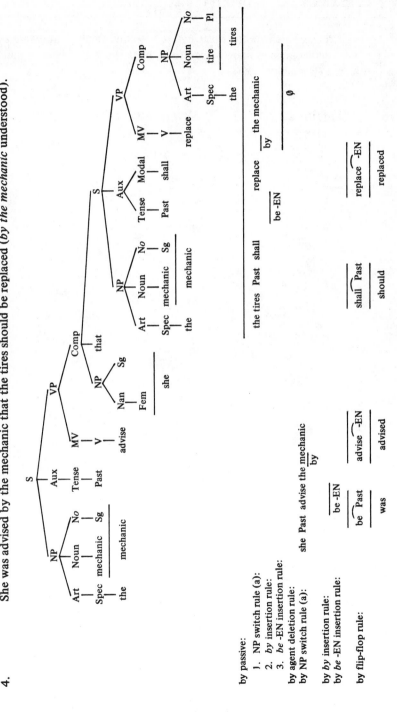

by passive:
  1. NP switch rule (a):
  2. *by* insertion rule:
  3. *be* -EN insertion rule:

by agent deletion rule:
by NP switch rule (a):   she Past advise the mechanic
                                              by

by *by* insertion rule:
by *be* -EN insertion rule:

by flip-flop rule:

Note: With embedded sentences we will normally apply the optional rules to the embedded sentence *before* we apply them to the main sentence.

227

Answers to Exercise 8.2   *IT* DELETION RULE

The noun in the NP part of the NP *(that)* S complement is an *animate* noun. Thus the noun phrase cannot be replaced by *it*, since *it* replaces noun phrases containing an animate noun.

Answers to Exercise 8.3   *IT (THAT)* S COMPLEMENTS

1.   We understood it that you would cooperate with us.

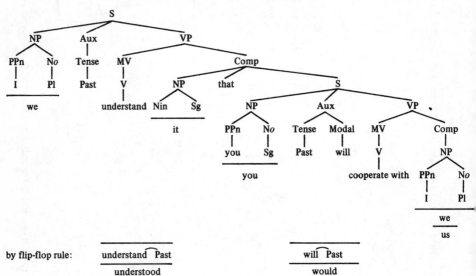

2.   Aunt Sally said that it had been nice.

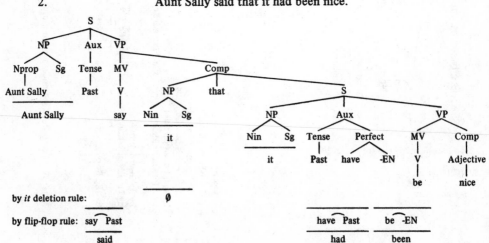

3.   The Captain discovered the ship to be sinking.

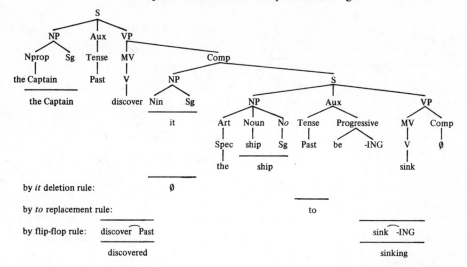

4.   It was shown (*by the government* understood) that John had not paid his taxes.

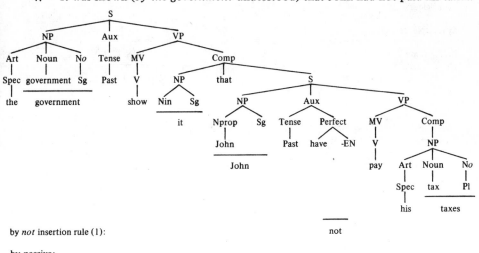

5.   She knew them to be alarmed by the accusations.

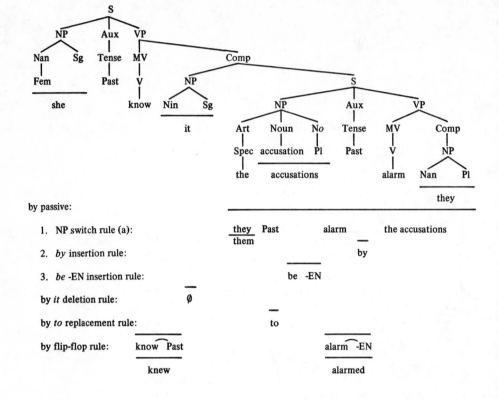

by passive:

1. NP switch rule (a):   they   Past   alarm   the accusations
                              them

2. *by* insertion rule: by

3. *be* -EN insertion rule: be -EN

by *it* deletion rule: Ø

by *to* replacement rule: to

by flip-flop rule: know Past   alarm -EN

                        knew   alarmed

Answers to Exercise 8.4   *TO* NP DELETION RULE

it to NP (that) S ⟹ *it (that) S*

The *to* NP deletion rule is applied first. Why?

Answers to Exercise 8.5 IT $\frown$ TO $\frown$ NP $\frown$ (THAT) $\frown$ S COMPLEMENTS

1.

We suggested it to John that he might join the Army.

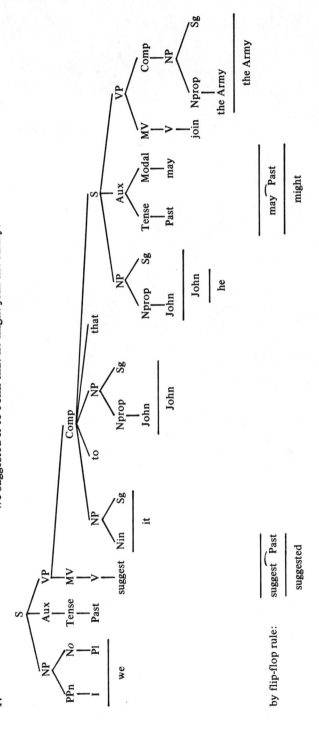

by flip-flop rule:

$$\frac{\text{suggest} \frown \text{Past}}{\text{suggested}}$$

2. It was reported (*by them* understood) to the police that they had wrecked the car.

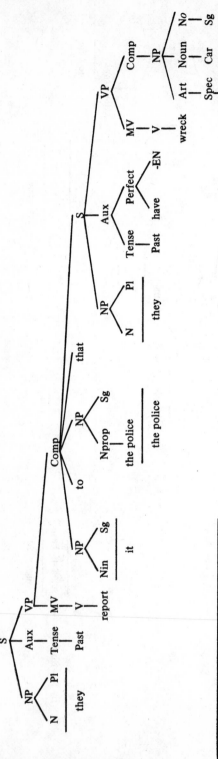

by passive:

1. NP switch rule (a): It Past report $\dfrac{\text{they}}{\text{them}}$ by ____

2. *by* insertion rule: ____ by

3. *be* -EN insertion rule: be -EN ____ Ø

by agent deletion rule:

by flip-flop rule: be⌢Past report⌢-EN   have⌢Past   wreck⌢-EN

was   reported   had   wrecked

3.

May I point out to you that your dog ruined my flowers?

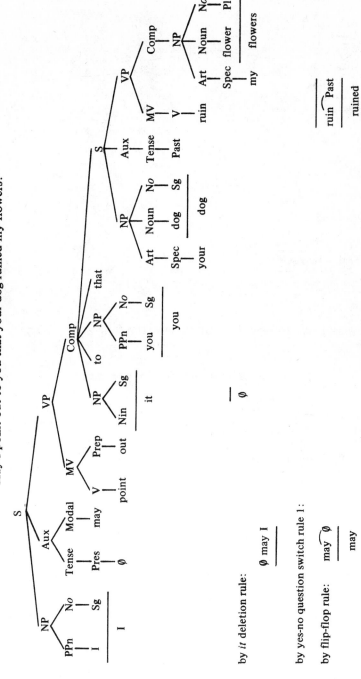

by *it* deletion rule:

$$\frac{\emptyset \text{ may I}}{}$$

by yes-no question switch rule 1 :

by flip-flop rule: $\dfrac{\text{may} \frown \emptyset}{\text{may}}$

4.   Aunt Sally acknowledged (*to us* understood) the criticism to be fair.

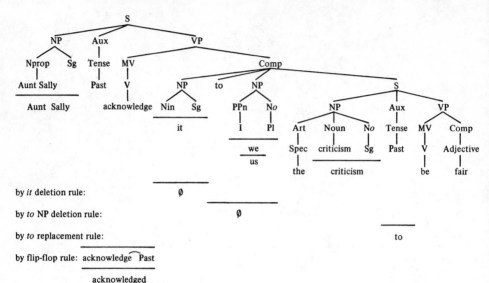

by *it* deletion rule: Ø

by *to* NP deletion rule: Ø

by *to* replacement rule: to

by flip-flop rule: acknowledge Past

                    acknowledged

Answers to Exercise 8.6   ADJECTIVE (THAT) S COMPLEMENTS

1.   Aunt Sally was grateful that you came.

by flip-flop rule: be Past   come Past

                      was   came

2.

It is well known that John is afraid of the dark.

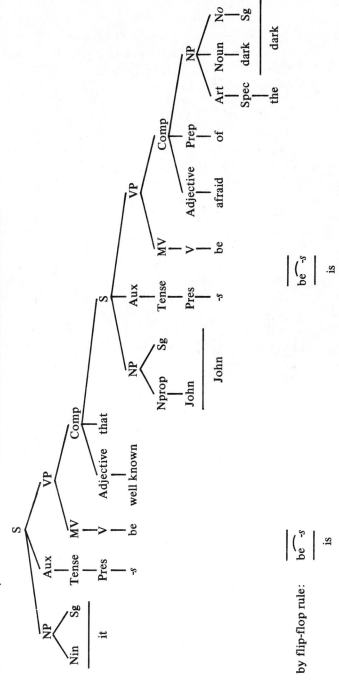

by flip-flop rule:

3.   We were astonished that the computer knew the answer.

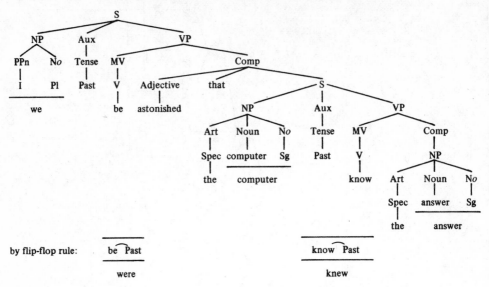

4.   It was disappointing that we did not win.

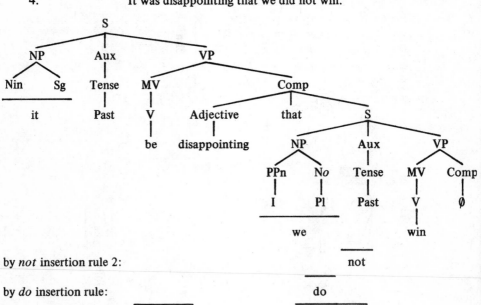

Answers to Exercise 8.7   REVIEW

1. We complained to Aunt Sally that she was neglecting us.
   it to NP (that) S
2. I was disturbed that you would think that. *Adjective (that) S*
3. It was hoped (*by us* understood) that you would cooperate. *it (that) S*
4. We informed him that his contract had been canceled (*by us* understood).
   NP (that) S
5. He is mistaken in his beliefs. *Adjective Prep NP*
6. She expected the guests to be on time. *it (that) S*
7. John confessed to us that he was ashamed of himself. *it to NP (that) S*
8. He warned them that the bridge was unsafe. *NP (that) S*
9. I introduced John to Mary. *NP Prep NP*
10. It was proposed (*by them* understood) to me that we should sell out.
    it to NP (that) S
11. John persuaded Aunt Sally that she should leave her umbrella at home.
    NP (that) S
12. It is annoying that they did not finish the job. *Adjective (that) S*
13. We saw that we had been tricked by them. *it (that) S*
14. He is adverse to criticism. *Adjective Prep NP*
15. He declared to us that he would give up peanut butter. *it to NP (that) S*
16. We were not aware that the ship was sinking. *Adjective (that) S*
17. It was denied (*by everyone* understood) that the world was round.
    it (that) S
18. They reminded us that we had promised to go. *NP (that) S*
19. We promised the job to John. *NP NP*
20. It is necessary that you leave as soon as possible. *Adjective (that) S*

CHAPTER 9

Sentences Embedded in the Verb Phrase Complement: Phrases

OVERVIEW

In the preceding chapter we dealt with sentences embedded within the verb phrase complements that came to the surface as clauses, that is, as intact sentences. In this chapter we will deal with sentences embedded within the verb phrase complement that come to the surface as phrases. You will recall that a phrase is missing one or more of the three essential elements that must be present to make up a sentence: a subject noun phrase, tense, and a verb phrase (complete with main verb and complement). All of the examples of embeddings that we shall deal with in this chapter lose their tense in the surface form, and many lose the subject noun phrase besides.

The chapter is organized around the three ways the tense can be lost: (1) deleted outright, (2) replaced by -ING, and (3) replaced by to. We will represent those embedded sentences that come to the surface with their tenses deleted outright this way: $S_\emptyset$. Following the same pattern, those embedded sentences that come to the surface with their tenses replaced by -ING or to will be marked as S_{-ING} and S_{to}, respectively.

A constant theme running through the chapter is what happens to the subject noun phrase in the embedded sentence. In each of the complement types we shall examine, one group of verbs will permit a complement with a different subject noun phrase in the embedded sentence from the subject noun phrase in the main sentence, while another group of verbs permits only subject noun phrases in the complement that are identical with the subject noun phrase of the main sentence. For this latter group, the subject noun phrase in the embedded sentence is deleted by what is called the identical noun phrase deletion rule.

There are four different types of complements in this chapter: one type each for $S_\emptyset$ and S_{-ING} embedded sentences and two types for S_{to}, one preceded by an adjective and one standing by itself. The four types are symbolized as follows:

$$\text{Comp} \longrightarrow \left\{ \begin{matrix} S_\emptyset \\ S_{-ING} \\ \text{Adjective } \overset{\frown}{S_{to}} \\ S_{to} \end{matrix} \right\}$$

Here are example sentences for each complement type, first with a different subject noun phrase in the main and embedded sentences and then with the subject noun phrases deleted from the embedded sentence because it was identical with the subject noun phrase in the main sentence:

$S_\emptyset$:

 Aunt Sally watched me work.
 Aunt Sally heard the telephone ring.

[handwritten note: Can't do it with same Aunt Sally the NP]

S_{-ING}:

 Aunt Sally found me working.
 Aunt Sally stopped working.

ADJECTIVE $\overset{\frown}{S_{to}}$:

 Aunt Sally is afraid for you to work.
 Aunt Sally is afraid to work.

S_{to}:

 Aunt Sally wanted you to work.
 Aunt Sally applied for you to work.
 Aunt Sally planned to work.

In this chapter we will examine those sentences embedded in the complement which come to the surface as a phrase, not as a clause. A phrase lacks one or more of the three essential elements of a sentence (or clause): subject noun phrase, tense, verb phrase. In all the cases we shall examine in this chapter, the tense is deleted from the embedded sentence. It might be more accurate to say, however, that the tense is either deleted outright and replaced with nothing or is replaced with either *to* or -ING. Accordingly, we will organize this chapter around the three things that can happen to the tense in the embedded sentence: (1) it can be deleted outright; (2) it can be replaced by *-ING*; (3) it can be replaced by *to*.

TENSE DELETED OUTRIGHT

Only a very limited number of verbs take a complement in which the tense is deleted outright. Here are some examples with the words from the embedded sentence in italics:

We let him *mail the package*.
They heard *us come in*.
The devil made *me do it*.

A basic question about phrases in the complement is how do we know they come from embedded sentences? Couldn't we argue that certain verbs are followed by a NP̂ VP complement? There are two main reasons for saying the phrase comes from an embedded sentence. The first reason is that the co-occurrence relation between the noun and the verb in the phrase is exactly the same as that between a subject noun and the main verb in a free-standing sentence. For example, the following sentences are both grammatical:

They heard *us come in*.   us come in = we came in
They heard *the glass break*.   the glass break = the glass broke

However, if we try to switch the embedded noun phrases in the two sentences, the resulting sentences are ungrammatical because of the relation of the noun and the verb in the phrase:

*They heard *the glass come in*.   the glass come in = *the glass came in
*They heard *us break*.   us break = *we broke

The second reason is that with many phrases, the noun phrase that precedes the verb phrase in the complement of the embedded sentence has been moved into that position as the result of the passive transformation and thus could not have been the object of the verb in the main sentence. For example, compare the active and passive versions of the same basic sentence:

We let his relatives meet him at the station.
We let him be met at the station (by his relatives).

Let us agree to label the embedded sentence this way: S_ϕ. In other words, the sentence derived from the S_ϕ node will appear on the surface with the tense deleted, and in turn the rule that deletes tense will apply only to tense derived from a S$_\phi$ node. The rule, which we will call the *tense deletion rule* is simply

Tense $\Longrightarrow \emptyset$.

Here is a sample derivation of a sentence containing a S$_\phi$ complement:

Aunt Sally watched John clean out the attic.

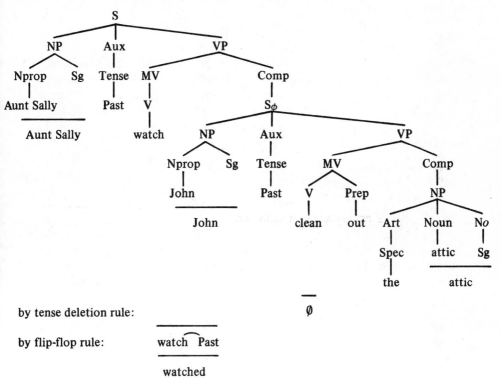

by tense deletion rule: $\emptyset$

by flip-flop rule: watch ⌢ Past

watched

There are only five verbs that take this complement: *hear, let, make, see,* and *watch.*

EXERCISE 9.1   S$_\phi$ **Complements**

Draw phrase structure trees and apply the necessary transformational rules to produce the following sentences:
1. John saw the Giants play the Dodgers.
2. They made the children bake the cookies.
3. We let it be known (*by everybody* understood) that we were having a party.

TENSE REPLACED BY -ING

There are a large number of verbs that occur with an embedded sentence complement in which the tense of the embedded sentence is replaced by -ING. Here are some examples:

Aunt Sally stopped going to parties.
Elliot shunned eating a peach.
I escaped doing the dishes.
He postponed taking the test.
John avoided being on the panel.

As you can see, the subject noun phrase has been deleted from the embedded sentence. For all but a handful of verbs that take this complement type, the subject noun phrase of the embedded sentence must be identical with the subject noun phrase of the main sentence. The subject noun phrase of the embedded sentence is not replaced by a reflexive, but must be deleted. All of the above sentences are ungrammatical if we retain the subject of the embedded sentence as a reflexive:

*Aunt Sally stopped herself going to parties.
*Elliot shunned himself eating a peach.
*I escaped myself doing the dishes.
*He postponed himself taking the test.
*John avoided himself being on the panel.

Consequently, for the large group of verbs that take this complement type, the tense and the identical subject noun phrase in the embedded sentence must both be deleted. We will call the rule that deletes the subject noun phrase from the embedded sentence the *identical NP deletion rule*. The rule may be formulated as a simple deletion:

$$NP \Longrightarrow \emptyset$$

However, to apply the rule properly, a full grammar would have to specify which noun phrase is being deleted. That is, it would specify that only the subject noun phrase that (1) is in an embedded sentence derived from an S_{-ING} complement (plus a few other complement types), and (2) is identical with the subject noun phrase of the main sentence, can be deleted.

There are, however, a few verbs that take this complement type which permit the subject noun phrase of the embedded sentence to be different from the subject noun phrase of the main sentence. Since the two noun phrases are different, by definition the identical NP deletion rule cannot apply. Here are some examples:

We saw Mr. Brown working in the backyard.
They found John studying in the library.
The police caught him opening the safe.
We watched him polishing the brasswork.

Since these verbs permit the embedded sentence to have a different subject noun phrase from the subject noun phrase in the main sentence, what happens if the two subject noun phrases are identical? If we then apply the identical NP deletion rule, the result is ungrammatical:

> Mr. Brown saw (Mr. Brown Past work in the backyard) ⟹ *Mr. Brown saw working in the backyard.
> They found (they Past study in the library) ⟹ *They found studying in the library.
> The police caught (the police Past open the safe) ⟹ *The police caught opening the safe.
> We watched (we Past polish the brasswork) ⟹ *We watched polishing the brasswork.

However, if we replace the subject noun phrase in the embedded sentence by the appropriate reflexive pronoun, then the surface sentences are grammatical:

> Mr. Brown saw himself working in the backyard.
> They found themselves studying in the library.
> The police caught themselves opening the safe.
> We watched ourselves polishing the brasswork.

We see that it is necessary to distinguish between two classes of verbs that take this complement type: one class which requires that the subject noun phrase of the embedded sentence be identical with the subject noun phrase of the main sentence (and thus deleted by the identical NP deletion rule); and a second class which permits the two noun phrases to be different, and when they are the same, does not apply the identical NP deletion rule, but instead turns the subject noun phrase in the embedded sentence into the corresponding reflexive pronoun.

Let us agree to identify this complement type this way: the rule that replaces the tense in the embedded sentence is simply

Tense ⟹ -ING

We will call this rule the -ING replacement rule. It applies only to the tense node that is contained in sentences derived from S$_{-ING}$. We will indicate the replacement of the subject noun phrase by the proper reflexive pronoun by drawing a line under the noun phrase and entering the reflexive pronoun underneath. For pronouns:

he	she	it	they	we	you (Sg)	you (Pl)
himself	herself	itself	themselves	ourselves	yourself	yourselves

When the noun phrase is not a pronoun, the reflexive is determined by the gender of the noun and the number, for example:

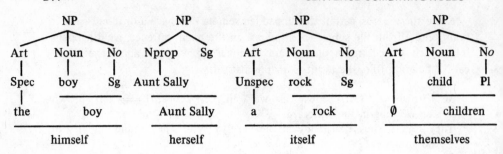

Here are some sample derivations of sentences that use this complement type:

He finished fixing the sink.

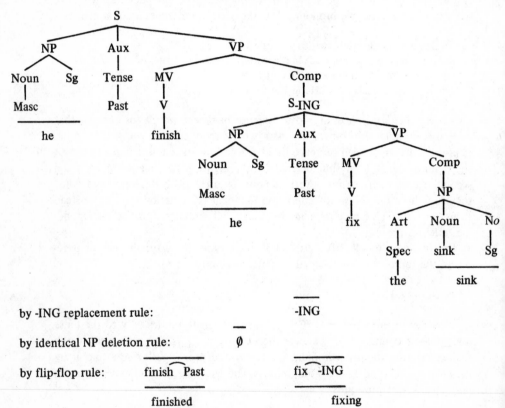

Carmen heard herself snoring.

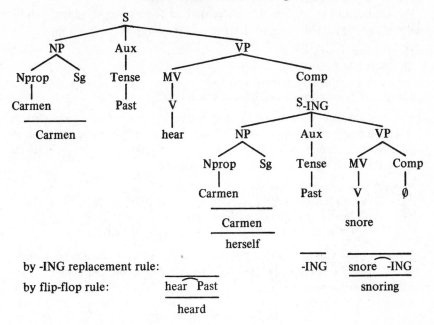

EXERCISE 9.2 S$_{-ING}$ **Complements**

Draw phrase structure trees and apply the necessary transformational rules to produce the following sentences:
1. John started crying.
2. Aunt Sally felt herself becoming angry.
3. The candidate put off being interviewed by the reporters.
4. They kept on talking.
5. I kept them talking about their work.

TENSE REPLACED BY *TO*

In the preceding chapter we encountered a *to* replacement rule which replaced the tense in an embedded sentence with *to*. However, in that case the *to* replacement rule was optional. In the two complement types we will consider here, the *to* replacement rule is obligatory.

Following the pattern we have used for the other two complement types in which the tense of the embedded sentence does not come to the surface, let us label embedded sentences in which the tense is replaced by *to* this way: S$_{to}$. There are two complement types that contain S$_{to}$. One complement type has an adjective in front of the embedded sentence, while in the other complement type the embedded sentence appears by itself. Since the adjective type is much simpler, we will deal with it first.

Adjective $\overset{\frown}{S}_{to}$ Complement

Many adjectives (as well as adjectives derived from past participles) can be used with an embedded sentence. Here are some examples:

He is clever to go.
She is certain to do it.
John will be delighted to help you.
Mr. Brown was lucky to be chosen by Aunt Sally.

The embedded sentences in all these examples contain subject noun phrases that are identical with subject noun phrases in the main sentences. If we attempt to retain the subject noun phrases in the embedded sentences as reflexives, the resulting sentences are ungrammatical:

*He is clever himself to go.
*She is certain herself to do it.
*John will be delighted himself to help you.
*Mr. Brown was lucky himself to be chosen by Aunt Sally.

The grammatical sentences above are produced by the *to* replacement rule and the identical NP deletion rule. Here is a sample derivation of a sentence containing this complement type:

They are fortunate to have you.

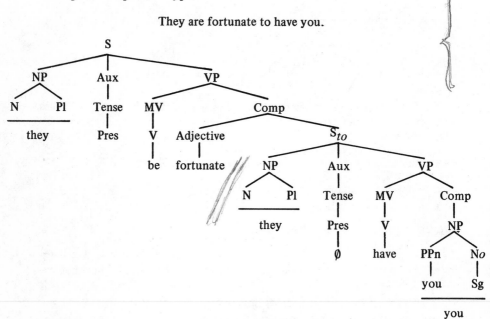

by *to* replacement rule: to

by identical NP deletion rule: ∅

by flip-flop rule: be͡ Pres

                                   are

There are a few adjectives that can also be used with embedded sentences that contain subject noun phrases different from the subject noun phrases of the main sentence. Compare the following sentences:

He is afraid to go.
He is afraid for her to go.

We are prepared to undertake the mission.
We are prepared for him to undertake the mission.

John was delighted to come to the party.
John was delighted for us to come to the party.

When the subject noun phrase of the embedded sentence is different from the subject noun phrase of the main sentence, we must put *for* in front of the embedded sentence. Let us call this the *for insertion rule* and formalize it this way:

Adjective $\overgroup{S_{to}} \Longrightarrow$ Adjective $\overgroup{for\ S_{to}}$

Here is an example of a sentence employing this rule:

The chairman was ready for the meeting to begin.

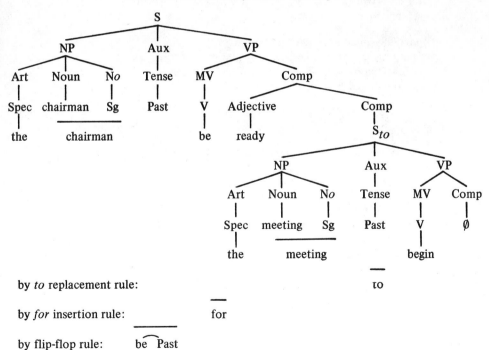

EXERCISE 9.3   **Adjective** S_{to} **Complements**

Draw phrase structure trees and apply the necessary transformational rules to produce the following sentences:
1. He is sure to be at home now.
2. Everyone was pleased for them to win.
3. Is John ready for us to turn the lights on?
4. They were proud to be named by the judge.

S_{to} Complement

A number of verbs are used with S_{to} complements in which the subject noun phrases of the embedded sentences must be deleted. That is, the subject noun phrases of the embedded sentences must (1) be identical with the subject noun phrases of the main sentences and (2) be deleted by the identical noun phrase deletion rule. Here are some sentences that contain S_{to} complements:

Aunt Sally plans to give a party.
I failed to see the humor in the situation.
He hesitated to give his name.
John pretended to be hurt.

The embedded subject noun phrases cannot be retained as reflexives in these sentences:

*Aunt Sally plans herself to give a party.
*I failed myself to see the humor in the situation.
*He hesitated himself to give his name.
*John pretended himself to be hurt.

Sometimes a completely different use of the reflexive is confused with the subject of the embedded noun phrase; for example, consider the following:

I, myself, failed to see the humor in the situation.
I failed to see the humor in the situation, myself.
I failed, myself, to see the humor in the situation.

In these sentences, the reflexive is used for emphasis. This reflexive has nothing to do with the subject of the embedded sentence.

Here is a sample phrase structure tree for a sentence with a S_{to} complement:

John decided to go.

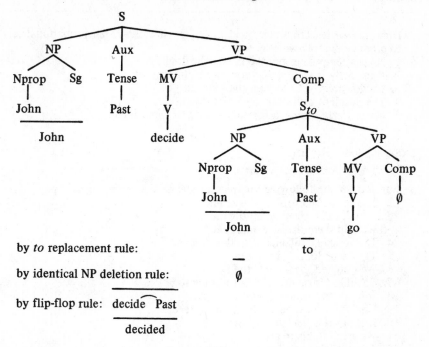

by *to* replacement rule:

by identical NP deletion rule:

by flip-flop rule: decide⁀Past

decided

A few verbs permit the subject noun phrases of the embedded sentences to be different from the subject noun phrases of the main sentences. Compare the following sentences:

I applied to go.
I applied for you to go.

They planned to take the children with them.
They planned for us to take the children.

We asked to be invited.
We asked for John to be invited.

When the subject noun phrases in the embedded sentences are different from the subject noun phrases of the main sentences, we put *for* in front of them, just as we did with Adjective⁀S_{to} complements.

Even fewer verbs permit the subject of the embedded noun phrase to come to the surface without the *for*. Compare the following sentences:

Aunt Sally expected to go.
Aunt Sally expected you to go.
(?)*Aunt Sally expected for you to go.

They wanted to see the movie.
They wanted us to see the movie.
(?)*They wanted for us to see the movie.

EXERCISE 9.4 S_{to} Complements

Draw phrase structure trees and apply the necessary transformational rules to produce the following sentences:
1. John attempted to pin the tail on the donkey.
2. Aunt Sally is waiting for you to fix the drinks.
3. We got everybody to sign the petition.
4. The accident caused us to be late.
5. Uncle Harry arranged for the movers to come today.

EXERCISE 9.5 **Review**

For each of the following sentences, indicate the complement type:
1. They managed to start the engines.
2. I don't mind cleaning up the kitchen.
3. We told them that it would rain.
4. The teacher explained it to the class.
5. They sent John to his room.
6. We watched them move the piano.
7. I couldn't imagine Aunt Sally going to jail.
8. John is eager for us to return.
9. Uncle Harry expected the water to recede.
10. It is obvious that she is lying.
11. We are not able to go.
12. John pleaded for them to reopen the case.
13. They discovered the solution to be correct.
14. It was hoped that he would come.
15. They let us make the changes.

Answers to Exercise 9.1   S_∅ COMPLEMENTS

1.   John saw the Giants play the Dodgers.

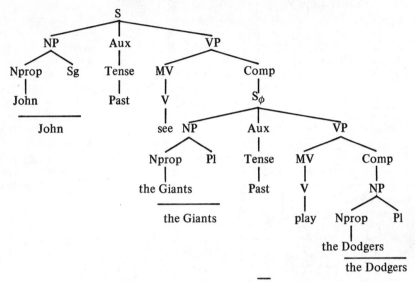

by tense deletion rule: ∅

by flip-flop rule: see͡ Past
                                              saw

2.   They made the children bake the cookies.

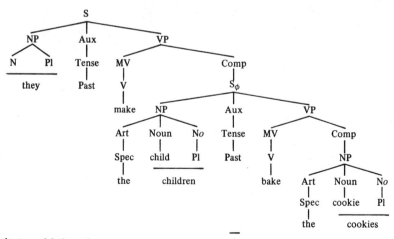

by tense deletion rule: ∅

by flip-flop rule: make͡ Past
                                  made

3.

We let it be known (*by everybody* understood) that we were having a party.

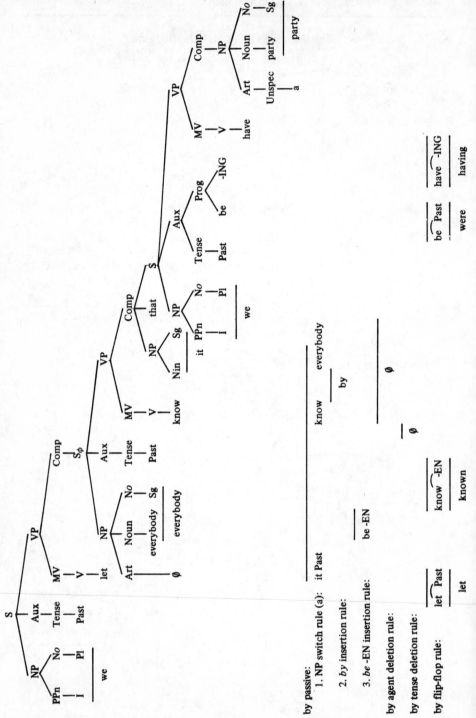

Answers to Exercise 9.2   S$_{-ING}$ COMPLEMENTS

1.   John started crying.

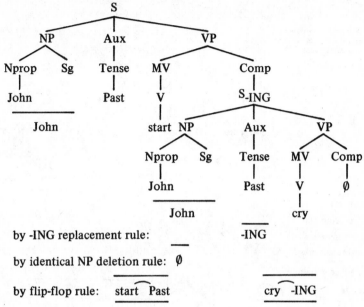

by -ING replacement rule: -ING

by identical NP deletion rule: ∅

by flip-flop rule: start͡ Past   cry͡ -ING

                           started   crying

2.   Aunt Sally felt herself becoming angry.

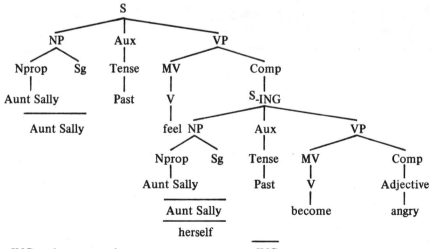

by -ING replacement rule: -ING

by flip-flop rule: feel͡ Past   become͡ -ING

                              felt   becoming

3.   The candidate put off being interviewed by the reporters.

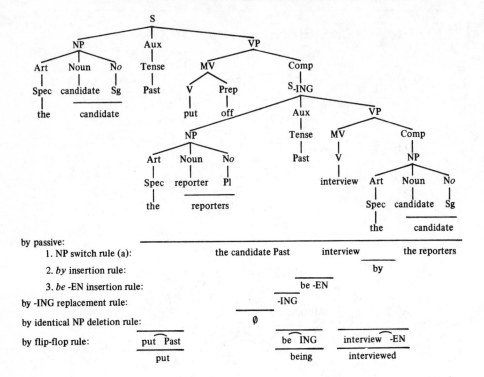

<table>
<tr><td>by passive:</td></tr>
<tr><td>   1. NP switch rule (a):</td><td>the candidate Past</td><td>interview</td><td>the reporters</td></tr>
<tr><td>   2. by insertion rule:</td><td></td><td>by</td><td></td></tr>
<tr><td>   3. be -EN insertion rule:</td><td>be -EN</td></tr>
<tr><td>by -ING replacement rule:</td><td>-ING</td></tr>
<tr><td>by identical NP deletion rule:</td><td>∅</td></tr>
<tr><td>by flip-flop rule:</td><td>put Past</td><td>be ING</td><td>interview -EN</td></tr>
<tr><td></td><td>put</td><td>being</td><td>interviewed</td></tr>
</table>

4.   They kept on talking.

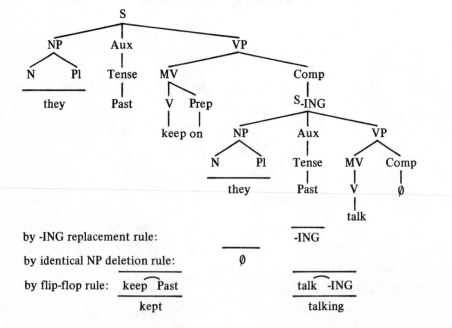

by -ING replacement rule:		-ING
by identical NP deletion rule:	∅	
by flip-flop rule:	keep Past	talk -ING
	kept	talking

5.   I kept them talking about their work.

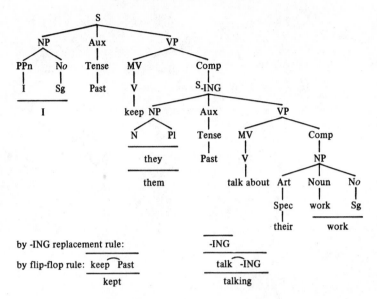

by -ING replacement rule: -ING

by flip-flop rule: keep   Past   talk -ING

                kept   talking

Answers to Exercise 9.3   ADJECTIVE S_{to} COMPLEMENTS

1.   He is sure to be at home now.

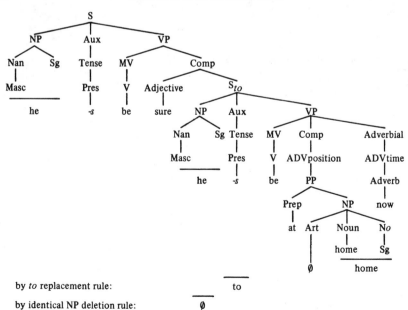

by *to* replacement rule: to

by identical NP deletion rule: Ø

by flip-flop rule: be -s

                  is

2.   Everyone was pleased for them to win.

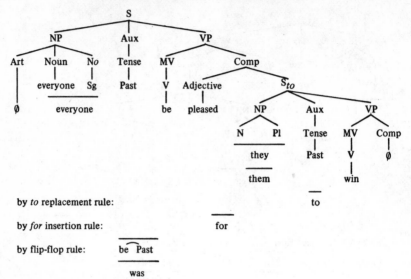

by *to* replacement rule: to

by *for* insertion rule: for

by flip-flop rule: be Past

                              was

3.   Is John ready for us to turn the lights on?

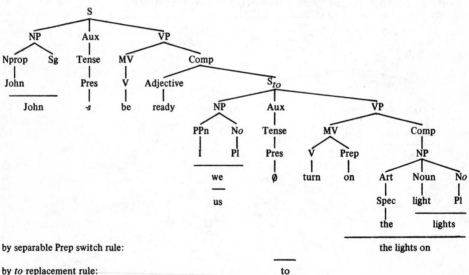

by separable Prep switch rule: the lights on

by *to* replacement rule: to

by *for* insertion rule: for

by *yes-no* question switch rule 1:

by flip-flop rule: -*s* be John

                              be -*s*

                                is

4.   They were proud to be named by the judge.

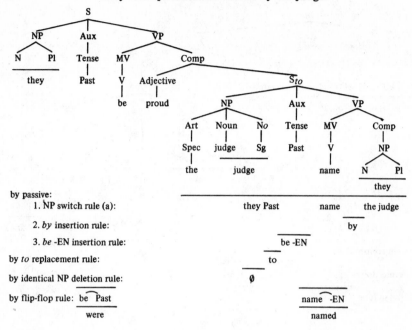

by passive:
    1. NP switch rule (a):   they Past   name   the judge

    2. *by* insertion rule: by

    3. *be* -EN insertion rule: be -EN

by *to* replacement rule: to

by identical NP deletion rule: ∅

by flip-flop rule: be⌢Past   name⌢-EN
           were   named

Answers to Exercise 9.4 S_{to} COMPLEMENTS

1.   John attempted to pin the tail on the donkey.

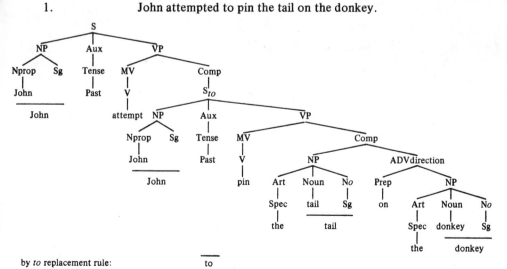

by *to* replacement rule: to

by identical NP deletion rule: ∅

by flip-flop rule: attempt⌢Past
          attempted

2.   Aunt Sally is waiting for you to fix the drinks.

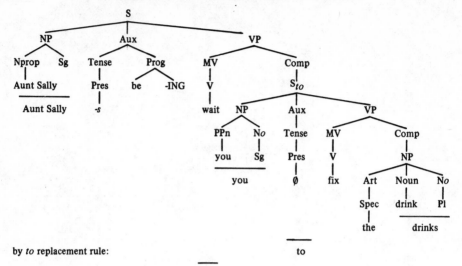

by *to* replacement rule: to

by *for* insertion rule: for

by flip-flop rule: be̲ ͡-s̲   wait ͡-ING

                         is   waiting

3.   We got everybody to sign the petition.

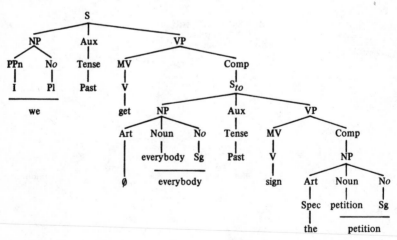

by *to* replacement rule: to

by flip-flop rule: get ͡ Past

                    got

4.   The accident caused us to be late.

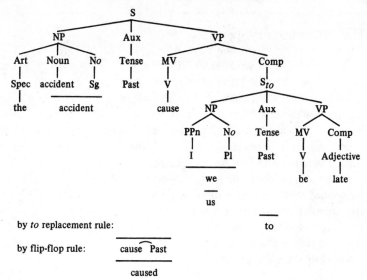

by *to* replacement rule: to

by flip-flop rule: cause Past

                            caused

5.   Uncle Harry arranged for the movers to come today.

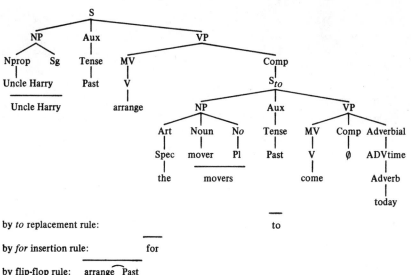

by *to* replacement rule: to

by *for* insertion rule: for

by flip-flop rule: arrange Past

                       arranged

Answers to Exercise 9.5   REVIEW

1. They managed to start the engines. S_{to}
2. I don't mind cleaning up the kitchen. S_{-ING}
3. We told them that it would rain. NP *(that)* S
4. The teacher explained it to the class. NP Prep NP
5. They sent John to his room. NP ADVposition
6. We watched them move the piano. $S_\emptyset$
7. I couldn't imagine Aunt Sally going to jail. S_{-ING}
8. John is eager for us to return. Adjective S_{to}
9. Uncle Harry expected the water to recede. S_{to}
10. It is obvious that she is lying. Adjective *(that)* S
11. We are not able to go. Adjective S_{to}
12. John pleaded for them to reopen the case. S_{to}
13. They discovered the solution to be correct. *it (that)* S
14. It was hoped that he would come. *it (that)* S
15. They let us make the changes. $S_\emptyset$

CHAPTER 10

Noun Modification

OVERVIEW

In a transformational grammar, noun modifiers are derived from underlying full sentences that make an assertion about the noun. For example, the sentence

The *tall young* man *wearing a beret whom you introduced me to* borrowed my car last night.

contains four assertions about *man*:

The *man* is tall.
The *man* is young.
The *man* was wearing a beret.
You introduced me to the *man.*

Noun modification is built into the grammar by a recursive phrase structure rule which permits a noun to be modified by one or more embedded sentences. We can formalize this rule in the following way:

NP $\longrightarrow$ Art $\frown$ Noun $\frown$ No $\frown$ (S)$_1$ $\frown$ (S)$_2$ $\frown$ (S)$_3$ . . . .

The only restraint on the embedded sentences is that they must contain within them the noun being modified (or else the embedded sentences would not be an assertion about the noun).

There are three different types of noun modification, depending on how the embedded sentence comes to the surface. In the first type, adjectival clauses, the noun phrase in the embedded sentence that is identical with the noun being modified in the main sentence is moved to the first position in the embedded sentence by the *identical noun phrase switch rule*. This noun phrase is then either replaced by the appropriate relative pronoun or is deleted. Thus, from the underlying sentence

I met the man (your mother -s know the man)

we can produce either of these surface sentences:

I met the man whom your mother knows.
I met the man your mother knows.

The second type of noun modification produces adjectives, appositives, and prepositional phrases. All of these modifiers come from embedded sentences that have *be* as the main verb. If the embedded sentence contains the main verb *be* followed by an adjective, we can delete everything in the embedded sentence except the adjective. For example, from the underlying sentence

The man *the man is tall* borrowed my car last night.

we can delete the subject noun phrase, tense, and *be* (by what is called the *adjectival clause deletion rule*), producing:

The man *tall* borrowed my car last night.

We now need a second rule (called the *adjective switch rule*) to switch the order of the noun and adjective to produce the proper surface word order for English:

The *tall* man borrowed my car last night.

If the embedded modifying sentence contains the main verb *be* followed by a noun phrase, we can produce an appositive by deleting the subject noun phrase, tense, and *be* through the use of the adjectival clause deletion rule. For example, if we take as an underlying sentence

The man *the man is an old friend of mine* borrowed my car last night.

We can reduce the modifying sentence to an appositive:

The man, *an old friend of mine*, borrowed my car last night.

If the embedded modifying sentence contains the main verb *be* followed by a prepositional phrase, we can produce a grammatical surface sentence by again applying the adjectival clause deletion rule. For example, from the underlying sentence

The man *the man is near the door* borrowed my car last night.

we can derive the sentence

The man *near the door* borrowed my car last night.

The third type of modification is participial phrases. A phrase, as you recall, has one or more of the three elements of the sentence missing. In the case of participial phrases, the subject noun phrase and the tense are deleted from the embedded sentence. The difference between this type and the second type is that the main verb of the embedded sentence does not have to be the verb *be* and the embedded verb comes to the surface with either -ING or -EN attached. The participial phrases that contain the -ING are called present participial phrases, for example,

The children, carrying their toys, came into the room.

The participial phrases that contain the -EN are called past participial phrases, for example,

The children, attracted by the voices, came into the room.

In the present participial phrase, the -ING affix comes from a progressive in the underlying sentence. In the past participial phrase, the -EN comes from the operation of the passive rules. By stretching the adjectival clause deletion rule to apply to *be* used as a helping verb, we can delete the subject noun phrase, tense, and verb *be* from the underlying sentence, leaving just the participial phrases, that is, either -ING or -EN plus the verb phrase.

Under certain conditions, both present and past participial phrases may be moved to a position in front of the noun phrases they modify. For example, the two sample sentences given above can be changed to

Carrying their toys, the children came into the room.
Attracted by the voices, the children came into the room.

If the participial phrase consists of only the main verb (with the -ING or -EN attached), we treat the participial phrase as though it were an adjective and move it to a position in front of the noun. Thus, for example, the modifier *reassuring* in the noun phrase *a reassuring statement* comes from an embedded sentence containing reassure as a main verb preceded by a progressive: *a statement is reassuring*.

The chapter closes with a brief discussion of *restrictive* and *nonrestrictive* modifiers. A restrictive modifier is one that, together with the noun it modifies, makes up a new semantic unit different in kind from the noun by itself. A nonrestrictive modifier is one that can be deleted from the sentence without radically changing the meaning of the whole sentence. A good example of a restrictive modifier is found in the adage

People *who live in glass houses* shouldn't throw stones.

If we were to take out the modifying clause, we would have a very different sentence:

People shouldn't throw stones.

Appositives are usually nonrestrictive modifiers. For example, the appositive in the following sentence could be deleted without changing the basic sentence:

Mr. Mann, *my English teacher*, took a trip to Venice.

NOUN MODIFICATION

In the chapter on the noun phrase, the NP was seen to consist of three obligatory elements: Art Noun No. This is correct as far as it goes, but we now need to account for the expansion of the noun phrase through the process of modification. The basic idea of the transformational approach to noun modification is that all true modifiers make an assertion about the noun that they modify, and that this assertion can be expressed as a complete underlying sentence. For example, the italicized adjective in the sentence

A *slender* boy stuck his head into the back room.

asserts that *the boy was slender*.
Similarly, the modifying adverb of place in the sentence

The picture *next to the window* needs to be straightened.

asserts that *the picture is next to the window*.
With adjectival participial phrases, the nature of the underlying assertion is easily seen; for example, in the sentence

The tree, *being quite weather-beaten*, was uprooted.

it is clear that the phrase is understood as asserting that *the tree was quite weather-beaten*.
Finally, when an adjectival clause is used, the assertion appears on the surface of the sentence; for example,

The girl *whom you met last night* is a friend of my sister's.

We know that the *whom* could refer only to *the girl*. Thus the underlying assertion is *you met the girl last night*.
There is no upper limit on the number of times that a noun can be modified; for example, the sentence

The *tall young* man *wearing a beret whom you introduced me to* borrowed my car last night.

contains four underlying assertions about *the man*:

The man is tall.
The man is young.
The man wore a beret.
You introduced me to the man.

The one restriction on the underlying assertion is that it must contain the noun being modified (or else it would not be an assertion about that noun). Modification is usually optional; that is, a sentence will not normally be ungrammatical solely because of the presence or absence of a modifier. We may incorporate all the above discussion into our rule for the development of the noun phrase by deriving the modifiers from an indefinite number of optional sentences. The new rule for the development of noun phrases would then look like this:

$$NP \longrightarrow Art \frown Noun \frown No \frown (S)_1, \frown (S)_2, \frown (S)_3 \ldots$$

The embedded sentence can come to the surface in any of three different ways: (1) as an adjectival clause; (2) as an adjective, appositive, or prepositional phrase; or (3) as an adjectival participial phrase. In adjectival clauses all of the elements of the embedded sentence can come to the surface. In adjectives, appositives, and prepositional phrases, the only element from the embedded sentence that comes to the surface is the complement. In participial phrases, the verb from the embedded sentence comes to the surface with either -ING or -EN attached.

ADJECTIVAL CLAUSES

Here are sentences containing adjectival clauses. The clauses are in italics:

I met the man *who knows your mother.*
I met the man *whom your mother knows.*
I saw the trees *which you told me about.*
I saw the tree *that you told me about.*
We visited the island *where they grow pepper.*
I remember the night *when you pushed me into the pool.*

Our assumption is that all modifiers come from an embedded sentence that contains within it an assertion about the noun being modified. Here are the same sentences with the embedded sentence in parentheses:

I met the man (the man Pres know your mother).
I met the man (your mother Pres know the man).
I saw the trees (you Past tell me about the trees).

I saw the tree (you Past tell me about the tree).
We visited the island (they ∅ grow pepper on the island).
I remember the night (you Past push me into the pool the night).

There are two basic changes necessary to convert the underlying embedded sentence into an adjectival clause: (1) the noun in the embedded sentence that is identical with the noun being modified in the main sentence is moved to the first position in the embedded sentence, that is, next to the noun phrase being modified; and (2) the identical noun phrase in the embedded sentence is replaced by the appropriate relative pronoun (*who/whom, which/that, where, when . . .*).

We will call the rule that moves the identical noun phrase to the first position in the embedded sentence the identical noun phrase switch rule and formalize it this way: Q Word p. 17

$$X_1 \ X_2 \ldots NP \ldots X_n \Longrightarrow NP \ X_1 \ X_2 \ldots X_n$$

(Question: this rule is virtually identical with a rule we had earlier. Do you recall what this rule was?)

The rule that replaces the noun phrase with the appropriate relative pronoun we will call the *relative pronoun replacement rule*. Note that the distinction between *who* and *whom* is based on the position of the noun phrase being replaced—*who* for the subject noun phrase, and *whom* for noun phrases after the verb (except *be*). *Which* and *that* are used for most nonhuman animate and all inanimate nouns, *who* and *whom* for human and some nonhuman animate nouns. *Where* is used for noun phrases that indicate place. *When* is used for noun phrases that indicate time.

Here are some sample derivations:

I met the man who knows your mother.

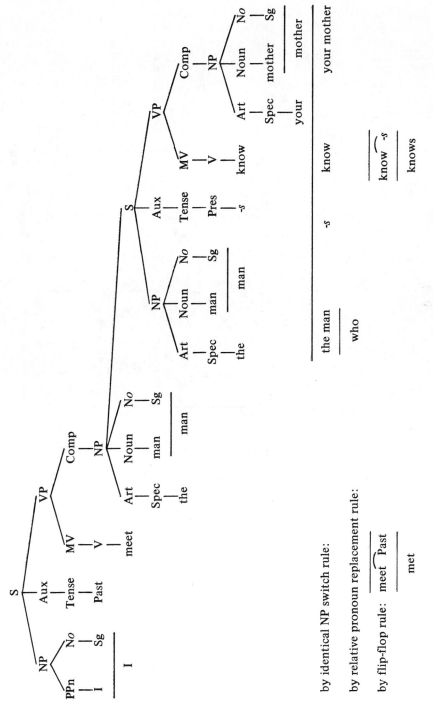

by identical NP switch rule:

the man   -s   know   your mother

by relative pronoun replacement rule:

who

by flip-flop rule: know -s
                       ———————
                       knows

(Notice that the identical NP switch rule has been applied even though the identical NP is already in the first position. Why is it simpler to do it this way?)

I met the man whom your mother knows.

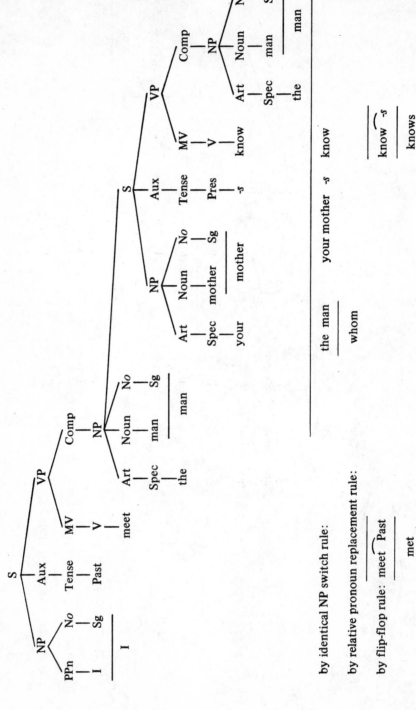

by identical NP switch rule:

$$\frac{\text{the man}}{\text{whom}}$$

by relative pronoun replacement rule:

by flip-flop rule: $\dfrac{\text{meet} \frown \text{Past}}{\text{met}}$

$$\frac{\text{your mother} \frown \text{know}}{\text{know} \frown \text{-s}}$$
$$\frac{}{\text{knows}}$$

268

I saw the trees that you told me about.

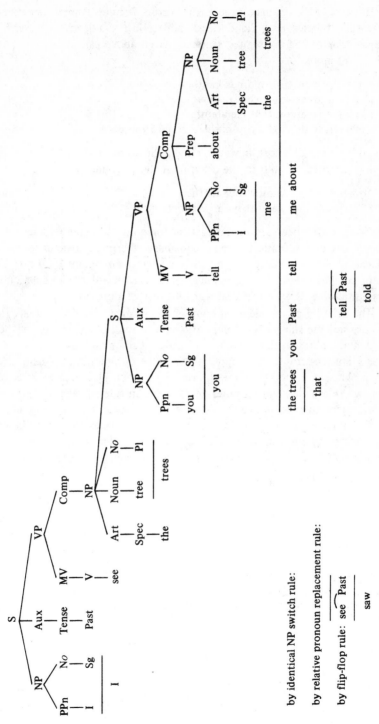

by identical NP switch rule:

by relative pronoun replacement rule:

by flip-flop rule: see ⌒ Past
                     ――――――
                       saw

269

However, as you might expect, the picture is more complicated than this. Often the relative pronoun does not appear in the adjectival clause. For example, four of the six sample sentences given above can be used without the relative pronoun:

> I met the man your mother knows.
> I saw the trees you told me about.
> I saw the tree you told me about.
> I remember the night you pushed me into the pool.

The other two sentences, however, require the presence of the relative pronoun. If they are used without it, the resulting sentence is ungrammatical:

> *I met the man knows your mother.
> *We visited the island they grow pepper.

These two sentences are ungrammatical for quite different reasons. The first sentence is ungrammatical because apparently there is a general restriction in adjectival clauses against deleting the subject noun phrase of the embedded sentence. The second sentence is ungrammatical because of the deletion of the preposition *on*—but we will deal with this matter a bit later.

The deletion of the identical noun phrase in the embedded sentence (as long as it is not the subject noun phrase) is simply another application of the identical noun phrase deletion rule we encountered in the last chapter. Since it seems unnecessary first to apply the relative pronoun replacement rule to a noun phrase and then to delete the very same noun phrase, let us agree to treat the two rules (the identical noun phrase deletion rule and the relative pronoun replacement rule) as mutually exclusive rules; that is, we can apply either one or the other, but not both. In technical terms the rules are said to be disjunctive (remember the similar discussion about the *yes-no* question switch rule?).

The only problem remaining is about the preposition. The sentence

> *We visited the island they grow pepper.

can be made grammatical (after a fashion) by restoring the preposition *on* that was in the original embedded sentence:

> We visited the island they grow pepper on.

If we retain the identical noun phrase from the embedded sentence and use *which* or *that* instead of *where* as the relative pronoun, we have two possible versions derived from the same underlying sentence:

> We visited the island on which they grow pepper.
> We visited the island which they grow pepper on.

Many people would prefer the first version over the second (especially in formal, written English) because it is considered (by some) to be bad form to end a sentence with a preposition (or as is sometimes said, it is bad grammar to use a preposition to end a sentence with). The avoidance of prepositions at the end of sentences is a matter of personal preference of style. It is easy to show that the restriction is a matter of style and not grammaticality since so many of the most careful writers use prepositions at the ends of sentences. Churchill, for example, is quoted as correcting an overeager editor who objected to Churchill's using a preposition at the end of a sentence by saying, "This is the kind of errant pedantry up with which I will not put."

Actually, the preposition is left at the end of the sentence because the identical noun phrase switch rule has moved the noun phrase that originally followed the preposition to the first position in the embedded sentence. In other words, in the deep structure, it is quite true that prepositions do not end sentences (except when the preposition is part of a two-word verb followed by a $\emptyset$ complement, as in the sentence *We finally gave in*). However, in the surface structure, it is possible for prepositions to be left stranded at the ends of sentences as a rather accidental outcome of a transformation applied to the noun phrase that originally followed the preposition.

In order to account for a sentence like

We visited the island on which they grow pepper.

in which the *on* has moved forward to the first position with the identical noun phrase, we would have to make a special version of the identical noun phrase switch rule that would permit the preposition in prepositional phrases to be carried along with the identical noun phrase.

EXERCISE 10.1 **Adjectival Clauses**

Draw phrase structure trees and apply the necessary transformational rules to produce the following sentences:
1. I broke the watch that you gave me.
2. The children who live upstairs are watching television.
3. The children we invited over are watching television.
4. The tree you pruned will live.
5. I know a place where you can get tortillas.

ADJECTIVES, APPOSITIVES, AND PREPOSITIONAL PHRASES

Modifying sentences that contain *be* as the main verb have a special status in the grammar. They undergo a transformational rule that deletes the subject noun phrase, the tense, and the *be*. For example, the underlying sentences

A man *the man was tall* saw our distress signal.
A man *the man was a lifeguard* saw our distress signal.
A man *the man was on the shore* saw our distress signal.

are converted into

*A man *tall* saw our distress signal.

A man, *a lifeguard*, saw our distress signal.

A man *on the shore* saw our distress signal.

The second and third sentences are grammatical as they stand. The modifying noun phrase *a lifeguard* in the second sentence is called an appositive.

The first sentence would be grammatical too if we were talking about French. In French, as you may know, most modifying adjectives occur after the noun they modify. A few survivals of the French order have continued into Modern English from the period after the Norman Conquest when French speakers ruled England. The clearest example is with pairs of adjectives. We can say

A girl, pretty and young, answered our knock.

as well as the more common

A pretty, young girl answered our knock.

For English, we ordinarily need to reverse the order of the adjective and noun.

Let us call the rule that deletes the subject noun phrase, the tense, and the main verb *be* the *adjectival clause deletion rule*. We may formalize the rule this way:

$$\text{Noun Phrase } \overbrace{\text{Tense}} \ be \Longrightarrow \emptyset$$

We will call the rule that moves the modifying adjectives from a position following the noun to a position preceding it the *adjective switch rule*. We may write the rule this way:

$$\overbrace{\text{Art } \text{Noun}} \ \overbrace{\text{N}o} \ \overbrace{\text{Adj}} \Longrightarrow \text{Art } \text{Adj } \overbrace{\text{Noun } \text{N}o}$$

Here are some sample derivations:

We fixed the crack in the chimney.

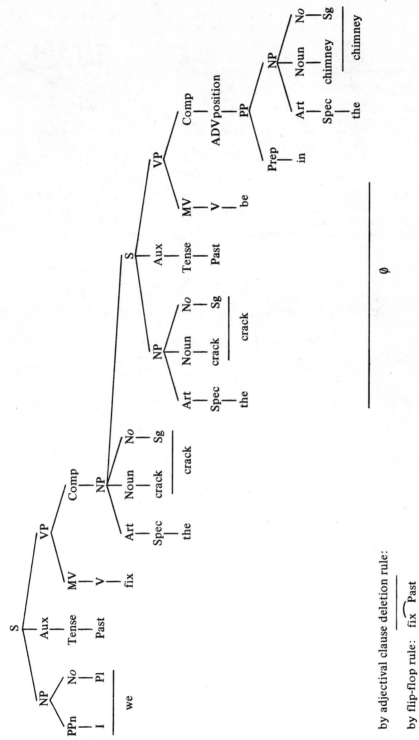

by adjectival clause deletion rule:

$$\frac{}{\text{fix} \frown \text{Past}}$$

by flip-flop rule:

$$\frac{\text{fix} \frown \text{Past}}{\text{fixed}}$$

A yellow owl stared at us.

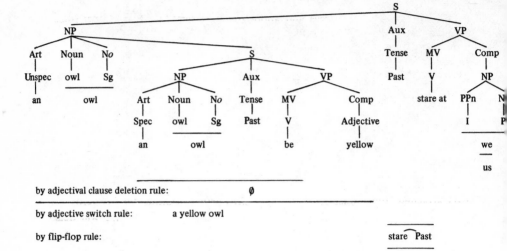

by adjectival clause deletion rule: ∅

by adjective switch rule: a yellow owl

by flip-flop rule: stare⌢Past

                                                         stared

Mr. Brown, my teacher, reported the accident.

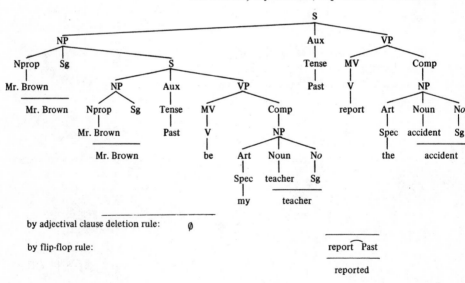

by adjectival clause deletion rule: ∅

by flip-flop rule: report⌢Past

                                                     reported

EXERCISE 10.2 Adjectives, Appositives, and Prepositional Phrases

Draw phrase structure trees and apply the necessary transformational rules to produce the following sentences:
1. The mailman delivered a brown envelope.
2. The train pulled onto a siding near the depot.
3. The tree, a huge oak, was uprooted by the storm.
4. The old house on the hill burned down.
5. You can't teach an old dog new tricks.

PARTICIPIAL PHRASES

A participial phrase is one in which the verb in the embedded sentence comes to the surface with either -ING or -EN attached. If the verb has the -ING attached, the phrase is called a *present participial phrase*; if the verb has the -EN attached, the phrase is called a *past participial phrase*. We will deal with present participial phrases first.

Present Participial Phrases

Here are some sample sentences containing present participial phrases (in italics):

The man, *having drunk far too much*, labored up the stairs.
The man, *swearing at each step*, labored up the stairs.
The man, *looking very red in the face*, labored up the stairs.

As you can see, the underlying embedded sentence has been changed in two ways: (1) the subject noun phrase (which must be identical with the noun being modified) has been deleted, and (2) the tense has been replaced by -ING.

EXERCISE 10.3 Rules for Present Participial Phrases

We have already seen rules that will make the two changes described above. What are they?   identical NP deletion 242

The Participial Switch Rule   ING replacement 243

One of the pecularities of the present participial phrase is that it can be moved in front of the noun phrase it modifies (however, only if the noun phrase it modifies is the subject noun phrase of the main sentence). For example, the three sample sentences above can all be transformed into the following versions:

Having drunk far too much, the man labored up the stairs.
Swearing at each step, the man labored up the stairs.
Looking very red in the face, the man labored up the stairs.

This rule, which we will call the participial switch rule, can be formalized this way:

$$\overparen{NP} \ \overparen{PresPart} \ \overparen{Aux} \ \overparen{VP} \Longrightarrow \overparen{PresPart} \ \overparen{NP} \ \overparen{Aux} \ \overparen{VP}$$
(where PresPart = a present participial phrase)

EXERCISE 10.4 **Present Participial Phrases**

Draw phrase structure trees and apply the necessary transformational rules to produce the following sentences:
1. The children, carrying their toys, rushed into the room.
2. Aunt Sally, having forgotten her glasses, asked me to read the menu to her.
3. Becoming angry at the situation, General Bluster called Headquarters.
4. Being ignored by the candidate, the reporters went to the bar.

Past Participial Phrases

The past participial phrase comes from an embedded sentence that has been made passive. Here are some examples with the past participial phrase in italics:

The police, *alerted by a passer-by*, caught them in the act.
The children, *attracted by the voices*, came into the room.
The class, *bored by the long lecture on participials*, lost their interest in the subject.
The cats, *startled by the sudden noise*, ran under the house.

Past participial phrases are often used with the agent deleted:

A mastodon skull, *discovered in Africa*, has attracted great attention.
A robbery *committed in New Jersey* has received nationwide publicity.

The underlying embedded sentence has had the subject noun phrase (the noun phrase that was the object before the NP switch rule was applied) deleted, along with the tense and the verb *be* that was introduced by the *be* -EN insertion rule. You recall that the *adjectival clause deletion rule* deleted the subject noun phrase, the tense, and the verb *be* from the embedded sentence—although *be* was the main verb, not a helping verb. Let us agree to extend the scope of the adjectival clause deletion rule to apply to *be* when *be* is produced by the *be* -EN insertion rule.

Notice that the past participial phrases in the sample sentences above can be moved in front of the noun phrase they modify:

Alerted by a passer-by, the police caught them in the act.
Attracted by the voices, the children came into the room.
Bored by the long lecture on participials, the class lost their interest in the subject.
Startled by the sudden noise, the cats ran under the house.

The first sentence with the agent deleted also permits the past participial phrase to be moved to the first position, although it sounds a bit odd:

Discovered in Africa, a mastodon skull has attracted great attention.

The other sentence with the agent deleted, however, is ungrammatical if the past participial phrase is moved to the first position, probably because the phrase is a restrictive modifier (see below):

*Committed in New Jersey, a robbery has received nationwide publicity.

(Question: what minor change do we have to make in the formalization of the participial switch rule to accommodate past participial phrases?)

use Past Part

EXERCISE 10.5 Past Participial Phrases

Draw phrase structure trees and apply the necessary transformational rules to produce the following sentences:
1. The customer, outraged by the bill, attacked the waiter.
2. Confused by the message, General Bluster returned to the base.
3. A story written by Aunt Sally was snapped up by *Playboy*.

Adjectives Derived from Participial Phrases

The adjectival clause deletion and adjective switch rules also can be used in deriving adjectives from verbs. Both the present and past participial forms of verbs can be turned into modifying adjectives, for example:

PRESENT PARTICIPIALS:

a *reassuring* statement
a *piercing* cry
a *weeping* girl
the *fleeing* outlaws
these *changing* times
a *sweeping* gesture

PAST PARTICIPIALS:

satisfied customers
a *broken* toy
an *unopened* letter
a *canceled* check
a *hidden* treasure
an *outraged* parent

The participial phrases above function as adjectives. However, many of them do not have the formal properties of adjectives; that is, they cannot be preceded by *very* or be used in a comparative statement, for example:

*A very weeping girl.	*The girl was more weeping than ever.
*The very fleeing outlaws.	*The outlaws were more fleeting than ever.
*A very canceled check.	*The check was more canceled than ever.
*A very hidden treasure.	*The treasure was more hidden than ever.

On the other hand, many of the participial phrases seem to have become full adjectives:

A very reassuring statement.	The statement was more reassuring than ever.
Very satisfied customers.	The customers were more satisfied than ever.

It seems natural to assume that these derived adjectives come from modifying embedded sentences in much the same way as other adjectives do. That is, the noun being modified must appear as the subject of an underlying sentence and the participial must occupy the position of a predicate adjective. Accordingly, we would derive the present participial adjectives from underlying sentences containing an intransitive verb in the progressive, for example:

EMBEDDED SENTENCE	BY ADJECTIVAL CLAUSE DELETION RULE:	BY ADJECTIVE SWITCH RULE:
a statement *the statement was reassuring* $\implies$	a statement *reassuring* $\implies$	a *reassuring* statement
a cry *the cry was piercing* $\implies$	a cry *piercing* $\implies$	a *piercing* cry
a girl *the girl was weeping* $\implies$	a girl *weeping* $\implies$	a *weeping* girl
The outlaws *the outlaws were fleeing* $\implies$	the outlaws *fleeing* $\implies$	the *fleeing* outlaws
these times *these times are changing* $\implies$	these times *changing* $\implies$	these *changing* times
a gesture *the gesture was sweeping* $\implies$	a gesture *sweeping* $\implies$	a *sweeping* gesture

The past participial adjectives are derived from passive sentences with the agent deleted. For example, *a broken toy* would be derived from

A toy *someone broke the toy*.

By the passive and agent deletion this would become

A toy *the toy was broken*.

The main verb of the embedded sentence now occupies the position of a predicate adjective, and the adjectival clause deletion and adjective switch rules may be applied. For example:

EMBEDDED SENTENCE (AFTER PASSIVE AND AGENT DELETION)	BY ADJECTIVAL CLAUSE DELETION RULE:	BY ADJECTIVE SWITCH RULE:
customers *customers were satisfied* $\implies$	customers *satisfied* $\implies$	*satisfied* customers
a toy *the toy was broken* $\implies$	the toy *broken* $\implies$	the *broken* toy
a letter *the letter was unopened* $\implies$	a letter *unopened* $\implies$	an *unopened* letter

a check *the check was* $\Longrightarrow$ a check *canceled* $\Longrightarrow$ a *canceled* check
canceled

a parent *the parent was* $\Longrightarrow$ a parent *outraged* $\Longrightarrow$ an *outraged* parent
outraged

The internal structures of present and past participial phrases are quite different. Despite their differences, however, the process by which the two different kinds of participial phrases are turned into derived adjectives is essentially identical. In both cases the main verb in the embedded sentence is preceded by the helping verb *be*. In the present participial phrase, the *be* comes from the progressive. In the past participial phrase, the *be* comes from the passive. In both cases the verb phrase consists of only a single overt element—the main verb. In the present participial phrase this is so because only intransitive verbs, that is, verbs with a $\emptyset$ complement, can be transformed into derived adjectives. In the past participial phrase this is because the agent deletion rule must be applied.

The adjectival clause deletion rule that deletes the subject noun phrase, the tense, and the verb *be* from the underlying embedded sentence applies to both types of embedded sentences: the ones containing a progressive and a $\emptyset$ complement (the source of present participial phrases) and the ones that have been made passive (the source of past participial phrases). Actually, this will require some further adjustment of the adjectival clause deletion rule. We have already broadened the rule to apply to *be* as a helping verb when the *be* comes from the operation of the *be* -EN insertion rule. Now we need to extend the rule to cover *be* when it comes from the progressive node in the auxiliary.

Moreover, we need to extend the adjective switch rule to apply to verb plus -ING (present participials) and verb plus -EN (past participials) elements. This, in turn requires that we apply the flip-flop rule to the sequences of -ING plus verb and -EN plus verb *before* we can apply the adjective switch rule. Can you rewrite the adjective switch rule to apply to present and past participles?

replace Adj (272) with -ING and -EN

EXERCISE 10.6 Adjectives Derived from Participial Phrases

Now that all this is perfectly clear, try your hand at drawing phrase structure trees and applying the necessary transformational rules to produce the following phrases:
1. A leaking shower.
2. An amused audience.
3. A sniveling urchin.
4. Modified nouns.

Restrictive and Nonrestrictive Modifiers

A final point about modification that needs mentioning is the difference between restrictive and nonrestrictive modifiers. Dorothy Parker's famous couplet is a clear illustration of a restrictive modifier:

Boys seldom make passes
At girls who wear glasses.

Who do boys seldom make passes at? *Girls* or *girls who wear glasses*? Obviously, the second interpretation is the one intended. As its name suggests, a restrictive modifier restricts or limits the meaning of the noun in such a way that the noun plus the modifier means something quite different than the noun without the modifier. Here is an example of a nonrestrictive modifier:

Mr. Mann, my English teacher, took a trip to Venice.

The appositive *my English teacher* helps identify who Mr. Mann is. It is a useful piece of information, but it does not really alter the meaning of the sentence in any basic way.

Sometimes, a modifier can be either restrictive or nonrestrictive, according to the way we choose to interpret the sentence. For example:

The policeman *the policeman knew the area best* led the search.

How many policemen were there? If we interpret the modifying sentence as being restrictive, there were several policemen, and the one policeman who knew the area better than the other policemen led the search. If the modifying sentence is interpreted as nonrestrictive, there was only one policeman, and the modifying sentence is just giving some additional useful information about why the policeman led the search.

Not only does it make a difference in meaning, but the choice between making the underlying sentence restrictive or nonrestrictive also governs the pronunciation of the sentence. If the modifying sentence is restrictive, the whole sentence is pronounced like this:

The policeman who knew the area best led the search.

If the modifying sentence is nonrestrictive, the whole sentence is pronounced like this:

The policeman _____ led the search.
　　　　　　who knew the area best

In the written sentence the nonrestrictive clause is set off by a pair of commas:

The policeman, who knew the area best, led the search.

EXERCISE 10.7 **Review**

Draw phrase structure trees and apply the necessary transformational rules to produce the following sentences:
1. The wreck, an overturned truck, blocked the intersection.
2. Alarmed by the recent events, General Bluster sent for a chaplain.
3. Aunt Sally, who dislikes miniskirts, looked at Miss Jones with obvious disapproval.
4. The campers, soaked by the heavy rain, built a roaring fire.
5. Bored by the long lecture about participials, the class was grateful for the interruption.

Answers to Exercise 10.1 ADJECTIVAL CLAUSES

1. I broke the watch that you gave me.

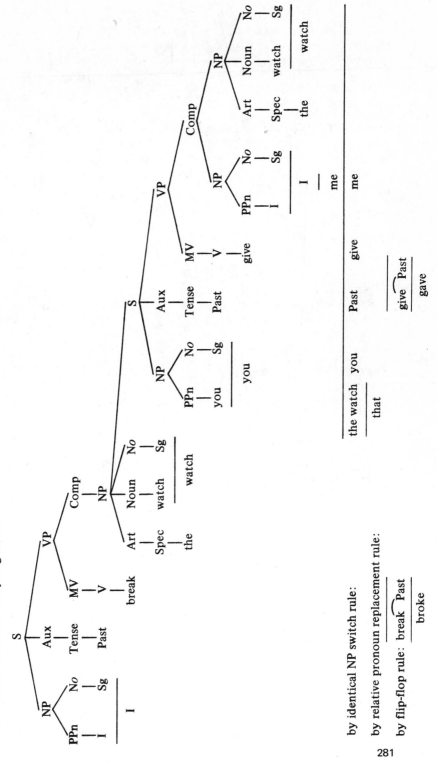

by identical NP switch rule:

the watch   you   Past   give

       that

by relative pronoun replacement rule:

I ——— me

   me

by flip-flop rule: break ⌢ Past

  broke

give ⌢ Past

  gave

2.

The children who live upstairs are watching television.

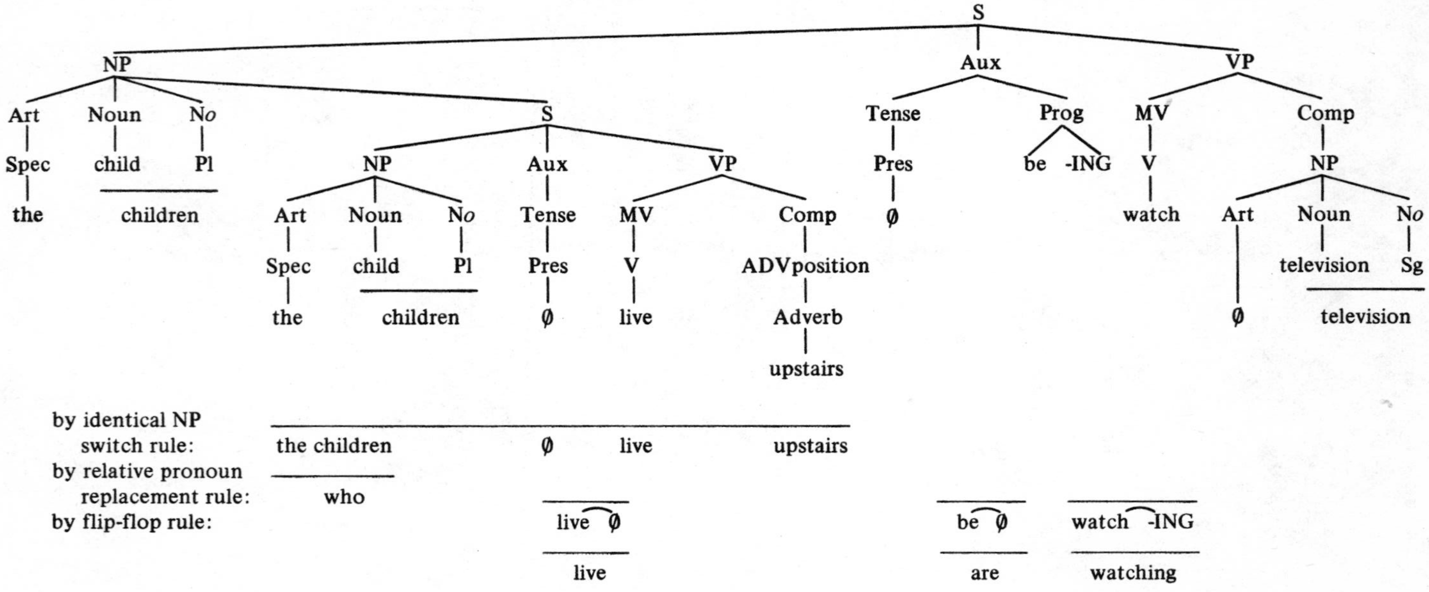

S

NP — Spec — Art — the
NP — Noun — child
NP — No — Pl — children

S
NP — Spec — Art — the
NP — Noun — child
NP — No — Pl — children
Aux — Tense — Pres — ∅
VP — MV — V — live
VP — Comp — ADVposition — Adverb — upstairs

Aux — Tense — Pres — ∅
Aux — Prog — be — -ING
VP — MV — V — watch
VP — Comp — NP — Art — ∅
VP — Comp — NP — Noun — television
VP — Comp — NP — No — Sg — television

by identical NP
switch rule: the children   ∅ live   upstairs
by relative pronoun
replacement rule: who

by flip-flop rule: live ∅ ⁀
live

be ∅ ⁀   watch⁀ -ING
are   watching

3.

The children we invited over are watching television.

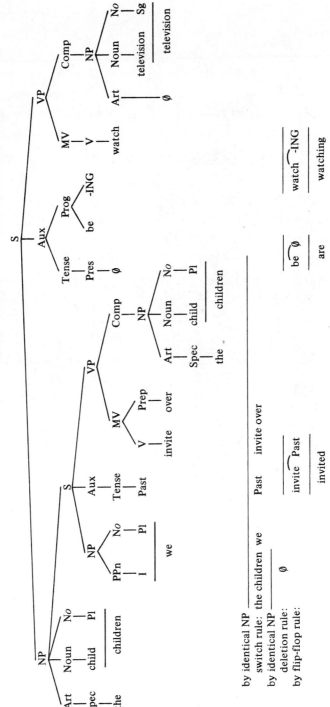

by identical NP
switch rule: the children we _____ Past _____ invite over

by identical NP
deletion rule: ∅

invite ⌢ Past
_____
invited

be ⌢ ∅
_____
are

watch ⌢ -ING
_____
watching

by flip-flop rule:

283

4.

The tree you pruned will live.

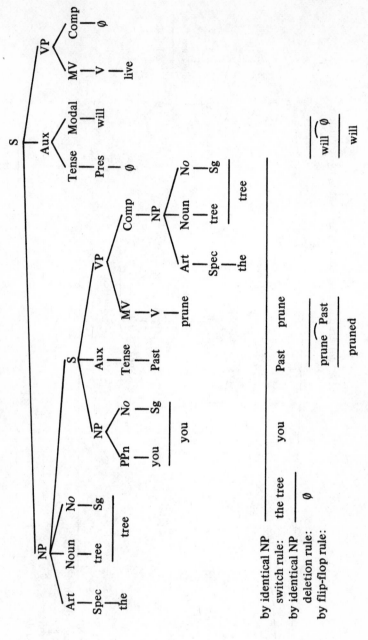

by identical NP switch rule: $\dfrac{\text{the tree} \quad \text{you} \quad \text{Past} \quad \text{prune}}{}$

by identical NP deletion rule: $\dfrac{\emptyset}{}$

by flip-flop rule: $\dfrac{\text{prune} \frown \text{Past}}{\text{pruned}}$ $\dfrac{\text{will} \frown \emptyset}{\text{will}}$

5.

I know a place where you can get tortillas.

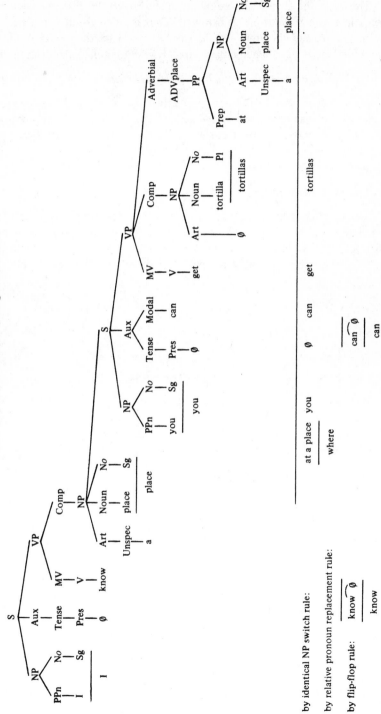

by identical NP switch rule:

by relative pronoun replacement rule:

by flip-flop rule:

285

The *at* in the deep structure of the analysis given here for sentence 5 raises some interesting questions. It can well be argued that the *at* is not part of the noun phrase, and therefore should not be moved by the identical NP switch rule. If we accept this argument, we are left with the following surface sentence:

(?)*I know a place where you can get tortillas at.

Even though this sentence is perfectly clear, it would be considered substandard by many because of the general stigma about using prepositions at the ends of sentences. We could easily deal with this state of affairs by creating a transformational rule that deletes final prepositions, thus producing the more standard

I know a place where you can get tortillas.

The counterargument is that *where* is not a replacement just for the noun phrase *a place* but for the whole adverbial of place. To properly formalize the identical NP switch rule so that it applies in this situation, we would have to broaden the rule to permit it to apply to prepositional phrases of place.

Answers to Exercise 10.2 ADJECTIVES, APPOSITIVES, AND PREPOSITIONAL PHRASES

1.   The mailman delivered a brown envelope.

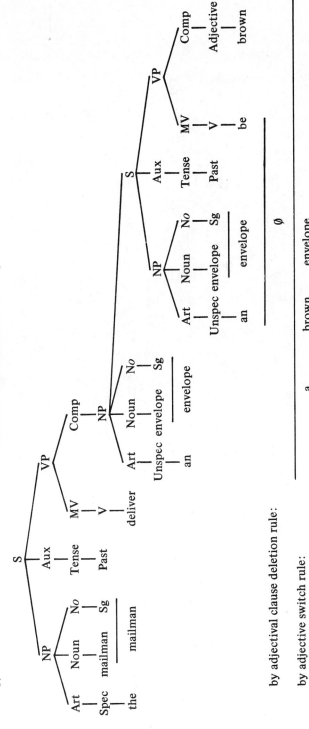

by adjectival clause deletion rule:

by adjective switch rule:

by flip-flop rule: $\overline{\text{deliver} \frown \text{Past}}$
          delivered

2.

The train pulled onto a siding near the depot.

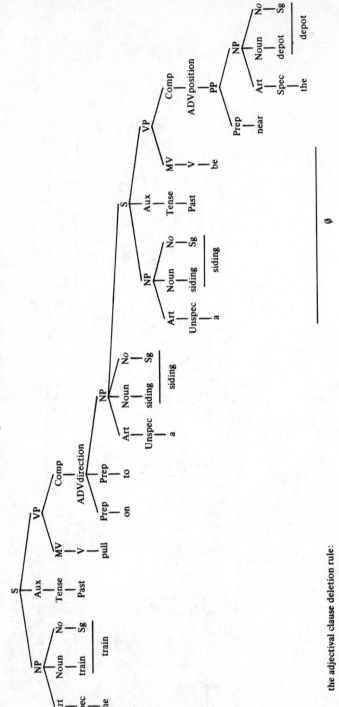

the adjectival clause deletion rule:

$$\frac{pull \frown Past}{pulled}$$

by flip-flop rule:

The tree, a huge oak, was uprooted by the storm.

3.

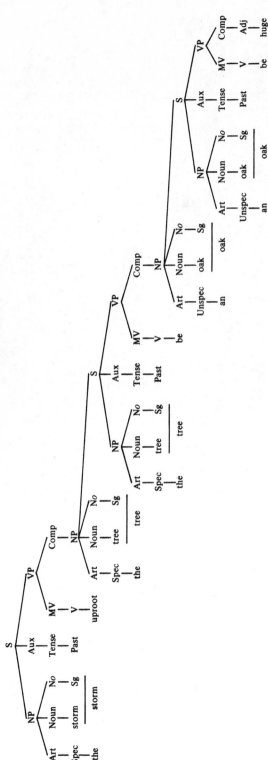

by adjectival clause deletion rule:

by adjective switch rule:

by adjectival clause deletion rule:

| | a | huge | oak | | |

by passive:
   1. NP switch rule (a): the tree a huge oak   Past uproot   the storm

   2. *by* insertion rule: by

   3. *be* -EN insertion rule: be -EN uproot -EN

by flip-flop rule: be Past uprooted

                                         was   uprooted

4.

The old house on the hill burned down.

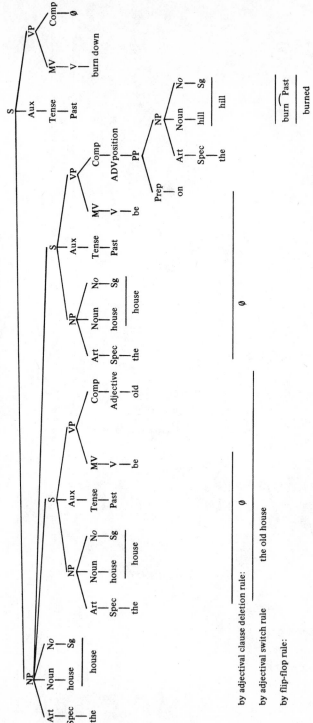

by adjectival clause deletion rule: ∅

by adjectival switch rule the old house

by flip-flop rule:

5.

You can't teach an old dog new tricks.

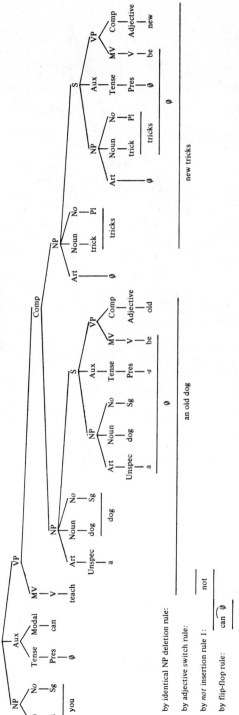

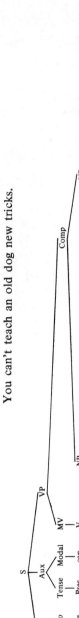

by identical NP deletion rule:

by adjective switch rule:

by *not* insertion rule 1 :   not

by flip-flop rule: can $\widehat{}$ ∅

                            can

Answers to Exercise 10.3 RULES FOR PRESENT PARTICIPIAL PHRASES

Identical noun phrase deletion rule and -ING replacement rule.

Answers to Exercise 10.4 PRESENT PARTICIPIAL PHRASES

1.   The children, carrying their toys, rushed into the room.

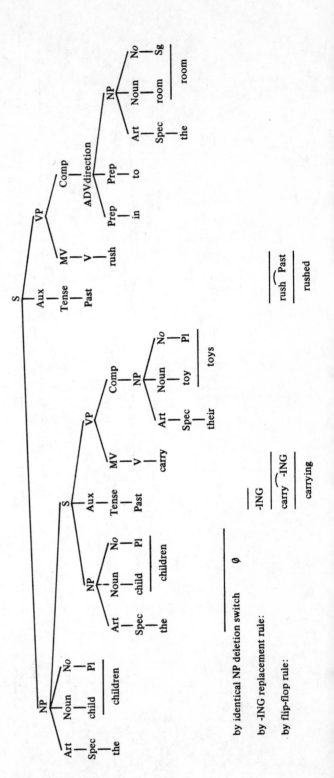

by identical NP deletion switch   ∅

by -ING replacement rule:

$$\frac{\text{-ING}}{\frac{\text{carry} \frown \text{-ING}}{\text{carrying}}}$$

by flip-flop rule:

$$\frac{\text{rush} \frown \text{Past}}{\text{rushed}}$$

2.

Aunt Sally, having forgotten her glasses, asked me to read the menu to her.

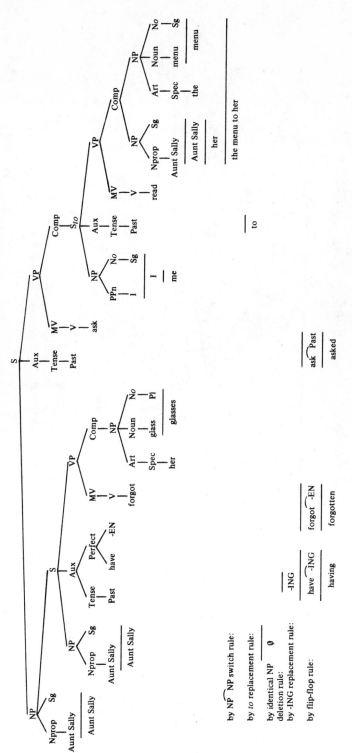

by NP⌢NP switch rule:

by *to* replacement rule:

by identical NP
deletion rule:

by -ING replacement rule:

by flip-flop rule:

3.

Becoming angry at the situation, General Bluster called Headquarters.

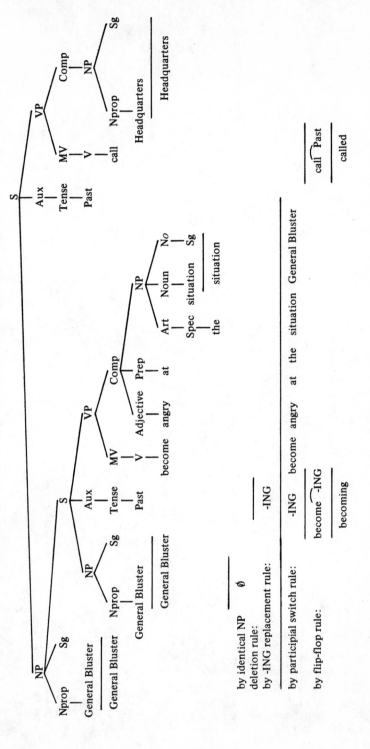

by identical NP deletion rule: ___ ∅

by -ING replacement rule: ___ -ING

by participial switch rule: -ING become angry at the situation General Bluster

by flip-flop rule: become ⌒ -ING

becoming

4.

Being ignored by the candidate, the reporters went to the bar.

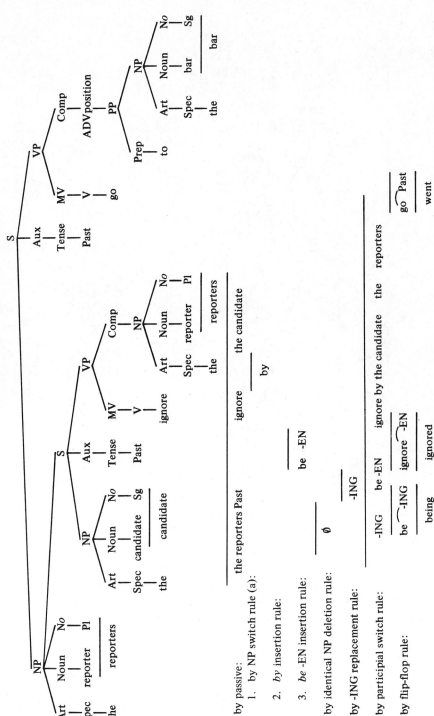

by passive: the reporters Past   ignore   the candidate
1. by NP switch rule (a):   by
2. *by* insertion rule:
3. *be* -EN insertion rule: be -EN
by identical NP deletion rule: Ø
by -ING replacement rule: -ING
by participial switch rule: -ING   be-EN   ignore by the candidate   the   reporters
by flip-flop rule: be⌒-ING ignore⌒-EN   go⌒Past
                                       being   ignored   went

295

Answers to Exercise 10.5 PAST PARTICIPIAL PHRASES

1.

The customer, outraged by the bill, attacked the waiter.

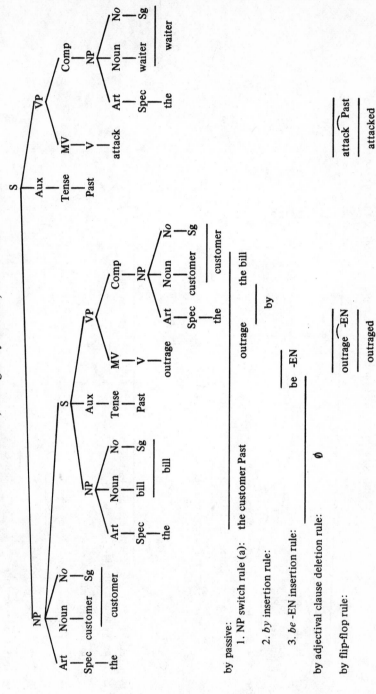

by passive:
  1. NP switch rule (a):   the customer Past
  2. *by* insertion rule:
  3. *be* -EN insertion rule: *be* -EN
by adjectival clause deletion rule: ∅
by flip-flop rule:

2.

Confused by the message, General Bluster returned to the base.

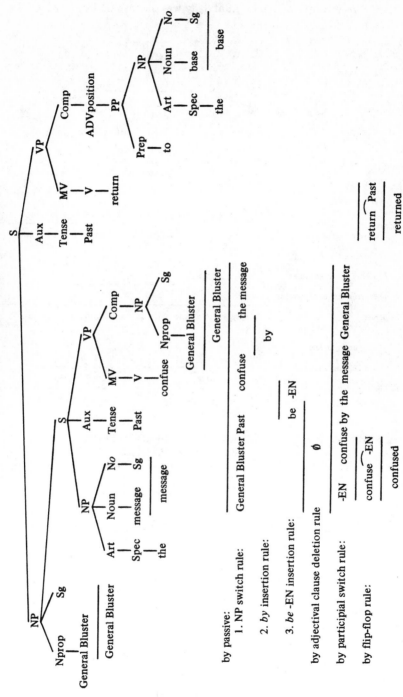

by passive:
  1. NP switch rule:
  2. *by* insertion rule:
  3. *be* -EN insertion rule:
by adjectival clause deletion rule
by participial switch rule:
by flip-flop rule:

3.   A story written by Aunt Sally was snapped up by *Playboy*.

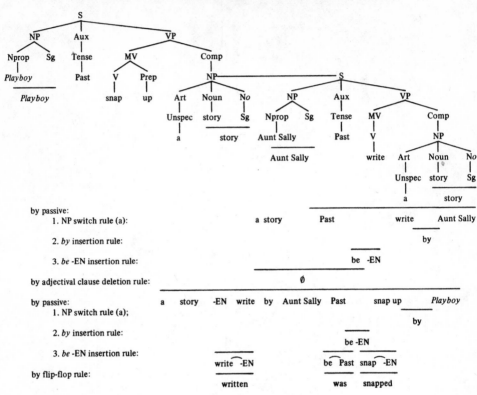

by passive:
   1. NP switch rule (a):   a story   Past   write   Aunt Sally

   2. *by* insertion rule: by

   3. *be* -EN insertion rule: be -EN

by adjectival clause deletion rule: ∅

by passive: a   story   -EN   write   by   Aunt Sally   Past   snap up   *Playboy*
   1. NP switch rule (a);   by

   2. *by* insertion rule:

   3. *be* -EN insertion rule: be -EN

                                    write⌢-EN   be⌢Past snap⌢-EN
by flip-flop rule:

                                    written   was   snapped

Answers to Exercise 10.6 ADJECTIVES DERIVED FROM
PARTICIPIAL PHRASES

1.   A leaking shower.

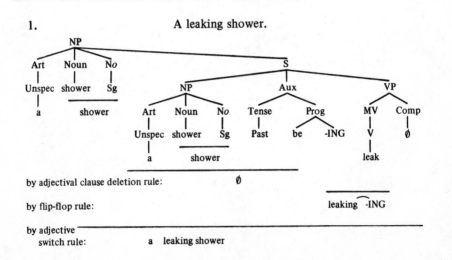

by adjectival clause deletion rule: ∅

by flip-flop rule: leaking⌢-ING

by adjective
   switch rule: a   leaking shower

2.   **An amused audience.**

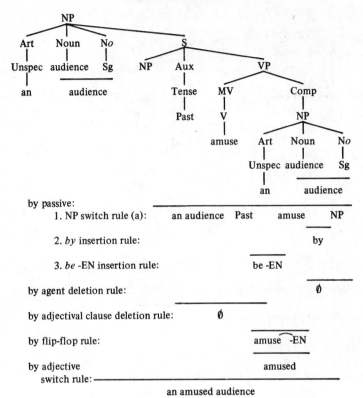

by passive:
    1. NP switch rule (a):   an audience   Past   amuse   NP

    2. *by* insertion rule: by

    3. *be* -EN insertion rule: be -EN

by agent deletion rule: Ø

by adjectival clause deletion rule: Ø

by flip-flop rule: amuse ⌒ -EN

by adjective
    switch rule: amused
                     an amused audience

3.   **A sniveling urchin.**

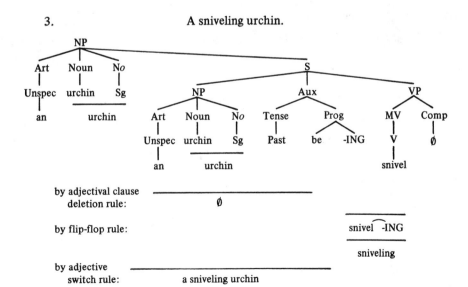

by adjectival clause
    deletion rule: Ø

by flip-flop rule: snivel ⌒ -ING

                          sniveling

by adjective
    switch rule: a sniveling urchin

4.   Modified nouns.

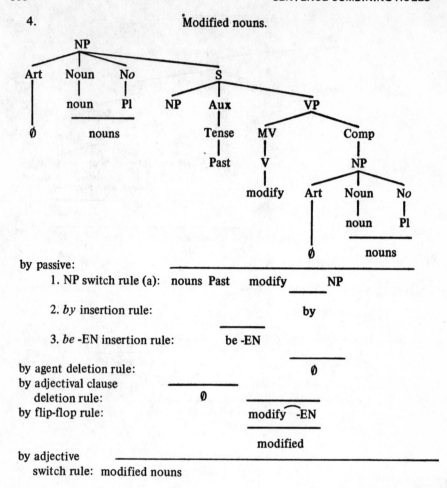

by passive:

    1. NP switch rule (a):   nouns Past   modify _____ NP

    2. *by* insertion rule: by

    3. *be* -EN insertion rule: be -EN

by agent deletion rule: Ø

by adjectival clause
  deletion rule: Ø

by flip-flop rule: modify -EN

                                         modified

by adjective
  switch rule: modified nouns

Answers to Exercise 10.7 REVIEW

1.

The wreck, an overturned truck, blocked the intersection.

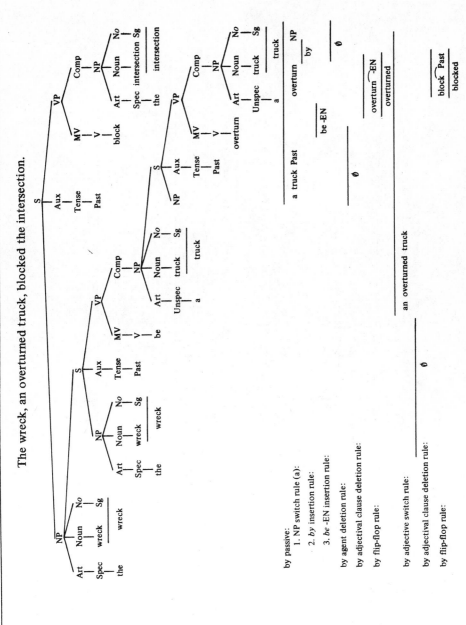

by passive:
  1. NP switch rule (a):
  2. *by* insertion rule:
  3. *be* -EN insertion rule:

by agent deletion rule:

by adjectival clause deletion rule:

by flip-flop rule:

by adjective switch rule:

by adjectival clause deletion rule:

by flip-flop rule:

302

Alarmed by the recent events, General Bluster sent for a chaplain.

2.

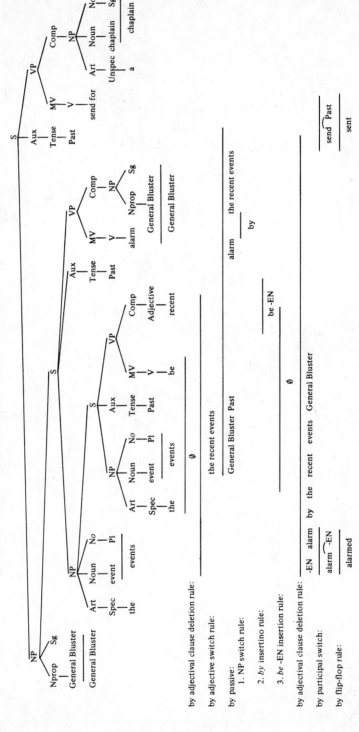

by adjectival clause deletion rule:

by adjective switch rule:

by passive:
1. NP switch rule:

2. *by* insertino rule:

3. *be* -EN insertion rule:

by adjectival clause deletion rule:

by participal switch:

by flip-flop rule:

3.   Aunt Sally, who dislikes miniskirts, looked at Miss Jones with obvious disapproval.

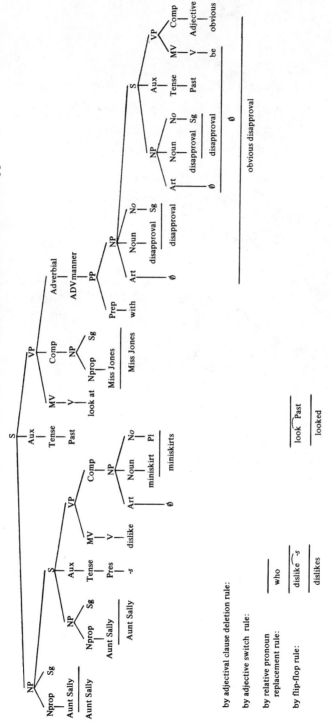

by adjectival clause deletion rule:

by adjective switch rule:

by relative pronoun
replacement rule:

by flip-flop rule:

4.

The campers, soaked by the heavy rain, built a roaring fire.

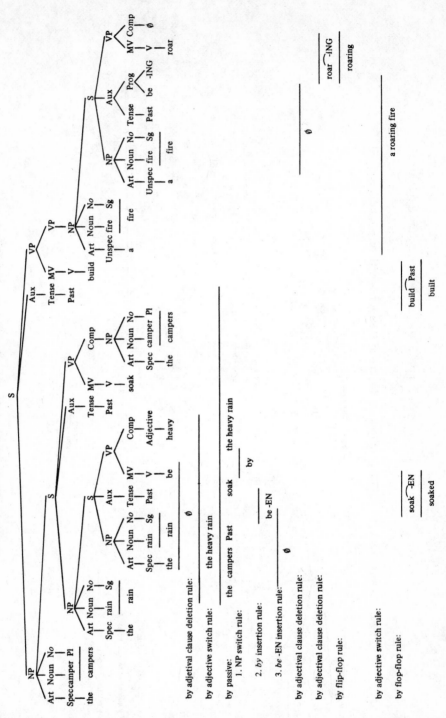

5.   Bored by the long lecture about participials, the class was grateful for the interruption.

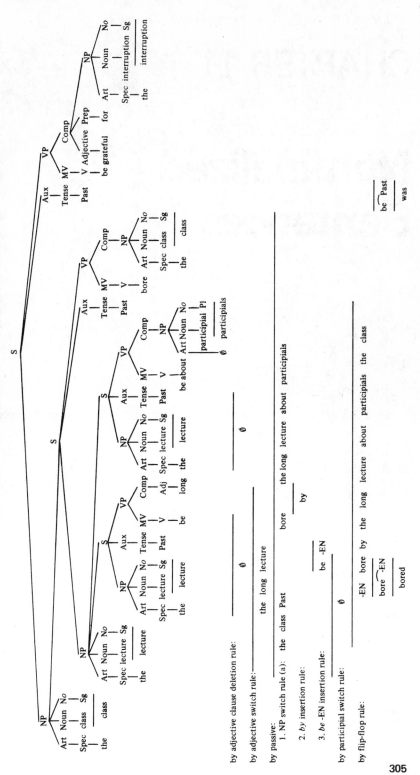

by adjective clause deletion rule:

by adjective switch rule:

by passive:
1. NP switch rule (a):
2. *by* insertion rule:
3. *be* -EN insertion rule:

by participial switch rule:

by flip-flop rule:

305

CHAPTER 11

Nominalized Sentences

OVERVIEW

When the grammar of a sentence will permit the use of a singular, abstract noun, the entire noun phrase of which that noun is a part can be replaced by an embedded sentence, which can come to the surface in a variety of superficially different forms. Let us take as an example the main sentence

   NP amused the audience.

Since *amuse* permits a singular, abstract noun as subject, we may substitute a nominalized sentence for the noun phrase, for example,

   John's rebutting (of) the speaker
   John's rebuttal of the speaker
   For John to rebut the speaker   } amused the audience.
   That John rebutted the speaker
   How John rebutted the speaker

These five different nominalized sentences can be classified into three main types of nominalizations according to what happens to the tense in the underlying embedded sentence: it can be (1) lost, (2) replaced by *to*, or (3) retained.

In all but the last example, the nominalized sentences are all derived from the same underlying embedded sentence:

   John Past rebut the speaker.

As you can see, in the first two example sentences,

John's rebutting (of) the speaker
John's rebuttal of the speaker

the tense of the embedded sentence has been lost. At first glance *rebutting* looks like a verb with -ING added. It is true that -ING has been added, but *rebutting* is no longer a verb, it is a *gerund*, a noun derived from a verb.

The third sentence,

For John to rebut the speaker

has had the tense replaced by *to*. The fourth sentence,

That John rebutted the speaker

has retained the tense. The fifth sentence has also retained tense, but it is not derived from the same underlying embedded sentence as the other sentences. It is derived from

John rebutted the speaker ADVmanner.

The adverb of manner has been replaced by *how*, which in turn was moved to the first position in its sentence by the question-word switch rule. (Why, then, isn't the nominalized sentence a question?) no yes/no switch rule

The last three sample sentences can undergo an optional rule which adds an *it* as a dummy subject and inverts the rest of the sentence. This rule, the *it* inversion rule, transforms

For John to rebut the speaker ⎤
That John rebutted the speaker ⎬ amused the audience.
How John rebutted the speaker ⎦

into

It amused the audience ⎰ for John to rebut the speaker.
⎱ that John rebutted the speaker.
⎱ how John rebutted the speaker.

Nominalized sentences have an additional pecularity—not all the forms that can be used as a substitute for a subject noun phrase can be used as a substitute for an object noun phrase. For example, using the main sentence

The audience applauded NP.

the following nominalizations are grammatical:

The audience applauded ⎰ John's rebutting (of) the speaker.
⎱ John's rebuttal of the speaker.
⎱ how John rebutted the speaker.

However, the following two nominalizations are ungrammatical:

*The audience applauded $\begin{cases} \text{for John to rebut the speaker.} \\ \text{that John rebutted the speaker.} \end{cases}$

NOMINALIZED SENTENCES

A nominalized sentence is a sentence used as a noun phrase. For example, in the sentence

The audience applauded John's rebutting the speaker.

the noun phrase object of the transitive verb *applaud* is *John's rebutting the speaker*. This noun phrase comes from an underlying sentence:

John rebutted the speaker.

There are many restrictions as to which noun phrases can be developed as nominalized sentences. Perhaps the most important restraint is that the noun in the noun phrase be abstract. For example, all of the following uses of the same nominalized sentence are ungrammatical because they are used in a position where an animate noun must be used:

*John's rebutting the speaker applauded the audience.
*John's rebutting the speaker was hungry.
*The event surprised John's rebutting the speaker.

When a nominalized sentence is used in place of a concrete noun, the results are even more outlandish:

*John's rebutting the speaker tipped over.
*The fisherman hooked his line on John's rebutting the speaker.

A key restriction of nominalized sentences, then, is that they can be used only in positions where abstract nouns are grammatical. A useful test word is *outcome*. *Outcome* is an abstract noun that is semantically compatible with almost any verb that will take abstract nouns. It can be used, for example, in the first sentence in this section:

The audience applauded the outcome.

A second restraint on the use of nominalized sentences is that they can be used only in the singular. For example, the verbs in the following sentences will accept abstract nouns, but the sentences are ungrammatical because the nominalized sentences cannot be made plural to agree with the verb:

*John's rebutting the speaker are surprising.
*John's rebutting the speaker were announced over the radio.

Another advantage in using the word *outcome* as a test case is that it is a mass (or noncount) noun, and consequently is inherently singular. In summary, any sentence that will accept a singular abstract noun will also accept a nominalized sentence in that same position.

The source of nominalized sentences is simplicity itself:

$$NP \longrightarrow S.$$

This completes the development of the noun phrase. The full phrase structure rule is now

$$NP \rightarrow \begin{cases} \text{Art} & \text{Noun} & \text{No} & (S)_1 & (S)_2 & \ldots \\ S & & & & \end{cases}$$

The noun phrase rule has two different types of embedded sentences. The "$(S)_1$ $(S)_2$ ..." in the first line of the rule is the source of all noun modification, while the S in the second line is the source of all nominalized sentences.

We can categorize nominalized surface sentences on the basis of what happens to the tense of the underlying embedded sentence in a manner quite similar to the way we categorized sentences embedded in the verb phrase complement. In the case of nominalized sentences we need to make a three-way distinction: (1) embedded sentences which lose their tense when they come to the surface, (2) embedded sentences which have their tense replaced by *to*, and (3) embedded sentences which retain their tense in their surface forms.

Nominalized Sentences Without Tense

This type of nominalization can come to the surface in two slightly different ways:

1. The subject noun is changed to a possessive noun and the main verb is changed to a *gerund*, a noun derived from a verb by adding *-ing* (transitive verbs may be followed by *of*).

The outcome
John's dying
His answering (of) the phone $\Big\}$ surprised us.
The company's publishing (of) the book
Aunt Sally's refusing (of) the offer

2. The subject noun is changed to a possessive noun and the main verb is changed into an abstract noun (followed by *of* if the verb is transitive).

The outcome
John's death
The company's publication of the book $\Big\}$ surprised us.
Aunt Sally's refusal of the offer

The first way is the most general; that is, all verbs can be turned into gerunds, but not all verbs can be turned into abstract nouns. For example, compare the following sentences:

The company printed the book.
The company published the book.

Both can be turned into nominalized sentences using gerunds:

The company's printing of the book.
The company's publishing of the book.

However, while we can turn *publish* into *publication*, there does not exist any abstract noun that we can turn *print* into.

To derive nominalized sentences of type 1, we need a rule, which we will call the *possessive replacement rule*, that replaces the subject noun phrase of the embedded sentence with the appropriate possessive noun or pronoun. This rule will merely add *'s* to singular nouns, *'* to plural regular nouns, and *'s* to plural irregular nouns, and convert the pronouns to the proper possessive form, for example:

John	the boys	the women	I	you	he	she	it	we	they
John's	the boys'	the women's	my	your	his	her	its	our	their

The rule that converts a verb to a gerund is basically the -ING replacement rule. However, since the gerund is often followed by *of*, let us create a new -ING *replacement rule:*

Tense $\Longrightarrow$ -ING *(of)*

Furthermore, let us agree to stretch the flip-flop rule to treat -ING *of* as a single unit and move it to the right-hand side of the verb. Here is an example of a derivation applying these rules:

His answering of the phone surprised me.

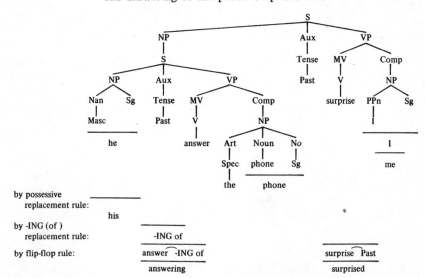

Nominalized sentences of this type can be ambiguous. The classic case of an ambiguous gerund is

the shooting of the hunters

from Chomsky's *Syntactic Structures.* This nominalized sentence can be derived from either: (1) *the hunters shot something* or (2) *someone shot the hunters.* A similar-looking nominalization,

The growling of the lions

is not ambiguous because in the underlying sentence *lions* can only be the subject noun phrase because the verb *growl* is intransitive: *lions growl*. In order for the nominalized sentence to be ambiguous it would have to have this possible underlying sentence:

*Something growls lions.

The contrast between the two nominalized sentences,

The shooting of the hunters
The growling of the lions

is a clear illustration of the need to interpret surface forms in terms of their underlying source sentences. A grammar that did not incorporate such abstract information would be totally incapable of telling *why* the first nominalized sentence was ambiguous and the second one was not, since on their surface, the two nominalized sentences appear to have exactly the same structure.

The second way that nominalized sentences of this type come to the surface is by changing the main verb of the embedded sentence into an abstract noun, followed by *of* if the verb is transitive. We will call the rule that converts a verb into an abstract noun the *abstract noun replacement rule*. We may formulize this rule in the following way:

V $\Longrightarrow$ Nab (of)
(where Nab = an abstract noun)

As was mentioned above, this rule can apply only if there exists an abstract noun that corresponds to the verb. The tense must also be deleted from the sentence by the application of the tense deletion rule. Here is an example of a derivation applying these rules:

The company's publication of the book surprised me.

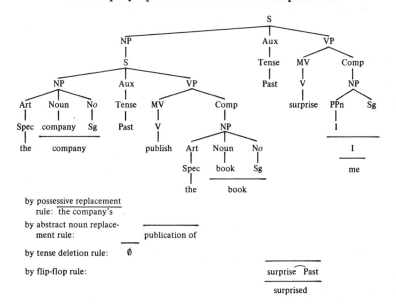

When the main verb in the embedded sentence is the verb *be* and it is followed by an adjective, the adjective turns into the abstract noun and the verb *be* is deleted. For example, compare the following pairs of sentences:

EMBEDDED SENTENCE (DEEP STRUCTURE)	NOMINALIZED SENTENCE (SURFACE STRUCTURE)
The boy is tall	The boy's tallness
Aunt Sally is able to go	Aunt Sally's ability to go
John is happy about his grades	John's happiness about his grades

In order to produce these sentences we must add a second part to the abstract noun replacement rule:

$$be \frown Adjective \Longrightarrow Nab$$

Here is a sample derivation using this rule:

The boy's tallness surprised us.

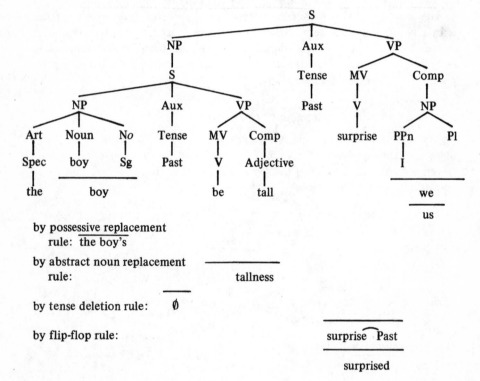

EXERCISE 11.1 **Nominalized Sentences Without Tense**

Draw phrase structure trees and apply the necessary rules to produce the following sentences:
1. Aunt Sally's having a cold spoiled her day.
2. The judge's postponement of the decision surprised everyone.
3. The record's being broken by John delighted the crowd.

4. His reluctance to answer the question bothered us.
5. The crowd was amused by John's refutation of the argument.

Nominalized Sentences with Tense Replaced by *to*

The second way in which the embedded sentence can come to the surface is by replacing the tense with *to* and inserting *for*. Here are some examples of sentences containing this type of nominalization:

The outcome
For John to die
For him to answer the phone
For them to have the answer
For the company to publish the book
For Aunt Sally to refuse the offer
} surprised us.

(Notice that the pronouns change from the subject form to the object form because they now follow the preposition *for*.)

Since this type of nominalization requires no new rules (other than allowing the *for* insertion rule to apply in this new context), we can move directly to a sample derivation:

For him to answer the phone surprised us.

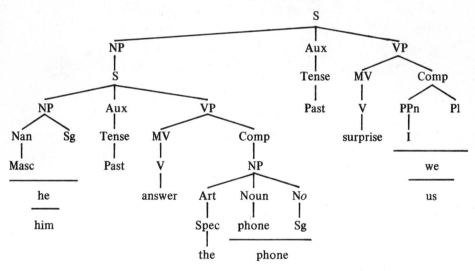

by *to* replacement rule: to

by *for* insertion rule:
for
by tense deletion rule

∅

by flip-flop rule:

surprise Past

surprised

Nominalized Sentences with Tense Retained

The third way in which the embedded sentence can come to the surface is by retaining the tense. There are two different types of nominalized sentences with retained tense. The first type merely adds *that* to the embedded sentence so that the embedded sentence comes to the surface like any other sentence (except, of course, it has *that* in front of it). Here are some examples:

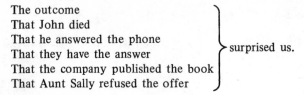

The outcome
That John died
That he answered the phone
That they have the answer
That the company published the book
That Aunt Sally refused the offer
} surprised us.

We will call the rule that inserts *that* in front of the embedded sentence the *that insertion rule* and formalize it thus:

$$S \Longrightarrow that \frown S$$

Here is a sample derivation for a sentence containing a nominalization of this type:

That Aunt Sally refused the offer surprised us.

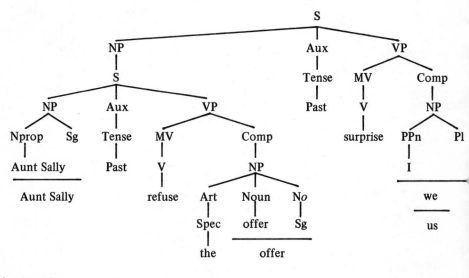

The second type of nominalized sentence with retained tense is a little more complicated. In this type, the question word switch rule is applied to the embedded sentence, producing sentences like the following:

Where Aunt Sally went
What John said
Why they did that   } surprised us.
Whom Aunt Sally invited
When the party began

The embedded sentences do not come to the surface as questions because the *yes-no* question switch rule has not been applied, as it must be to produce a question. That is, from the underlying sentence

John Past say what

we can derive the question form *What did John say?* by using both the *yes-no* question switch rule and the question word switch rule or we can derive the nominalized form *What John said* by using the question word switch rule alone. Here is a sample derivation of a sentence with a nominalized sentence of this type:

What John said surprised us.

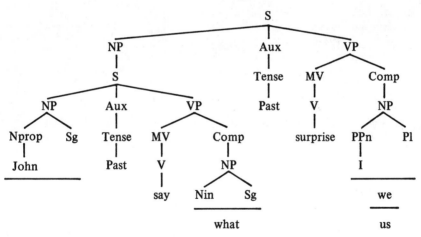

by question word
  switch rule:

| what | John | Past | say |

by flip-flop rule: say Past   surprise Past

                said   surprised

EXERCISE 11.2 **Nominalized Sentences**

Draw phrase structure trees and apply the necessary transformational rules
to produce the following sentences:
1. For us to go was a pleasant change.
2. That Aunt Sally came was a surprise.
3. Who he is is a mystery.
4. For him to eat liver is a miracle.
5. What was said by the lawyer disturbed the judge.

It Inversion

Nominalized sentences which retain their tense and nominalized sentences
which replace their tense with *to* can undergo an optional transformational
rule that inverts the sentence and supplies an *it* as the surface subject. For
example, we can transform the sentences

That John refused the offer surprised me.
Who refused the offer surprised me.
Why John refused the offer surprised me.
For John to refuse the offer surprised me.

into the following inverted sentences:

It surprised me that John refused the offer.
It surprised me who refused the offer.
It surprised me why John refused the offer.
It surprised me for John to refuse the offer.

The nominalized sentences that have lost their tense do not have any corresponding inverted form; for example, for the sentences

His answering the phone surprised me.
Aunt Sally's refusal of the offer surprised me.

there is no corresponding inverted sentence:

?*It surprised me his answering the phone.
  *It surprised me Aunt Sally's refusal of the offer.

The *it inversion rule* is a combination of an insertion rule (for the *it*) and a
switch rule for the rest of the sentence. We may formalize the *it* inversion rule
in the following way:

NP͡ Aux͡ VP $\Longrightarrow$ *it*͡ Aux͡ VP͡ NP
(where NP contains a nominalized sentence that has either retained tense or
replaced tense with *to*)

Here is a sample derivation employing this rule:

It surprised me that John refused the offer.

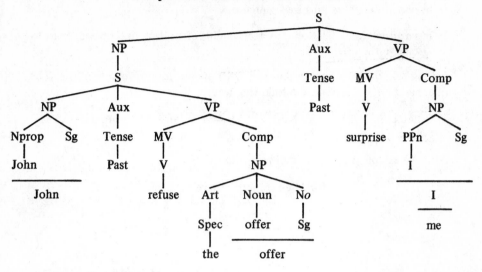

by *that* insertion rule:
that

by *it* inversion rule:
it Past surprise me that John Past refuse the offer

by flip-flop rule: surprise Past refuse Past

surprised refused

It inversion for nominalized sentences with tense replaced by *to* have an additional peculiarity. When the subject noun phrase of the nominalized sentence is the same as the object noun phrase of the main sentence, the subject noun phrase of the nominalized sentence is deleted (along with the preceding *for*). For example, starting with the sentence

For John to receive the offer surprised John

the *it* inversion rule produces

It surprised John for John to receive the offer.

While this may not be ungrammatical, it is certainly stilted. If we replace the second occurrence of the noun phrase with a pronoun we get

It surprised John for him to receive the offer.

This is a perfectly grammatical sentence, but it does not mean the same thing; the *him* does not refer to John, but to somebody else. In order for the surface sentence to have the meaning we want, we must delete the *for* and the subject noun phrase of the nominalized sentence:

It surprised John for John to receive the offer $\Longrightarrow$ It surprised John to receive the offer.

Let us call the rule that makes this deletion the *for NP deletion rule*. The rule may be formalized in the following way:

it Aux MV NP₁ *for* NP₂ *to* VP $\Longrightarrow$ *it* Aux MV NP₁ *to* VP
(where NP₁ = NP₂)

Here is a sample derivation employing this rule:

It surprised John to receive the offer.

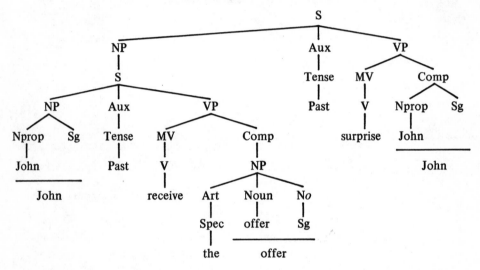

by *to* replacement
   rule: to

by *for* insertion rule:
for

by *it* inversion rule:
             it   Past   surprise John for John to receive the offer

by *for* NP deletion switch rule: Ø

by flip-flop rule: surprise Past

                 surprised

EXERCISE 11.3 *It* **Inversion**

Draw phrase structure trees and apply the necessary transformational rules to produce the following sentences:
1. It tickled me that John wouldn't come.
2. It overwhelmed Cinderella to get the invitation.
3. It amused me for John to be afraid to go.
4. It pleases Aunt Sally when he comes.
5. It angered me to be insulted by John.

Nominalized Sentences as Objects

All of the examples of nominalized sentences that we have discussed to this point have been the subject in the main sentence. When a nominalized sentence is embedded as an object noun phrase, not all forms that we have described for the subject position can be used. Let us take the following group of nominalized sentences to be representative of the three main types we have already seen:

Aunt Sally's refusing the offer
Aunt Sally's refusal of the offer } (tense lost)
For Aunt Sally to refuse the offer   (tense replaced by *to*)
That Aunt Sally refused the offer
Why Aunt Sally refused the offer } (tense retained)

The verb *complain about* can take an abstract noun as object, for example,

John complained about the outcome.

Now let us see what happens when we use the five nominalized sentences above as object of *complain about:*

John complained about {
Aunt Sally's refusing the offer.
Aunt Sally's refusal of the offer.
*For Aunt Sally to refuse the offer.
*That Aunt Sally refused the offer.
Why Aunt Sally refused the offer.
}

As you can see, the nominalizations beginning with *for* and *that* are ungrammatical.

We need to distinguish carefully between nominalized sentences and complements that contain embedded sentences of the *it ͡(that)* S type. Many verbs that take this type of complement delete the *it* (either optionally or obligatorily). The resulting sentence looks exactly like a nominalization beginning with *that*. For example, the verb *complain* takes an *it ͡(that)* S complement. When we apply the *it* deletion rule we can produce the following surface sentence:

John complained that Aunt Sally refused the offer.

We can establish that *that Aunt Sally refused the offer* is not a nominalized sentence by attempting to substitute nominalized sentences that have lost tense:

$$
\text{John complained} \begin{cases} \text{*Aunt Sally's refusing the offer} \\ \text{*Aunt Sally's refusal of the offer} \end{cases}
$$

A second kind of evidence that *complain* is not followed by a nominalized sentence is that *complain* cannot be followed by an abstract noun:

*John complained the outcome.

EXERCISE 11.4 Review

Draw phrase structure trees and apply the necessary transformational rules to produce the following sentences:
1. I can't repeat what he said.
2. We admired Aunt Sally's arrangement of the flowers.
3. It was a surprise for him to fly.
4. Their forgetting to bring the beer was unforgivable.
5. She hoped that we would change our minds.
6. It seemed unfair that he should criticize our being unprepared.

Answers to Exercise 11.1 NOMINALIZED SENTENCES WITHOUT TENSE

1.   Aunt Sally's having a cold spoiled her day.

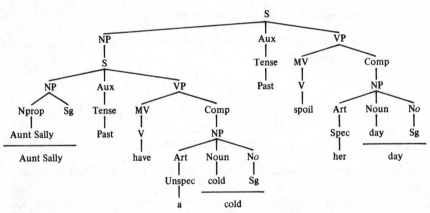

by possessive replacement rule:
 Aunt Sally's

by -ING (of) replacement
 rule: -ING

by flip-flop rule: have⌢-ING   spoil⌢Past

                          having   spoiled

2.   **The judge's postponement of the decision surprised everyone.**

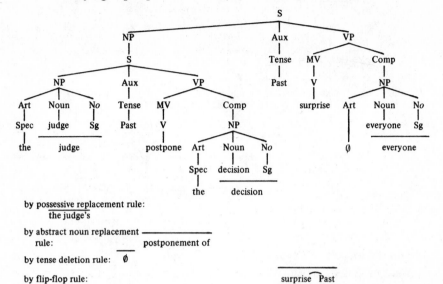

by possessive replacement rule:
    the judge's

by abstract noun replacement ───────────
  rule: postponement of

by tense deletion rule: Ø

by flip-flop rule: surprise͡ Past

                                   surprised

3.   **The record's being broken by John delighted the crowd.**

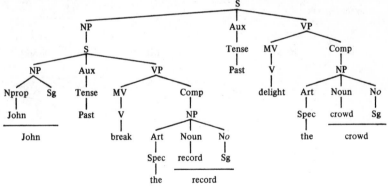

by passive:
  1. NP switch rule: the record Past   break   John

  2. *by* insertion rule: by

  3. *be* -EN insertion rule: be -EN

by possessive *replacement* ───────────
  rule: the record's

by -ING (of) replacement
  rule: -ING

by flip-flop rule: be͡ -ING break͡ -EN   delight͡ Past

                  being   broken   delighted

4.   His reluctance to answer the question bothered us.

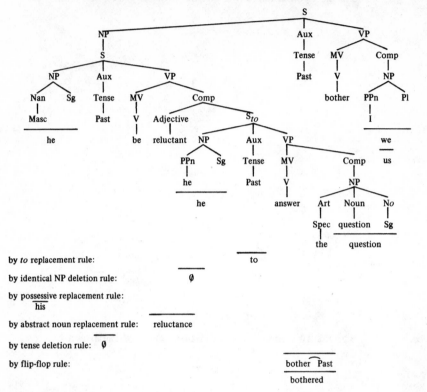

by *to* replacement rule:		to
by identical NP deletion rule:	∅	
by possessive replacement rule: his		
by abstract noun replacement rule:	reluctance	
by tense deletion rule: ∅		
by flip-flop rule:		bother ⌢ Past bothered

5.   The crowd was amused by John's refutation of the argument.

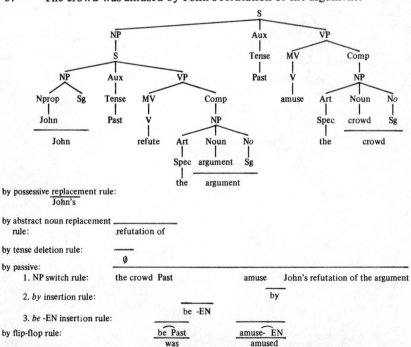

by possessive replacement rule: John's		
by abstract noun replacement rule:	refutation of	
by tense deletion rule:	∅	
by passive:		
1. NP switch rule:	the crowd Past	amuse John's refutation of the argument
2. *by* insertion rule:		by
3. *be* -EN insertion rule:	be -EN	
by flip-flop rule:	be ⌢ Past was	amuse- ⌢ EN amused

Answers to Exercise 11.2 NOMINALIZED SENTENCES

1.

For us to go was a pleasant change.

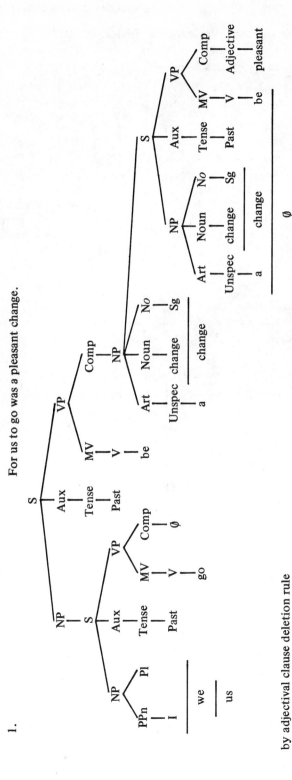

by adjectival clause deletion rule

by adjective switch rule:

by *to* replacement rule: to

by *for* insertion rule:
for

by flip-flop rule:

be Past
was

2.   That Aunt Sally came was a surprise.

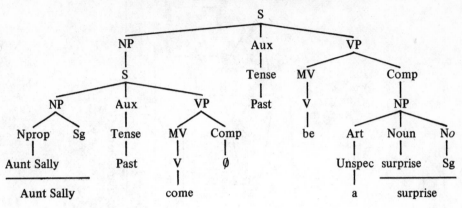

by *that* insertion
rule: $\overline{that}$

by flip-flop rule: come⌢Past   be⌢Past

                               came   was

3.   Who he is is a mystery.

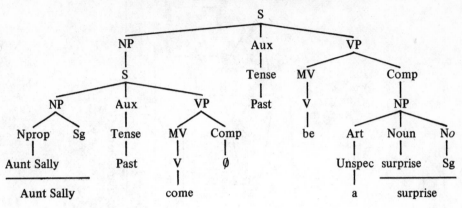

by question word
switch rule: _____
                  who   he   -s   be

by flip-flop rule: be⌢-s   be⌢-s

                        is   is

4. **For him to eat liver is a miracle.**

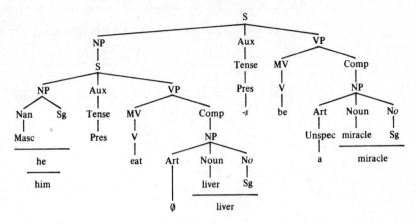

by to replacement
rule: to

by *for* insertion
rule: for

by flip-flop rule:

$$\widehat{be \ \text{-}s}$$

is

5. **What was said by the lawyer disturbed the judge.**

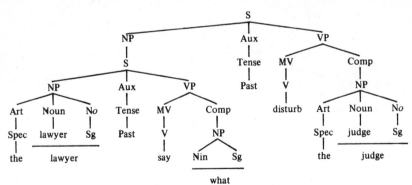

by passive:
   1. NP switch rule:
               what   Past   say   the lawyer

   2. *by* insertion rule: by

   3. *be* -EN insertion rule: be -EN

by flip-flop rule: $\widehat{be \ \text{Past}}$ $\widehat{say \ \text{-EN}}$ $\widehat{disturb \ \text{Past}}$

                       was   said   disturbed

Answers to Exercise 11.3 *IT* INVERSION

1.   It tickled me that John wouldn't come.

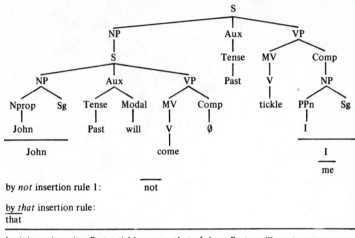

by *not* insertion rule 1:   not

by *that* insertion rule:
that

by *it* inversion: it   Past   tickle   me   that   John   Past   will   not   come

by flip-flop rule: tickle ⌒ Past   will ⌒ Past

                              tickled   would

2.   It overwhelmed Cinderella to get the invitation.

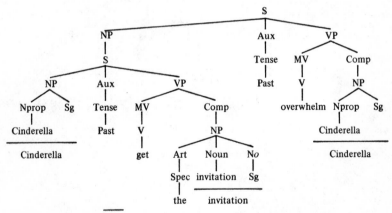

by *to* replacement rule: to

by *for* insertion rule:
for

by *it* inversion rule:
          it   Past   overwhelm   Cinderella   for   Cinderella   to   get   the   invitation

by *for* ⌒ NP deletion rule: ∅

by flip-flop rule:_____
                overwhelm ⌒ Past
                overwhelmed

3.   It amused me for John to be afraid to go.

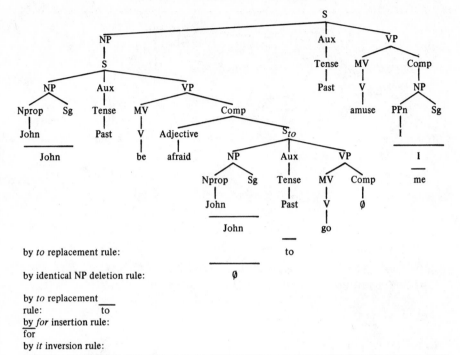

by *to* replacement rule: to

by identical NP deletion rule: ∅

by *to* replacement rule: to
by *for* insertion rule: for
by *it* inversion rule:

it   Past amuse me for John to be afraid to go

by flip-flop rule: amuse͡ Past

               amused

4.   It pleases Aunt Sally when he comes.

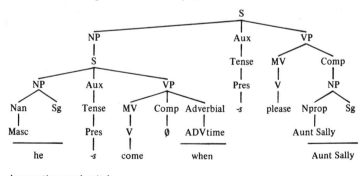

by question word switch rule: when he -s come

by *it* inversion rule:
       it -s please Aunt Sally when he -s come

by flip-flop rule: please͡ -s   come͡ -s

           pleases   comes

5.   It angered me to be insulted by John.

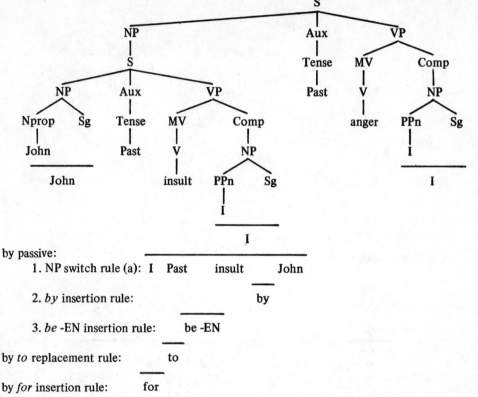

by passive: _____
   1. NP switch rule (a): I   Past   insult   John

   2. *by* insertion rule: by

   3. *be* -EN insertion rule: be -EN

by *to* replacement rule: to

by *for* insertion rule: for

by *it* inversion rule: it   Past   anger   I   for I   to be -EN   insult   by   John
                                                    me̲   me̲

by *for* NP deletion rule: ∅

by flip-flop rule: anger ⌢ Past   insult ⌢ -EN

                                    angered   insulted

Answers to Exercise 11.4 REVIEW

1.   I can't repeat what he said.

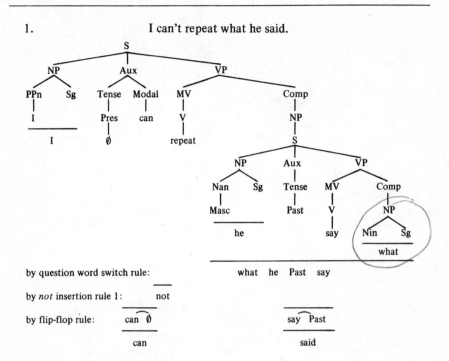

by question word switch rule: what he Past say

by *not* insertion rule 1:   not

by flip-flop rule: can̆ ∅   say̆ Past

                         can   said

2.   We admired Aunt Sally's arrangement of the flowers.

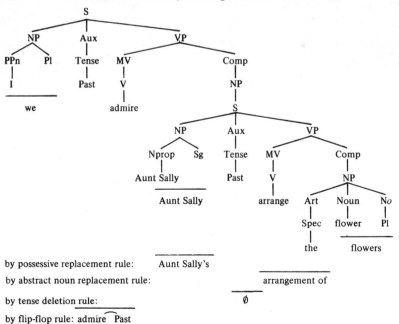

by possessive replacement rule: Aunt Sally's
by abstract noun replacement rule: arrangement of
by tense deletion rule: ∅
by flip-flop rule: admirĕ Past
                   admired

3.   It was a surprise for him to fly.

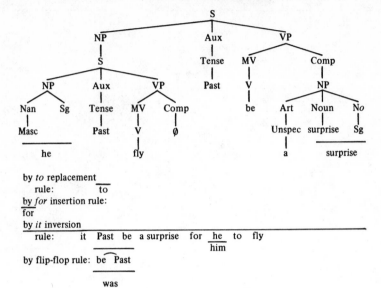

by *to* replacement
   rule: to
by *for* insertion rule:
for
by *it* inversion
   rule: it Past be a surprise for he to fly
                               him
by flip-flop rule: be Past

                 was

4.   Their forgetting to bring the beer was unforgivable.

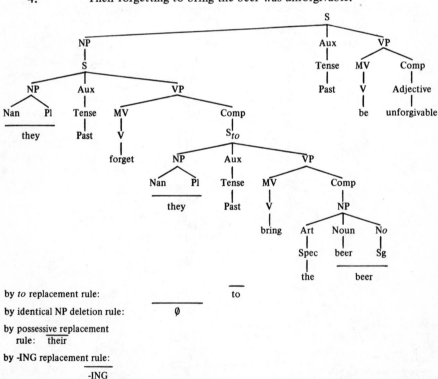

by *to* replacement rule: to

by identical NP deletion rule: ∅

by possessive replacement
   rule: their

by -ING replacement rule:

       -ING

by flip-flop rule: forget -ING   be Past

       forgetting   was

5.   She hoped that we would change our minds.

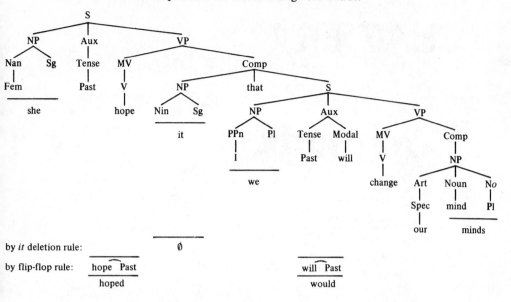

6.   It seemed unfair that he should criticize our being unprepared.

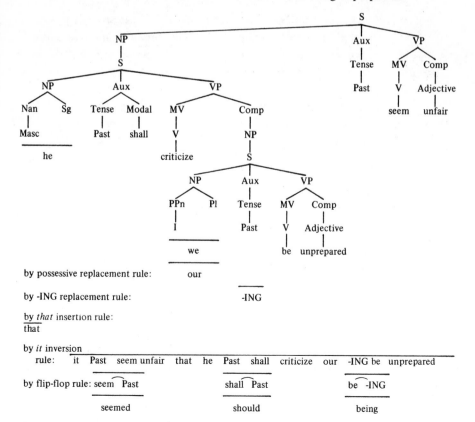

CHAPTER 12

Conjunction

OVERVIEW

For the last four chapters we have examined ways in which sentences can be combined by the process of embedding to produce more complex sentences. In this chapter we will examine yet another way of combining sentences: by conjunction. The process of conjunction does not usually embed one sentence inside another sentence. Instead, conjunction links two surface sentences together to form a longer single-surface sentence. In this chapter we will examine three different types of conjunctions: (1) coordinating conjunctions, (2) subordinating conjunctions, and (3) conjunctive adverbs.

Conjunction is the process of joining two sentences together. The most common type of conjunction is coordination. In this chapter we examine some of the ways that sentences can be joined by the coordinating conjunction *and*. *And* can be used to join two totally different sentences, for example, *John sang and Mary danced*. *And* can also be used to join sentences that have identical parts, for example, identical subjects, *John and Mary sang*, or identical objects, *John sang and danced*.

Coordination involves deleting the elements from the second sentence that are identical with the corresponding elements in the first sentence, and then joining the different elements with *and*. Thus, *John sang and danced* is derived from two sentences, *John sang* and *John danced*. The element in the second sentence that is identical with the corresponding element in the first sentence is *John*. *John* is then deleted and the differing elements (*sang* and *danced* in this case) are joined by *and*, producing *John sang and danced*.

The chapter also examines two easily confused types of conjunctions, subordinating conjunctions and conjunctive adverbs. Subordinating conjunctions, words like *because* and *although*, join two sentences, for example, *He took an umbrella because it looked like it might rain*. The distinguishing characteristic of subordinating conjunctions is that they, and the sentence following them, can be moved to the first position of the sentence, for example, *Because it looked like it might rain, he took an umbrella*.

Conjunctive adverbs, words like *therefore* and *however*, behave in a quite different way. They can move around in the sentences they introduce. For example, instead of merely occurring between the two sentences, as in *It's getting late; therefore, I must be going*, the conjunctive adverb can be used in the middle of the second sentence, *It's getting late; I must, therefore, be going*, or even at the end, *It's getting late; I must be going, therefore*.

CONJUNCTION

Coordinating Conjunctions

Coordination means joining two sentences with the coordinating conjunctions *and*, *or*, *but*. Each of the three coordinating conjunctions has its own special range of meanings and privileges of occurrence. In this discussion we will be concerned only with *and*.

The basic process of coordination is simple: the two sentences being coordinated are matched with each other. All elements of the second sentence that are the same as the corresponding elements of the first sentence are deleted, while all elements of the second sentence that are different from the corresponding element in the first sentence are retained. Let us take as our first example a pair of sentences that have no elements in common.

S_1: John sang.
S_2: Mary danced.
S_1 and S_2: John sang and Mary danced.

Here is an example where the subject noun phrases of the two sentences are identical, while the verb phrases are not:

S_1: John sang.
S_2: John danced.
S_1 and S_2: John sang and John danced $\Longrightarrow$ John sang and danced.

Here is an example with identical verb phrases:

S_1: John sang.
S_2: Mary sang.
S_1 and S_2: John sang and Mary sang $\Longrightarrow$ John and Mary sang.

Here is an example with identical subjects and identical verb phrases, but with different modal auxiliaries:

S_1: John can sing.
S_2: John will sing.
S_1 and S_2: John can sing and John will sing $\Longrightarrow$ John can and will sing.

The process of coordination depends on our ability to recognize when an element in one sentence "corresponds" to an element in the second sentence. Chomsky gives an example in *Syntactic Structures* of a pair of sentences that cannot be grammatically coordinated because the corresponding elements play different grammatical roles in their underlying sentences:

S_1: The scene of the movie was in Chicago.
S_2: The scene that I wrote was in Chicago.
S_1 and S_2: The scene of the movie was in Chicago and the scene that I wrote was in Chicago $\Longrightarrow$ *The scene of the movie and that I wrote was in Chicago.

One of the side effects of coordination is that the resulting sentence is often ambiguous. One type of ambiguity results from two different underlying second sentences producing the same surface. A classic example is the phrase *old men and women*, which is ambiguous because *old* may modify both *men* and *women* or just *men* alone. The surface sentence

Save the old men and women first!

has two different interpretations depending on the nature of the second underlying sentence. One interpretation would derive from this pair of underlying sentences containing *old* in the second sentence:

S_1: Save the old men first!
S_2: Save the old women first!
S_1 and S_2: Save the old men first and save the old women first! $\Longrightarrow$

Save the old men and women first!

The other interpretation would derive from an underlying second sentence that did not contain *old* at all:

S_1: Save the old men first!
S_2: Save the women first!
S_1 and S_2: Save the old men and save the women first! $\Longrightarrow$

Save the old men and women first!

We will employ two new transformational rules in joining sentences together with *and*. The first rule we will call the *coordination deletion rule*. This rule deletes any element in the second sentence which is identical (both in function and actual words) with a corresponding element in the first sentence. We can formalize this rule in the following way:

$$\#X_{a_1} \frown X_{a_2} \frown X_{a_3} \#\#X_{b_1} \frown X_{b_2} \frown X_{b_3} \# \Longrightarrow \#X_{a_1} \frown X_{a_2} \frown X_{a_3} \#\#X_{b_2} \#$$

(where $X_{a_2} \neq X_{b_2}$; $X_{a_1} = X_{b_1}$; and $X_{a_3} = X_{b_3}$)

#...# are sentence boundaries

X_a is any grammatical element in sentence *a*

X_b is any grammatical element in sentence *b*

The second rule we need is the *coordination insertion rule*. This rule does two things. It inserts the surviving element from the second sentence (remember that all the elements in the second sentence that were identical with their corresponding elements in the first sentence have been deleted) into the first sentence after its corresponding elements. The second thing the rule does is to insert an *and* between the two corresponding elements. This rule can be formalized in the following way:

$$\#X_{a_1} \overgroup{X_{a_2}} \overgroup{X_{a_3}} \#\#X_{b_2}\# \Longrightarrow \#X_{a_1} \overgroup{X_{a_2}} \text{ and } \overgroup{X_{b_2}} \overgroup{X_{a_3}} \#.$$

Here are some sample derivations using these two rules:

> John sang and danced.
> John sang. John danced.

by coordination deletion rule: $\emptyset$

by coordination insertion rule: John sang and danced.

> John and Mary sang.
> John sang. Mary sang.

by coordination deletion rule: $\emptyset$

by coordination insertion rule: John and Mary sang.

> John can and will sing.
> John can sing. John will sing.

by coordination deletion rule: $\emptyset$ $\emptyset$

by coordination insertion rule: John can and will sing.

> John sang and Mary danced.
> John sang. Mary danced.

by coordination insertion rule: John sang and Mary danced.

EXERCISE 12.1 Coordinating Conjunctions

Using the format developed in the sample derivations above, derive the following sentences:

1. I bought some cement and a shovel.
2. John and Mary saw the accident.
3. John smiled and shrugged his shoulders.
4. Aunt Sally was exhausted and discouraged by her defeat at Monopoly. (Can you give two different derivations for this same sentence?)

Subordinating Conjunctions

Subordinating conjunctions are used to join two sentences together. However, unlike coordinating conjunctions, the two sentences are kept intact and separate. Subordinating conjunctions have a wide range of meaning; however, the most common types are reason (*since, because*), condition (*if, unless*), time (*when, after*), and place (*where, wherever*). Here are some examples of sentences joined by subordinating conjunctions:

I stopped off for a hamburger *since* I had missed my dinner.
I decided to help him out *although* it was against my better judgment.
Drop over *whenever* you are free.
They bought fresh supplies *wherever* they could.
He took an umbrella *because* it looked like it might rain.
I will come *even if* I have to walk.
The phone started to ring *as soon as* I came in the door.

The rule that joins the two sentences is an elementary rule that we will call the *subordinating conjunction insertion rule*:

$$\#S_1 \#\#S_2 \# \Longrightarrow \#S_1 \frown \text{Subconj} \frown S_2 \#$$

(where Subconj = subordinating conjunction)

The distinguishing characteristic of subordinating conjunctions is that the subordinating conjunction and the following sentence can be moved to the first position in the sentence. For example, we can move the subordinating conjunction and the second sentence in all of the sample sentences above:

Since I had missed my dinner, I stopped off for a hamburger.
Although it was against my better judgment, I decided to help him out.
Whenever you are free, drop over.
Whenever they could, they bought fresh supplies.
Because it looked like it might rain, he took an umbrella.
Even if I have to walk, I will come.
As soon as I came in the door, the phone started to ring.

We will call the rule that inverts the two sentences the *subordinating conjunction switch rule*:

$$S_1 \frown \text{Subconj} \frown S_2 \Longrightarrow \text{Subconj} \frown S_2 \frown S_1$$

Here is a sample derivation employing this rule:

When I am 65, I will retire.
I will retire. I am 65.

by subordinating conjunction insertion rule:	
	I will retire when I am 65.
by subordinating conjunction switch rule:	
	When I am 65, I will retire.

Conjunctive Adverbs

Conjunctive adverbs, like subordinating conjunctions, are used to join together two independent sentences. Here are some examples of sentences joined by conjunctive adverbs:

John was at the scene; *however,* he did not see the accident.
John was at the scene; *moreover,* he saw the accident.
John was at the scene; *therefore,* he must have seen the accident.

As you can see, conjunctive adverbs look very much like subordinating conjunctions. However, there are several differences. Conjunctive adverbs cannot undergo the subordinating conjunction switch rule. Thus the following sentences are ungrammatical when we attempt to apply this rule:

*However he did not see the accident, John was at the scene.
*Consequently he must have seen the accident, John was at the scene.
*Therefore he must have seen the accident, John was at the scene.

The distinguishing characteristic of conjunctive adverbs is that conjunctive adverbs can be moved about within the second sentence. For example, taking the three sample sentences above, we can put the conjunctive adverb in the middle of the second sentence,

John was at the scene; he did not, *however,* see the accident.
John was at the scene; he, *moreover,* saw the accident.
John was at the scene; he must, *therefore,* have seen the accident.

or at the end,

John was at the scene; he did not see the accident, *however.*
John was at the scene; he saw the accident, *moreover.*
John was at the scene; he must have seen the accident, *therefore.*

If we attempt to move a subordinating conjunction around within the second sentence, the result is ungrammatical, for example,

**I stopped off for a hamburger, I had, *since,* missed my dinner.
**I stopped off for a hamburger, I had missed my dinner, *since.*

The rule that joins the two sentences together by means of a conjunctive adverb is very similar to the subordinating conjunction insertion rule. We will call this new rule the *conjunctive adverb insertion rule* and formalize it this way:

$$\#S_1 \#\#S_2 \# \Longrightarrow \#S_1 \frown \text{Conjadv} \frown S_2 \#$$

(where Conjadv = conjunctive adverb)

The rule that moves the conjunctive adverb to different positions within the second sentence is more complicated because the conjunctive adverb can be used in several places in the middle of the second sentence depending on the nature of the sentence. Nevertheless, the two most common places for the conjunctive adverb are (1) after the first auxiliary verb (if there is one, if not, then immediately in front of the main verb) and (2) at the end of the sentence. We may formalize the placement of the conjunctive adverb by the *conjunctive adverb switch rule*:

$$S_1 \text{ Conjadv NP } (AV)_1 \ (AV)_2 \ (AV)_3 \text{ VP} \Longrightarrow$$

$$\begin{Bmatrix} S_1 \text{ NP } (AV)_1 \text{ Conjadv } (AV)_2 \ (AV)_3 \text{ VP} \\ S_1 \text{ NP } (AV)_1 \ (AV)_2 \ (AV)_3 \text{ VP Conjadv} \end{Bmatrix}$$

(where AV = auxiliary verb)

Here is a sample derivation using this rule:

He said the sentence backwards; it was, therefore, quite ungrammatical.

He said the sentence backwards. It was quite ungrammatical.

by conjunctive
adverb inser-
tion rule: He said the sentence backwards therefore it was quite un-
                                                                  grammatical.

by conjunctive
adverb
switch rule: it was therefore quite un-
                                                                  grammatical.

EXERCISE 12.2 Subordinating Conjunctions and Conjunctive Adverbs

Using the subordinating conjunction and conjunctive adverb switch rules, can you tell which of the following italicized words is a subordinating conjunction and which is a conjunctive adverb?
1. John answered the phone   *as*   he knew it wasn't for him.
                                therefore
                                although
                                however
                                nevertheless
                                even though
                                since
2. I was discouraged *consequently* I was coming down with a cold.
                                because
                                also
                                while
                                moreover
                                after

EXERCISE 12.3 Review

Derive the following sentences:
1. I think; therefore, I am.
2. She found a pair of socks and an old skate key in the drawer.
3. Although Aunt Sally normally can't stand swiss chard, she ate it without complaining last night.

4. He passed Go; he was, nonetheless, forced to sell his railroads.
5. While you were out, he called you twice.
6. Time and tide wait for no man.

Answers to Exercise 12.1 COORDINATION

---

1. I bought some cement and a shovel.

I bought some cement. I bought a shovel.

by coordination deletion rule: $\emptyset$

by coordination insertion rule: I bought some cement and a shovel.

2. John and Mary saw the accident.

John saw the accident. Mary saw the accident.

by coordination deletion rule: ϕ

by coordination insertion rule: John and Mary saw the accident.

3. John smiled and shrugged his shoulders.

John smiled. John shrugged his shoulders.

by coordination deletion rule: $\emptyset$

by coordination insertion rule: John smiled and shrugged his shoulders.

4. Aunt Sally was exhausted and discouraged by her defeat at Monopoly.

(a) Aunt Sally was exhausted. Aunt Sally was discouraged by her defeat at Monopoly.

by coordination
deletion rule: $\emptyset$

by coordination
insertion rule: Aunt Sally was exhausted and discouraged by her defeat at Monopoly.

(b) Aunt Sally was exhausted by her defeat at Monopoly. Aunt Sally was discouraged by her defeat at Monopoly.

by coordination
deletion rule: $\emptyset$ $\emptyset$

by coordination
insertion rule: Aunt Sally was exhausted and discouraged by her defeat at Monopoly.

Answers to Exercise 12.2 SUBORDINATING CONJUNCTIONS AND CONJUNCTIVE ADVERBS

---

1. *as* —subordinating conjunction
therefore—conjunctive adverb
although—subordinating conjunction

however—conjunctive adverb
nevertheless—conjunctive adverb
even though—subordinating conjunction
since- subordinating conjunction

2. *consequently*—conjunctive adverb
because—subordinating conjunction
also—conjunctive adverb
while—subordinating conjunction
moreover—conjunctive adverb
after—subordinating conjunction

Answers to Exercise 12.3 REVIEW

1.   I think; therefore, I am.

I think. I am.

by conjunctive adverb insertion rule: I think therefore I am.

2.   She found a pair of socks and an old skate key in the drawer.

She found a pair of socks in the drawer.
She found an old skate key in the drawer.

by coordination
deletion rule: Ø   Ø
by coordination
insertion rule: She found a pair of socks and an old skate key in the drawer.

3.   Although Aunt Sally normally can't stand swiss chard,
        she ate it without complaining last night.

She ate it without complaining last night. Aunt Sally normally can't stand swiss chard.

by subordinating
conjunction
insertion rule: She ate it without complaining last night although Aunt
Sally normally can't stand swiss chard.
by subordinating
conjunction
switch rule: Although Aunt Sally normally can't stand swiss chard she
ate it without complaining last night.

4.   He passed Go; he was, nonetheless, forced to sell his railroads.

He passed Go. He was forced to sell his railroads.

by conjunctive adverb
insertion rule: He passed Go nonetheless he was forced to sell his
railroads.

by conjunctive adverb
   switch rule: He passed Go he was nonetheless forced to sell his
                                                     railroads.

5.   While you were out, he called you twice.

                      He called you twice. You were out.

by subordinating conjunction
   insertion rule: He called you twice while you were out.
by subordinating conjunction
   switch rule: While you were out he called you twice.

6.   Time and tide wait for no man.

                      Time waits for no man. Tide waits for no man.

by coordination deletion
   rule: ∅
by coordination insertion
   rule: Time and tide wait for no man.

APPENDIX

Summary of Rules

PART I PHRASE STRUCTURE RULES

S $\longrightarrow$ NP Aux VP   (p. 23)

Chapter 1 The Noun Phrase

NP $\longrightarrow$ $\left\{\begin{array}{l}\text{Article Noun Number}\\\text{Proper Noun }\left\{\begin{array}{l}\text{Singular}\\\text{Plural}\end{array}\right\}\\\text{Personal Pronoun Number}\end{array}\right\}$ (p. 26; for revised forms see pp. 265 and 309)

Article (Art) $\longrightarrow$ $\left\{\begin{array}{l}\text{Specified}\\\text{Unspecified}\\\emptyset\end{array}\right\}$ (p. 26)

Specified (Spec) $\longrightarrow$ $\left\{\begin{array}{l}\textit{the, this, that, these, those};\\\text{possessive nouns and possessive}\\\text{pronouns; numbers}\end{array}\right\}$ (p. 26)

Unspecified (Unspec) $\longrightarrow$ $\left\{\begin{array}{l}\textit{a/an, some, a few, a couple,}\\\textit{several, much, many, . . .}\end{array}\right\}$ (p. 26)

Noun $\longrightarrow$ $\left\{\textit{boy, tree, idea, elephant, . . .}\right\}$ (p. 26)

$$\text{Proper Noun (Nprop)} \longrightarrow \begin{cases} \textit{Mr. Brown, Mary, America,} \\ \textit{the Alps, the Colorado River,} \\ \textit{the Hawaiian Islands, . . .} \end{cases} \quad \text{(p. 26)}$$

$$\text{Number (N}o) \longrightarrow \begin{cases} \text{Singular} \\ \text{Plural} \end{cases} \quad \text{(p. 26)}$$

Personal Pronoun (PPn)⟶ *I, you*   (p. 26)

Chapter 2   The Auxiliary

Auxiliary (Aux) ⟶ Tense (Modal) (Perfect) (Progressive)   (p. 49)

$$\text{Tense} \longrightarrow \begin{cases} \text{Present} \\ \text{Past} \end{cases}$$

$$\text{Modal} \longrightarrow \left\{ \textit{can, may, must, shall, will} \right\}$$

Perfect ⟶ *have* -EN

Prog ⟶ *be* -ING

flip-flop rule (a)   (p. 54; for general form see p. 65)
Tense Verb ⟹ Verb Tense
Example: John -s sing ⟹ John sing -s

flip-flop rule (b)   (p. 60; for general form see p. 65)
-EN Verb ⟹ Verb -EN
Example: He Past have -EN eat ⟹ He Past have eat -EN

flip-flop rule (c)   (p. 63; for general form see p. 65)
-ING Verb ⟹ Verb -ING
Example: I Pres be -ING work ⟹ I Pres be work -ING

flip-flop rule   (p. 65)
Af Verb ⟹ Verb Af (where Af = Tense, -EN, or -ING)
Example: He Past have -EN be -ING sing ⟹ He have Past be -EN sing -ING

IF Pres Modal, THEN Pres ⟶ ∅

IF N Sg Pres, THEN Pres ⟶ *-s/-es*

IF PPn Sg Pres, THEN Pres ⟶ ∅

IF Pl Pres, THEN Pres ⟶ ∅   (p. 50)

Chapter 3   The Verb Phrase

Verb Phrase (VP) ⟶ Main Verb Complement (Adverbial)   (p. 83)

$$\text{Main Verb (MV)} \longrightarrow \begin{cases} \textit{be, run, laugh,} \\ \textit{have think, . . .} \end{cases} \quad \text{(p. 85)}$$

$$\text{Adverbial} \longrightarrow \begin{cases} \text{Adverbial of time} \\ \text{Adverbial of position} \\ \text{Adverbial of direction} \\ \text{Adverbial of manner} \end{cases} \quad \text{(p. 87)}$$

$$\left\{\begin{array}{l}\text{Adverbial of time} \\ \quad \text{(ADVtime)} \\ \text{Adverbial of position} \\ \quad \text{(ADVposition)} \\ \text{Adverbial of direction} \\ \quad \text{(ADVdirection)} \\ \text{Adverbial of manner} \\ \quad \text{(ADVmanner)}\end{array}\right\} \longrightarrow \left\{\begin{array}{l}\text{Prepositional} \\ \quad \text{Phrase} \\ \text{Adverb}\end{array}\right\} \quad \text{(p. 87)}$$

Prepositional
Phrase (PP) $\longrightarrow$ Preposition $\frown$ NP   (p. 87)

Preposition (Prep) $\longrightarrow$ *at, in, on, to,*
with, . . .   (p. 87)

Adverb $\longrightarrow$ *away, have, soon, grandly, . . .*   (p. 87)

$$\text{Complement} \atop \text{(Comp)} \longrightarrow \left\{\begin{array}{l}\emptyset \\ \text{NP} \\ \text{Adjective} \\ \text{(NP)} \frown \text{ADVposition} \\ \text{(NP)} \frown \text{ADVdirection} \\ \text{Adjective} \frown \text{Prep} \frown \text{NP} \\ \text{NP} \frown \text{NP} \\ \text{NP} \frown \text{Prep} \frown \text{NP}\end{array}\right\} \begin{array}{l}\text{(p. 90; for} \\ \text{other com-} \\ \text{plement} \\ \text{types, see} \\ \text{pp. 217} \\ \text{and 239)}\end{array}$$

Adjective $\longrightarrow$ $\left\{\begin{array}{l}\textit{brave, cheerful, thrifty,} \\ \textit{courteous, interesting,} \\ \textit{worried, . . .}\end{array}\right\}$ (p. 95)

adverbial of direction deletion rule   (p. 100; for revised form see p. 127)
MV $\frown$ Prep$_1$ $\frown$ Prep$_2$ $\frown$ NP $\Longrightarrow$ MV $\frown$ Prep$_1$
Example: The car Past pull away from the curb $\Longrightarrow$
The car Past pull away

MV $\longrightarrow$ $\left\{\begin{array}{l}\text{V} \\ \text{V} \frown \text{Prep}\end{array}\right\}$ (p. 110)

V $\longrightarrow$ $\{$ *be, have, talk, depend on, talk back to, . . .* $\}$ (p. 110)

adverbial of direction deletion rule   (p. 127; for initial form see p. 100)
MV $\frown$ (NP$_1$) $\frown$ Prep $\frown$ (Prep$_2$) $\frown$ NP$_2$ $\Longrightarrow$ MV $\frown$ (NP$_1$) $\frown$ Prep$_1$
Example: The truck Past pull the car out of the mud $\Longrightarrow$
The truck Past pull the car out

NP $\frown$ NP switch rule   (p. 130)
NP$_1$ $\frown$ NP$_2$ $\Longrightarrow$ NP$_2$ $\frown$ $\left\{\begin{array}{l}\textit{to} \\ \textit{for}\end{array}\right\}$ $\frown$ NP$_1$
Example: She Past read the children a story $\Longrightarrow$
She Past read a story to the children

separable preposition switch rule   (p. 133)
V $\frown$ Prep $\frown$ NP $\Longrightarrow$ V $\frown$ NP $\frown$ Prep
Example: The general Past look over the situation $\Longrightarrow$
The general Past look the situation over

PART II SIMPLE TRANSFORMATIONAL RULES

Chapter 4 The Passive

agent deletion rule (p. 147)
$$by\ NP_1 \Longrightarrow \emptyset$$
Example: The message Past be -EN receive by John $\Longrightarrow$
The message Past be -EN receive

NP switch rule (a)   (p. 153)
$$NP_1\ Aux\ MV\ NP_2 \Longrightarrow NP_2\ Aux\ MV\ NP_1$$
Example: Everybody Pres respect he $\Longrightarrow$
He Pres respect everybody

NP switch rule (b)   (p. 149)
$$NP_1\ Aux\ MV\ NP_2\ ADV \begin{Bmatrix} direction \\ position \end{Bmatrix} (Adverbial) \Longrightarrow NP_2\ Aux\ MV$$
$$ADV \begin{Bmatrix} direction \\ position \end{Bmatrix} NP_1\ (Adverbial)$$
Example: John Past stand the broom in the corner $\Longrightarrow$
The broom Past stand in the corner John

NP switch rule (c)   (p. 149)
$$NP_1\ Aux\ MV\ NP_2\ NP_3 \Longrightarrow NP_2\ Aux\ MV\ NP_3\ NP_1$$
Example: The wizard Past grant the knight a wish $\Longrightarrow$
The knight Past grant a wish the wizard

NP switch rule (d)   (p. 150)
$$NP_1\ Aux\ MV\ NP_2\ NP_3 \Longrightarrow NP_3\ Aux\ MV\ NP_2\ NP_1$$
Example: The wizard Past grant the knight a wish $\Longrightarrow$
A wish Past grant the knight the wizard

NP switch rule (e)   (p. 151)
$$NP_1\ Aux\ MV\ NP_2 \begin{Bmatrix} to \\ for \end{Bmatrix} NP_3 \Longrightarrow NP_2\ Aux\ MV \begin{Bmatrix} to \\ for \end{Bmatrix} NP_3\ NP_1$$
Example: The wizard Past grant a wish to the knight $\Longrightarrow$
A wish Past grant to the knight the wizard

NP switch rule (f)   (p. 151)
$$NP_1\ Aux\ MV\ NP_2\ Prep\ NP_3 \Longrightarrow NP_2\ Aux\ MV\ Prep\ NP_3\ NP_1$$
Example: They Past inform him of the outcome $\Longrightarrow$
He Past inform of the outcome them

by insertion rule   (p. 153)
$$NP_1 \Longrightarrow by\ NP_1$$
Example: The school Past evaluate the board $\Longrightarrow$
The school Past evaluate by the board

be -EN insertion rule   (p. 153)
$$Aux\ MV \Longrightarrow Aux\ be\ -EN\ MV$$
Example: The school Past evaluate by the board $\Longrightarrow$
The school Past be -EN evaluate by the board

Chapter 5 Questions

yes-no question switch rule 1   (p. 166)

NP Tense $V_{Aux} \Longrightarrow$ Tense V_{Aux} NP (where V_{Aux} = the first optional element in the auxiliary or, if no optional element has been selected, the main verb *be*)

Example: John Past may come $\Longrightarrow$ Past may John come

yes-no question switch rule 2   (p. 166)

NP Tense $\Longrightarrow$ Tense NP

Example: John Past come $\Longrightarrow$ Past John come

do insertion rule   (p. 167)

Tense X $\Longrightarrow$ Tense *do* X (where X = any element except a verb)

Example: Past he bring the beer $\Longrightarrow$ Past do he bring the beer

question word switch rule   (p. 171)

X_1 X_2 ... QWord ... $X_n \Longrightarrow$ QWord X_1 X_2 ... X_n (where
QWord = *who/whom, what, where, when, why, ...*
X = any grammatical element except QWord)

Example: Pres have you -EN be where $\Longrightarrow$ Where Pres have you -EN be

Chapter 6 Negatives

not insertion rule 1   (p. 184)

Tense $V_{Aux} \Longrightarrow$ Tense V_{Aux} not

Example: John Pres be -ING go $\Longrightarrow$ John Pres be not -ING go

not insertion rule 2   (p. 184)

Tense $\Longrightarrow$ Tense not

Example: You Pres know what I mean $\Longrightarrow$
You Pres not know what I mean

question tag insertion rule   (p. 186)

NP Tense V_{Aux} X_1 X_2 ... $X_n \Longrightarrow$
NP Tense V_{Aux} X_1 X_2 ... X_n NP Tense V_{Aux}
(where V_{Aux} may be $\emptyset$)

Example: It -s be hot $\Longrightarrow$ It -s be hot, it -s be

Chapter 7 Emphasis and Commands

EMP insertion rule 1   (p. 201)

Tense $V_{Aux} \Longrightarrow$ Tense V_{Aux} EMP

Example: He Past can win, after all $\Longrightarrow$ He Past can EMP win, after all

EMP insertion rule 2   (p. 201)

Tense MV $\Longrightarrow$ Tense EMP MV

Example: I Past see a lawyer $\Longrightarrow$ I Past EMP see a lawyer

PART III SENTENCE-COMBINING RULES

Chapter 8 Sentences Embedded in the Verb Phrase Complement: Clauses

Comp $\rightarrow$ $\left\{ \begin{array}{l} \text{NP } (that) \text{ S} \\ it \ (that) \text{ S} \\ it \ to \text{ NP } (that) \text{ S} \\ \text{Adjective } (that) \text{ S} \end{array} \right\}$ (p. 217; for other complement types see pp. 90 and 239)

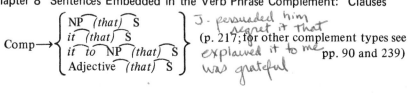

it deletion rule   (p. 219; for revised form see p. 223)
  it ⌢(that) S ⟹(that) S
  Example: He Past hope it that they Past will win ⟹
       He Past hope that they Past will win

to replacement rule   (p. 221)
  Tense ⟹ *to*
  Example: He Past guarantee the boat Past be sound ⟹
       He Past guarantee the boat to be sound

it deletion rule   (p. 223; for initial form see p. 219)
  it ⌢(to ⌢NP) ⌢(that) S ⟹(to ⌢NP) ⌢(that) S
  Example: John Past explain it to me that they Past have -EN be -EN
       lost ⟹ John Past explain to me that they Past have -EN be lost

to ⌢NP deletion rule   (p. 223)
  it ⌢to ⌢NP ⌢(that) S ⟹ it ⌢(that) S
  Example: John Past explain it to me that they Past have -EN be lost ⟹
       John Past explain it that they Past have -EN be lost

Chapter 9   Sentences Embedded in the Verb Phrase Complement: Phrases

$$\text{Comp} \longrightarrow \left\{ \begin{array}{l} S_\emptyset \\ S_{\text{-ING}} \\ \text{Adjective } \widehat{\ } S_{to} \\ S_{to} \end{array} \right\} \quad \text{(p. 239; for other complement types see pp. 90 and 217)}$$

tense deletion rule   (p. 241)
  Tense ⟹ ∅
  Example: Aunt Sally Past watch John Past clean out the attic ⟹
       Aunt Sally Past watch John clean out the attic

identical NP deletion rule   (p. 242)
  NP ⟹ ∅
  Example: Aunt Sally Past stop Aunt Sally -ING go to parties ⟹
       Aunt Sally Past stop -ING go to parties

-ING replacement rule   (p. 243) (for revised form see p. 310)
  Tense ⟹ -ING
  Example: He Past finish he Past fix the sink ⟹
       He Past finish he -ING fix the sink

for insertion rule   (p. 247)
  Adjective ⌢S_{to} ⟹ Adjective ⌢*for* ⌢S_{to}
  Example: The chairman Past be ready the meeting to begin ⟹
       The chairman Past be ready for the meeting to begin

Chapter 10   Noun Modification

  NP ⟶ Art ⌢Noun ⌢No ⌢(S)₁, ⌢(S)₂, ⌢(S)₃   (p. 265; for initial form see
                                    p. 26; for revised form see
                                    p. 309)

identical NP switch rule   (p. 266)
  X₁ ⌢X₂ ... NP ... Xₙ ⟹ NP ⌢X₁ ⌢X₂ ... Xₙ

Example: I Past meet the man (your mother -s know the man) ⟹
I Past meet the man (the man your mother -s know)

relative pronoun replacement rule   (p. 270)
Example: I met the man whom your mother knows⟹
I met the man your mother knows

adjectival clause deletion rule   (p. 272)
NP⌢Tense⌢be⟹∅
Example: We Past fix the crack (the crack Past be in the chimney)⟹
We Past fix the crack in the chimney

adjective switch rule   (p. 272; see p. 279 for revised form)
Art⌢Noun⌢No⌢Adj⟹Art⌢Adj⌢Noun⌢No
Example: An owl yellow Past stare at us⟹A yellow owl Past stare at us

participial switch rule   (p. 276)
NP⌢PresPart⌢Aux⌢VP⟹PresPart⌢NP⌢Aux⌢VP (where PresPart = a
present participial phrase)
Example: The man, having drunk far too much, labored up the stairs ⟹
Having drunk far too much, the man labored up the stairs

adjective switch rule   (p. 279; see p. 272 for initial form)

$$\text{Art⌢Noun⌢No} \left\{ \begin{array}{l} \text{Adj} \\ \text{V⌢-EN} \\ \text{V⌢-ING} \end{array} \right\} \Longrightarrow \text{Art} \left\{ \begin{array}{l} \text{Adj} \\ \text{V⌢-EN··} \\ \text{V⌢-ING} \end{array} \right\} \text{Noun⌢No}$$

Example: A shower leaking⟹A leaking shower

Chapter 11   Nominalized Sentences

$$\text{NP} \longrightarrow \left\{ \begin{array}{l} \text{Art⌢Noun⌢No⌢(S)}_1 \text{⌢(S)}_2 \ldots \\ \text{S} \end{array} \right\} \quad \text{(p. 309; for initial forms see pp. 26 and 265)}$$

possessive replacement rule   (p. 310)
Example: John ⟹ John's

-ING replacement rule   (p. 310; for initial form see p. 243)
Tense⟹-ING *(of)*
Example: His Past answer the phone Past surprise me ⟹
His -ING of answer the phone Past surprise me

abstract noun replacement rule
V⟹Nab⌢*(of)* (where Nab = an abstract noun)   (p. 311)
Example: The company's publish the book Past surprise me ⟹
The company's publication of the book Past surprise me

be⌢Adjective ⟹ Nab   (p. 312)
Example: The boy Tense be tall ⟹ The boy Tense tallness

that insertion rule   (p. 314)
S⟹*that*⌢S
Example: Aunt Sally Past refuse the offer Past surprise us ⟹
That Aunt Sally Past refuse the offer Past surprise us

it inversion rule   (p. 316)

$$\overset{\frown}{NP}\ \overset{\frown}{Aux}\ VP \Longrightarrow it\ \overset{\frown}{Aux}\ \overset{\frown}{VP}\ NP \quad \text{(where NP contains a nominalized}$$
$$\text{sentence that has either retained}$$
$$\text{tense or replaced tense with } to)$$

Example: That John Past refuse the offer Past surprise me $\Longrightarrow$
          It Past surprise me that John Past refuse the offer

for $\overset{\frown}{NP}$ deletion rule   (p. 318)

$$it\ \overset{\frown}{Aux}\ \overset{\frown}{MV}\ \overset{\frown}{NP_1}\ \overset{\frown}{for}\ \overset{\frown}{NP_2}\ \overset{\frown}{to}\ VP \Longrightarrow it\ \overset{\frown}{Aux}\ \overset{\frown}{MV}\ \overset{\frown}{NP_1}\ \overset{\frown}{to}\ VP$$
(where $NP_1 = NP_2$)

Example: It Past surprise John for John to receive the offer $\Longrightarrow$
          It Past surprise John to receive the offer

Chapter 12   Conjunction

coordination deletion rule   (p. 334)

$$\#\overset{\frown}{X_{a_1}}\ \overset{\frown}{X_{a_2}}\ \overset{\frown}{X_{a_3}}\#\ \#\overset{\frown}{X_{b_1}}\ \overset{\frown}{X_{b_2}}\ \overset{\frown}{X_{b_3}}\# \Longrightarrow \#\overset{\frown}{X_{a_1}}\ \overset{\frown}{X_{a_2}}\ X_{a_3}\#\#X_{b_2}\#$$
(where $X_{a_2} \neq X_{b_2}$, $X_{a_1} = X_{b_1}$, and $X_{a_3} = X_{b_3}$; $\#\dots\#$ are sentence
boundaries; X_a is any grammatical element in sentence a; X_b is any
grammatical element in sentence b)

Example: John sang. John danced. $\Longrightarrow$ John sang. danced.

coordination insertion rule   (p. 335)

$$\#\overset{\frown}{X_{a_1}}\ \overset{\frown}{X_{a_2}}\ \overset{\frown}{X_{a_3}}\#\ \#\overset{\frown}{X_{b_2}}\# \Longrightarrow \#\overset{\frown}{X_{a_1}}\ \overset{\frown}{X_{a_2}}\ and\ \overset{\frown}{X_{b_2}}\ X_{a_3}\#$$

Example: John sang. danced. $\Longrightarrow$ John sang and danced.

subordinating conjunction insertion rule   (p. 336)

$$\#S_1\#\#S_2\# \Longrightarrow \#S_1\ \overset{\frown}{Subconj}\ S_2\# \quad \text{(where Subconj = subordinating}$$
$$\text{conjunction)}$$

Example: I will come. I have to walk. $\Longrightarrow$
          I will come even if I have to walk.

subordinating conjunction switch rule   (p. 336)

$$S_1\ \overset{\frown}{Subconj}\ S_2 \Longrightarrow Subconj\ \overset{\frown}{S_2}\ S_1$$

Example: I will retire when I am 65. $\Longrightarrow$ When I am 65, I will retire.

conjunctive adverb insertion rule   (p. 337)

$$\#S_1\#\ \#S_2\# \Longrightarrow \#S_1\ \overset{\frown}{Conjadv}\ S_2\# \quad \text{(where Conjadv = conjunctive}$$
$$\text{adverb)}$$

Example: He said the sentence backwards. It was quite ungrammatical. $\Longrightarrow$
          He said the sentence backwards therefore it was quite ungram-
          matical.

conjunctive adverb switch rule   (p. 338)

$$S_1\ \overset{\frown}{Conjadv}\ \overset{\frown}{NP}\ \overset{\frown}{(AV)_1}\ \overset{\frown}{(AV)_2}\ \overset{\frown}{(AV)_3}\ VP \Longrightarrow$$
$$\begin{Bmatrix} S_1\ \overset{\frown}{NP}\ \overset{\frown}{(AV)_1}\ \overset{\frown}{Conjadv}\ \overset{\frown}{(AV)_2}\ \overset{\frown}{(AV)_3}\ VP \\ S_1\ \overset{\frown}{NP}\ \overset{\frown}{(AV)_1}\ \overset{\frown}{(AV)_2}\ \overset{\frown}{(AV)_3}\ VP\ Conjadv \end{Bmatrix}$$
(where AV = auxiliary verb)

Example: He said the sentence backwards; therefore it was quite ungram-
          matical. $\Longrightarrow$ He said the sentence backwards; it was therefore
          quite ungrammatical.

Index